Scotland and the Abolition of Black Slavery, 1756–1838

Scotland and the Abolition of Black Slavery, 1756–1838

Iain Whyte

Edinburgh University Press

For the unsung heroes of the struggle whose courageous resistance
to slavery advanced freedom for us all

Reprinted with corrections 2007

Edinburgh University Press Ltd
22 George Square, Edinburgh

Typeset in Adobe Sabon
by Servis Filmsetting Ltd, Manchester, and
printed and bound in Great Britain by
CPI Group (UK) Ltd, Croydon, CR0 4YY

A CIP record for this book is available from the British Library

ISBN-10   0 7486 2432 5 (hardback)
ISBN-13   978 0 7486 2432 4 (hardback)
ISBN-10   0 7486 2433 3 (paperback)
ISBN-13   978 0 7486 2433 1 (paperback)

The right of Iain Whyte to be identified as the author of this work
has been asserted in accordance with the Copyright, Designs and
Patents Act 1988.

Published with the support of the Edinburgh University
Scholarly Publishing Initiatives Fund.

CONTENTS

ACKNOWLEDGEMENTS

There have been many people who have provided encouragement, support and practical assistance during the research and writing of this book.

The staff of the university libraries in Edinburgh and Aberdeen and especially the Special Collections departments have been extremely helpful, as have been those in New College Library, Edinburgh, the National Library of Scotland, Edinburgh City Library, the Mitchell Library in Glasgow, and the National Archives of Scotland. More recently a pleasant few days were spent writing in a peaceful atmosphere at Gladstone's Library in Hawarden, Wales.

My friendship with Professor Geoff Palmer of Heriot Watt University goes back many years and he has continued to encourage me in this project that links his native Jamaica with his adopted Scotland. Dr Karina Williamson has allowed me to draw on her experience of literary sources. Professor John Cairns has generously given of his time and expertise in legal matters and provided access to certain papers. At an earlier stage Professor Duncan Rice and Professor George Shepperson gave encouragement and provided some helpful pointers from their extensive knowledge in this field.

I owe a particular debt to my two post-graduate supervisors, Professor Stewart J. Brown and Dr Alex Murdoch of the University of Edinburgh, who have given me invaluable assistance throughout my studies and well beyond them. Others whose support has been much appreciated are Mr Owen Dudley Edwards, Sir Lance and Lady Errington, Dr Polly Rewt and Mr James Robertson.

I am honoured and grateful that Archbishop Desmond Tutu, in the midst of a very crowded schedule, has agreed to write a brief foreword. The editorial staff at Edinburgh University Press have been full of support, advice and encouragement for this first-time author.

Finally I want to thank my family, Dave, Maggie and above all my wife Isabel. She has shared so much of my interest in issues of justice, has patiently listened to many a story on slavery and has made numerous helpful suggestions, especially when I have been obtuse. As in everything else, her support has meant everything to me.

Iain Whyte

ABBREVIATIONS

ALE	Advocates Library, Edinburgh
AUL	Aberdeen University Library
BL	British Library
EUL	Edinburgh University Library
MLG	Mitchell Library, Glasgow
NAS	National Archives of Scotland
NC	New College Library, Edinburgh
NLS	National Library of Scotland
RHO	Rhodes House Library, Oxford
ASR	*Anti-Slavery Reporter*
CI	*Christian Instructor*
CM	*Caledonian Mercury*
EA	*Edinburgh Advertiser*
EEC	*Edinburgh Evening Courant*
ER	*Edinburgh Review*
GA	*Glasgow Advertiser*
GC	*Glasgow Courier*
GCH	*Glasgow Chronicle*
GH	*Glasgow Herald*
JB	*John Bull*
JHC	*Journals of the House of Commons*
JHL	*Journals of the House of Lords*
KC	*Kelso Chronicle*
SC	*Scotsman*
SG	*Scottish Guardian*
SM	*Scots Magazine*
SMPR	*Scottish Missionary and Philanthropic Register*

FIGURES

FOREWORD

Apartheid was a system that required that some human beings be regarded as less than human. In that way they could control and, seemingly, the oppressor's conscience could be salved. Similarly, for slavery to exist demanded that certain people be regarded as less than human. Biological differences make it easier to instil an 'us' and 'them' mentality. This book asserts that there comes a time when people recognise that their humanity is dependent upon the acknowledgement of all people as God's children; that we are created for togetherness, for interdependence and to treat another person as less than a child of God is blasphemous.

The passion of the Scots for freedom and individuality is legendary. We enjoyed wonderful support from the Scottish people in our struggle against apartheid, for which we are deeply grateful. Thank you, Iain Whyte, for telling a history of which the Scots can be rightly proud.

Desmond M. Tutu
Anglican Archbishop Emeritus of Cape Town

INTRODUCTION

WHO BROUGHT ABOUT THE ABOLITION OF SLAVERY?

In the mid-eighteenth century the idea that Britain should abandon the slave trade, let alone plantation slavery, would have been all but unthinkable. Slavery had undoubtedly proved to be one of the most profitable commercial enterprises of the growing Empire and its maintenance had provided means of employment for Britons on land and sea. Later generations were to be shocked that it took twenty years from the first abolition campaign to secure even a partially effective ban on the slave trade in 1807 and that slavery itself was not abolished for a further twenty-seven years. But the real anomaly was not the years of frustration encountered by those who campaigned, but the eventual success of their efforts in the teeth of so much vested interest and obdurate resistance.

The answer to the question in the heading above would have been obvious to thinking people in the second half of the nineteenth century and the first half of the twentieth. Until the Second World War, historians writing about the abolition of the slave trade and slavery in the British Empire generally accepted that the principal influence lay in the work of a group of evangelical Christians living in South London at the turn of the eighteenth century, known collectively as the 'Clapham Sect' or 'The Saints', of whom the most prominent was William Wilberforce. The Oxford historian Sir Reginald Coupland, in a biography of Wilberforce and an account of the abolitionist movement, endorsed that view. Coupland claimed that the successful challenge to such a profitable area of imperial commerce came about through the untiring efforts of dedicated English humanitarians in the long eighteenth century.[1]

However, the publication in 1944 of *Capitalism and Slavery* by a young scholar from Trinidad provided the most fundamental challenge to that accepted wisdom.[2] Eric Williams, later to be prime minister of the island state, argued that economic factors rather than humanitarian pressure put an end to Caribbean slavery and that the Clapham Sect, with few exceptions, did not merit such credit. They were, for him, more of a hindrance than a help in the process of abolition. Williams contended that the slave trade was abolished when it became uneconomic, that the West Indian plantations were in terminal decline and that protection of the sugar industry, which depended on slavery, was abandoned by a Britain that was quickly embracing the new doctrine of free trade.

Today support for the Williams' thesis is founded largely, though not exclusively, amongst historians from Africa and the Caribbean. Seymour Carrington from the University of West Indies has claimed that the American Revolution made slavery unviable and Joseph Inikori from Nigeria has supported Williams in his view that the development of eighteenth-century British industrial capitalism was fuelled by slavery and that slavery was indeed abandoned when it no longer made economic sense.[3]

By contrast, two English historians, Roger Anstey and Howard Temperley, focused on what they saw as inconsistency in Williams' evidence. Temperley argued that anti-slavery and anti-monopolist concerns could not be linked,[4] while Anstey made a careful study of profitability and reasserted the case for the humanitarians.[5] But David Brion Davis, the American historian, whilst acknowledging Anstey's leading role in undermining the Williams case for economic motivation, sought a middle ground that rejected Williams' sweeping reductionism, but took account of the various interests which made up the equation.[6] Many scholars accept that the viability of the West Indian plantations was declining but another American historian, Seymour Drescher, provided a very detailed challenge to the automatic link of decline with abolition and provided possibly the most comprehensive response to Williams' ideas.[7] These three, along with James Walvin of York University[8] argued that there were many aspects to the eventual success of abolition and credit the part played by other religious and civic groups in the abolitionist cause. Until recently the place of individual women and women's groups was largely unrecognised until Clare Midgley's *Women Against Slavery* highlighted their contribution, which was made often in the face of male resistance.[9]

There were one or two celebrated ex-slaves who spoke on public platforms. Olaudah Equiano or Gustavus Vasa, perhaps the best-known of them, wrote and promoted his book *The Interesting Narrative and Other Writings* throughout Britain, even listening to a debate on the slave trade at the Church of Scotland's General Assembly.[10] But few gave recognition to the continual resistance to slavery from the black population in England in the long eighteenth century until it was chronicled by the Nigerian historian Folarin Shyllon in 1974.[11] There have been descriptive accounts based on eye witness reports of the effect of slave rebellions in the West Indies but both James Walvin and Michael Craton have demonstrated more recently the impact of varied and subtle resistance by West Indian slaves on a day-to-day basis in order to weaken and cripple the institution.[12]

All this indicates that there is no general agreement today that one group, one factor, and certainly no one individual, can claim sole responsibility for the abolition of British imperial slavery. When Nelson Mandela received the freedom of twelve British local authorities in Glasgow in 1993 he made the same point about the abolition of apartheid in South Africa. This was at a time when analysts were claiming that the collapse of the rand and secret meetings between local businessmen and the African National Congress had been the real catalyst for the reversal of government policy. Many Africans justifiably credit liberation movements on the continent itself as the most significant factor in the destruction of the old South Africa. But, without underestimating any of these elements, Mr Mandela stated his firm conviction that the boycott of South African goods and the campaigning of the anti-apartheid movement had been vital planks in the overthrow of apartheid.

So too with the anti-slavery movement 150 years beforehand. All logic suggested that with falling markets in the Caribbean and alternative sources of sugar in the East Indies, Britain could not indefinitely be expected to support the expensive protection of West Indian plantation, let alone commit military and naval protection to defend the rights of a few planters, whose contempt for the motherland was increasingly evident. Real or imagined slave plots and slave rebellions, so much part of the whites' concern on the islands were not only destabilising life there but were increasingly raising questions in Britain. Yet some of the most determined resistance to emancipation came from planters and their supporters in Britain in the twilight years of slavery, suggesting that that there was still an enormous amount to be done by the anti-slavery movement. Ironically, the slave-owners' unwillingness to give ground was to play into the hands of abolitionist propaganda. Few serious students of imperial slavery today would deny that without a sustained abolition campaign in Britain, which did indeed fuel the frustration of the victims of slavery in the Caribbean and led to both the threat and reality of more resistance, the abandonment of this profitable and enormous crime against humanity would have been considerably delayed.

SCOTLAND'S PART IN THE WIDER PICTURE

Despite recognizing the economic transformation of Glasgow through tobacco, sugar and cotton imports, and the growth of Edinburgh as a major financial centre, most histories of Scotland have at most a passing reference to the extensive involvement of the nation in the slave trade and on the West Indian plantations. Friends expressed surprise at my interest in linking Scotland and slavery, considering involvement in this infamous business the preserve of such places as Liverpool and Bristol, and something in which a freedom-loving nation had no part. A reference to Glasgow's sources of wealth sowed some doubts, though, and the balance has shifted in recent years as very different historians such as Angus Calder, Michael Fry and Tom Devine have given much weight to this aspect of Scotland's colonial involvement. There has also been an upsurge of interest in the media over what was described in a newspaper article in 2003 as 'Scotland's dark trade in slavery'.[13]

Yet Scottish involvement in the anti-slavery movement has only merited a few references in most of these accounts. Duncan Rice's *The Scots Abolitionists, 1833–1861* was mainly concerned with the Scottish anti-slavery focus on the United States after the Emancipation Act of 1833, and has only a brief chapter summarising abolitionist activity on Caribbean slavery up to that date. Professor Rice made an earlier study of abolitionists in his native Aberdeen, but published nothing that detailed similar activity in other parts of the country.[14] Edith Hurwitz, J. R. Oldfield and James Walvin all feature Scotland in their surveys of the popular movement in Britain, but the wide scope of these studies do not allow for more than spasmodic references to events north of the border.[15]

In 1756 the first case of a black slave in Scotland who sought freedom came before the Court of Session, Scotland's highest civil court. Two more were to follow before the judges were to declare by a majority that the legal authority of the West Indies, or even of England, held no writ to permit slavery in Scotland. Baptism was to play a part in this, as were biblical and theological concepts more familiar to ordinary Scots than to their southern neighbours. Such legal cases and the intermittent involvement of black slaves in Scottish communities provided a preparation for the upsurge of public petitions. The Apprenticeship Scheme, which followed the abolition of slavery in the British Empire, was brought to an end in 1838, closing one chapter in the struggle, yet opening another.

The roots of anti-slavery activity in Scotland go back to the presence of slaves in Scotland in the eighteenth century and the influence of the Enlightenment. In addition to the campaign in Scotland, the careers of a number of London Scots were to play vital roles in the British abolition movement. In the early nineteenth century, Scottish evangelical churchmen were to play a vital part in the transition between calling for gradual and then immediate abolition of slavery, in the same way that some of the more establishment voices in the Church of Scotland had been raised in opposition to the slave trade in the previous century.

The large Scottish stake in the slave trade and slavery, the theoretical hostility to slavery in the ideas of the Scottish Enlightenment, and the apparent tension between the two, has puzzled many of those exploring the issue. It has been suggested that the ideas of the Scottish Enlightenment and the Evangelical movement in the eighteenth century were in conflict. Certainly the Enlightenment optimism about human progress and the Evangelical emphasis on sin and human failing seemed to be in direct contradiction. The Enlightenment also laid an emphasis on reason and logic as avenues to truth, and while that was true of the religious figures of the Enlightenment, and even more so of the secular ones, the Evangelicals regarded truth as a direct revelation from God. Certainly the two could be in conflict over attitudes to slavery, especially when Evangelical fervour brought an urgency to action resisted by the more cautious. But abolitionist activity in Scotland required and received a blend of all of these seemingly opposing insights to be at its most effective. Nor could it be assumed that the ideas were all of a piece. Enthusiasm for enslaving vagrants, comments on racial inferiority and natural grading of races are all to be found amongst the figures of the Enlightenment, supporting the contention that Enlightenment ideas could be used to support slavery, as well as to oppose it.

At a sinister level, the constant fear of insurrection from the great black majority necessitated the maintenance of a brutal regime in the West Indies. Since most Scots there considered themselves temporary residents, they elected to keep quiet about it until they could return home. At home, a combination of ignorance of the facts, respect for the sanctity of property and fear of revolution combined to 'keep the lid' on any challenge to slavery.

Threats of opposition and diversion from the cause are threaded through this complex period. Nonetheless Scotland's churches and people made a highly significant contribution to the anti-slavery movement despite the many factors that worked against the cause. An early exposure to the issue through the presence of slaves in Scottish communities and the clear theological and moral challenge to the trafficking of human beings and holding them as property gave the Scottish anti-slavery movement a unique impetus. This was as true of the London Scots as it was of the anti-slavery leaders and activists in Scotland. The Evangelical doctrines of human creation in the image of God alongside fallen humanity were brought into the service of anti-slavery. Evangelical theology made common cause with some of the best values of the Scottish Enlightenment and with a simple, but not simplistic, conviction that slavery was cruel, uncivilised and wrong. This combination may not have been unique, but it formed the distinctive contribution that Scotland was to bring to the struggle against the slave trade and Caribbean slavery.

The visible Scottish contribution to anti-slavery in this period was almost exclusively a male one. In keeping with the attitudes of the time, women were not encouraged by the movement to speak, to write or to sign petitions. In one case, in Dundee in 1792, a petition was seen to be invalid since it contained the signatures of a few women as well as children. When the boycott of West Indian sugar became a tool in the campaign, clearly women played very direct, though unrecognised, part in abolitionist activity. In the 1830s separate women's abolitionist societies were formed and equally separate petitions from groups of men and women in Scottish towns were sent to Parliament, with one well-subscribed appeal from Scottish women to Queen Victoria. But few records of the women's societies are to be found until later in the nineteenth century.

This starting date for my account marks the escape of a young black slave who tricked his master into letting him go outside the house where he was held before being taken on board ship at Port Glasgow. The arguments heard over slavery at the Court of Session in this and subsequent cases could not have taken place without the initiative of the slaves. There were a number of others who reacted to their enslavement by simply running away from their masters. But apart from Olaudah Equiano's visit to Scotland in 1792 and the promotion of his book there, it would be forty-four years before there was any other record of a direct black contribution to the Scottish abolition movement. In 1836 James McCune Smith from New York became active in the Glasgow Emancipation Society, and in the 1840s Frederick Douglass, the celebrated African-American campaigner, delivered significant speeches in several Scottish cities appealing for help to rid the United States of slavery.

Slavery is a subject that occupies an increasingly wide canvas. Anti-Slavery International's stark contemporary assertion that there are more slaves in the world today than ever before is a reminder that this is an institution which is thousands of years old and whose presence has spread through many countries in the world. A West Indian friend cautions my enthusiasm for the Scottish abolition movement with a reminder that it took hundreds of years from Scotland's first involvement in black slavery to be effective. It could be argued with a great deal of justification that slavery existed in concrete form, if not in name, in European (including British colonial) enterprise even a century after its official ending. To examine the whole of Scottish involvement with it, attitudes towards it and activity against it would be the subject of many volumes. During the long eighteenth century, Scots served in the armed forces throughout the expanding Empire and their commercial interests often pioneered this expansion. A fascinating study could be made of Scottish attitudes within the East India Company or the sugar estates in Mauritius. Scots support for American anti-slavery activity overlapped with the final stages of West Indian abolitionism and indeed built on it. David Livingstone and others, who took up the struggle against the slave trade in Africa later in the nineteenth century, wrote a different chapter in Scots abolitionism and Livingstone certainly knew something of the earlier campaign.

A great deal of this history is interconnected, but the scope of this study is restricted to that earlier but key period between the awakening of white Scots at home to the issue of slavery and the final abandonment of British support for it within the Empire. There are now Scots at all levels of society whose history and ethnicity is drawn from many different racial and cultural roots. Scotland's own black history is being recognised now, celebrated and written about by those whose particular heritage it is. It needs to stand alongside this account in recognition of different parts of this small country's heritage that has elements of pride as well as shame, of courage as well as cruelty, of powerful spirituality as well as hard material greed.

Notes

1 Sir Reginald Coupland, *The British Anti-Slavery Movement* (Oxford, 1933); Sir Reginald Coupland, *Wilberforce* (Oxford, 1923).
2 Eric Williams, *Capitalism and Slavery* (London, [1944] 1964).
3 B. Solow and S. Engerman, eds, *British Capitalism and Caribbean Slavery: The Legacy of Eric Williams* (Cambridge, MA, 1987), pp. 79–102, 135–63.
4 Howard Temperley, *British Anti-Slavery 1833–40* (London, 1972).
5 Roger Anstey, *The Atlantic Trade and British Abolition, 1760–1810* (London, 1975); 'Capitalism and Slavery: A Critique', *Economic History Review*, 2nd Series, Vol. 21 No. 2 (1968).
6 David Brion Davis, 'Capitalism, Abolitionism and Hegenomy', in *British Capitalism and Caribbean Slavery*, B. Solow and S. Engerman, eds, (Cambridge, MA, 1987), p. 209.
7 Seymour Drescher, *Econocide: British Slavery in the Year of Abolition* (Pittsburg, 1977).
8 James Walvin, 'The Rise of British Popular Sentiment for Abolition', in *Anti-Slavery, Religion and Reform: Essays in Memory of Roger Anstey*, C. Bolt and S. Drescher, eds (Folkestone, 1980).
9 Clare Midgley, *Women Against Slavery: The British Campaign 1780–1870* (London, 1982).
10 Olaudah Equiano, *The Interesting Narrative and Other Writings*, ed. V. Carretta (London, [1789] 1995).
11 Folarin Shyllon, *Black Slaves in Britain* (Oxford, 1974).
12 Michael Craton, *Testing the Chains: Resistance to Slavery in the British West Indies* (Ithaca, NY, 1982); 'What and Who to Whom and What, The Significance of Slave Resistance', in *British Capitalism and Caribbean Slavery*, B. Solow and S. Engerman, eds, pp. 259–83.
13 *The Herald*, Weekend Review, 18 Oct 2003, p. 13.
14 C. Duncan Rice, *The Scots Abolitionists; 1833–1861* (Baton Rouge, LA, 1981); 'Abolitionists and Abolitionism in Aberdeen', *Northern Scotland*, No. 1 (1972).
15 Edith F. Hurwitz, *Politics and the Public Conscience: Slave Emancipation and the Abolitionist Movement in Britain* (London, 1973); J. R. Oldfield, *Popular Politics and British Anti-Slavery: The Mobilisation of Public Opinion against the Slave Trade 1787–1807* (Manchaester, 1995); James Walvin, *England, Slaves, and Freedom 1776–1838* (Jackson, MS, 1986).

1

BLACK SLAVES IN SCOTLAND AND BAPTISM

⎯

Although in the plantations they have laid hold of the poor blacks, and made slaves of them, yet I do not think that is agreeable to humanity, not to say to the Christian religion. Is a man a slave because he is black? No. He is our brother; and he is a man though not of our colour; he is in a land of liberty, with his wife and his child: let him remain there.
> Lord Auchinleck, Court of Session, Edinburgh, January 1778

In 1760 Dr David Dalrymple purchased a slave from a Grenada estate owned by fellow Scot Ninian Home, named him 'Black Tom' and brought him as his personal attendant to Methil in Fife eight years later. That this was a temporary situation is evident from Dalymple's clear intention to return the slave to Grenada. He had written to a friend in the island with directions for training 'Tom' in carpentry. The date fixed for his return was 11 September 1769. On the previous day, 'Tom' had requested leave to go to the minister of Wemyss Parish Church, Dr Harry Spens, to seek baptism. Dalrymple had agreed to this.[1] The parish records show that on that day 'Dr. Dalrymple's black in Methil was baptised and named David Spens.'[2] The next morning the newly baptised slave packed his clothes and left Dalrymple's house to take refuge in the home of John Henderson, a local Kirk elder and farmer at nearby Methelhill. Accompanied by Henderson, he returned to Dalrymple's house at Lindifferen and declared his right to freedom.

The speech that David made is hardly known beyond legal documents but must stand as one of the classics in any country. Far from begging for his freedom on bended knee, the statement echoes much more the Roman slave rebel Spartacus than the American fictional hero Uncle Tom. Although there is no doubt that it was drafted with the assistance of others, it stands as a remarkable statement in the history of liberty.

I David Spens formerly called Black Tom late slave to Dr. David Dalrymple of Lindifferen heareby intimate to you the said Dr. Dalrymple that being formerly an heathen slave to you and of consequence then at your disposal but being now instructed in the Christian Religion I have embraced the same and been publicly baptised to that faith by the Reverend Mr. Harry Spens, minister of the gospel at Wemyss and so admitted to the Church of Christ established in this Kingdom and of consequence I am now by the Christian Religion Liberate and set at freedom from my old yoke, bondage, and slavery and by the laws of this Christian land there is no slavery nor vestige of slavery allowed. Nevertheless you take it upon you to exercise your tyrannical power over me and would dispose of me arbitrally at your despotic will and pleasure and for that end you threaten to send me abroad out of this country to the West Indies and there dispose of me for money by which you subvert the ends and designs of the Christian institution which ransoms liberty to all its members but also you would deprive our sovereign Lord the King of a good subject. Therefore I heareby declare that from henceforth I am to leave your family and service and protest that if you shall put in execution your wicked intention or offer to put the same in execution or in any ways abetting aiding or assisting therein or any ways be accessory there or concerned in the same less or more you shall be liable in the pains and penalties of law inflicted on persons guilty of such crimes and in all the consequences of such a wicked practice and all damages or expenses for any of my Christian Brethren who shall aid and assist and protect, may be put to in prosecuting you and remedying ourselves at law and therefore take instruments.[3]

Others did not view the matter in such clear-cut terms. Ten days later Dalrymple formally demanded that Henderson hand Spens over to him. The response from the farmer was that if he delivered him up, 'the whole country would be inflamed'. Dalrymple then took legal steps against Spens and Henderson, and on 3 March 1770 a court order was served for David Spens' apprehension. Wisely, and no doubt acting on advice, the slave at liberty now sought to strengthen his status by travelling to Edinburgh. He thought that he had obtained security but on returning to Fife was arrested by a Mr Thomson, Messenger of the Court, and taken to Dysart jail. Far from lying quietly there, Spens, who had several sympathetic lawyers acting for him, not only obtained his release on a caution (bail) of £30 but was busy throughout his time in jail issuing writs for wrongful arrest and petitioning the Court of Session. Legal papers were prepared on both sides, but Dalrymple died later that year and in somewhat of an anticlimax David Spens gained his freedom by default before the judges had a chance to come to a decision over it.[4]

The *Dalrymple* v *Spens* case was one of three cases involving the recovery of slaves in Scotland that came before the Court of Session in the eighteenth century. In 1756 Robert Sheddan, a merchant from Morrishill in Ayrshire, sought to detain his runaway slave Jamie Montgomery, but this time it was the death of the slave in Edinburgh's Tolbooth jail that cut short the process of petitions and memorials presented by both sides. It would be another twenty-two years before the law would finally pronounce on whether slavery was permissible in Scotland. Joseph Knight, a slave brought from Jamaica by Sir John Wedderburn of Ballandean near Perth, resisted his master's attempt to keep him in permanent service and after a number of years of argument a majority of law lords in Scotland's highest court decided that there could be no such thing as slavery in Scotland.

Many strands are to be found in the saga of black slaves in Scotland in the eighteenth century – their conditions and treatment; the lure of freedom and the fear of return to the West Indies or America; baptism and its relationship to the church, society and, ultimately, to the decisions of the courts. Whilst Scottish law had different historic roots from that in England, this did not mean that baptism necessarily provided a passport to freedom for black slaves. Issues of property weighed as heavily in the minds of some Scottish judges as they would for many of those representing commercial interests. Nonetheless, for many citizens of Scotland the horrors of slavery and of the slave trade were becoming better known and even a comparatively small number of thinly distributed black slaves enabled them to be seen as individuals rather than as a group who might be a threat to white society. It was easier to see their plight as an unjust one and to appreciate the incongruity of slavery when slaves were encountered personally. Those who held high legal office often shared attitudes in common with the dominant Moderate party of the Kirk, many of whose members were their friends, and although they were by this time less bound by a biblical literalism that accepted slavery, it was ironically a return to zeal for the Bible that was to prove such a strong weapon against the institution.[5]

WHO WERE THE SLAVES IN SCOTLAND?

All the indications point to the presence at this time of about seventy black slaves in Scotland. England, by contrast, had a black population of around 15,000 by the end of the eighteenth century and the sizeable communities in ports such as Liverpool and Bristol[6] do not appear to be in any way replicated in Glasgow or Leith. Scotland's slaves were spread throughout the country and the great majority were in personal service. There is a wide variety of references to slaves in contemporary newspapers but with the exception of those featured in the three court cases under discussion here, we know very little about their lives beyond the odd reference. Some contemporary family portraits feature black attendants on the wealthy or aristocratic, one or two examples are found in literature and there are references in letters, court records and parish records of baptisms, marriages and the proceedings of Kirk Sessions. A very few gravestones provide further clues. Between 1719 and 1776, there were thirty-six newspaper advertisements for runaways who were brought from the Caribbean, the American colonies or the Indies, with nine notices of slaves for sale, four of these being in 1766.

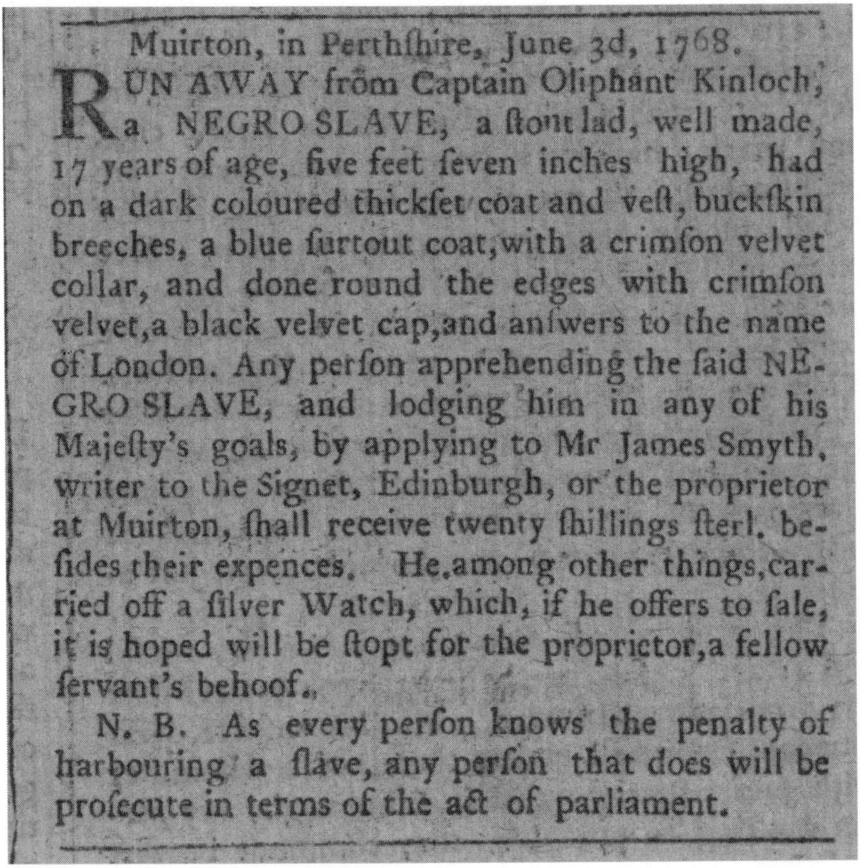

Muirton, in Perthſhire, June 3d, 1768.

RUN AWAY from Captain Oliphant Kinloch, a NEGRO SLAVE, a ſtout lad, well made, 17 years of age, five feet ſeven inches high, had on a dark coloured thickſet coat and veſt, buckſkin breeches, a blue ſurtout coat, with a crimſon velvet collar, and done round the edges with crimſon velvet, a black velvet cap, and anſwers to the name of London. Any perſon apprehending the ſaid NEGRO SLAVE, and lodging him in any of his Majeſty's goals, by applying to Mr James Smyth, writer to the Signet, Edinburgh, or the proprietor at Muirton, ſhall receive twenty ſhillings ſterl. beſides their expences. He, among other things, carried off a ſilver Watch, which, if he offers to ſale, it is hoped will be ſtopt for the proprietor, a fellow ſervant's behoof.

N. B. As every perſon knows the penalty of harbouring a ſlave, any perſon that does will be proſecute in terms of the act of parliament.

Figure 1 Advertisement in the Edinburgh Evening Courant *for a runaway slave,* 3 June 1768. © *The Trustees of the National Library of Scotland*

In the Scottish National Portrait Gallery a late seventeenth-century painting of the Duke of Perth features a young black boy looking up at his master. In similar vein is a painting of the same era of the Duchess of Buccleuch accompanied by her black page. A document in 1725 from Culzean Castle in Ayrshire is signed by 'Scipio', who had been in Scotland since 1705 as a slave to Sir John Kennedy.[7] Lady Stair, related by marriage to James Dalrymple, law lord and author of *Institutions of the Law of Scotland*, in which was stated that 'little of slavery remains elsewhere among Christians . . . in Scotland there is no such thing',[8] was reported in 1744 to have 'a black boy'.[9] In 1772 Lord Oliphant advertised a 'handsome' reward for the recovery of his slave John Louden, or 'Quashy', who had run away from his Perthshire estate,[10] and Lord Monboddo, who voted against Joseph Knight's freedom in 1788, had a black servant named 'Gory' who was probably a slave.[11] In 1762 the Duke of Gordon's factor, William Bell, recorded sums of over £33 paid to clothiers and a shoemaker in Huntly for 'the black boy Harry' who was clearly in the Duke's household.[12]

Yet well-dressed black personal servants in Scotland were not the sole preserve of the aristocracy. When Samuel Ramsay ran away from Almycross near Arbroath in July 1760, his master David Fraser described him as in 'a gentleman's livery'. In 1764 James Thomson fled from Baillie Hutton, a Glasgow merchant, wearing 'a blue broad coat, surbour coat and a good double broad goldlaced hat'. Four years later, 'London', a runaway slave owned by Captain Oliphant Kinloch of Muirton in Perthshire, was notable for a velvet collar on his coat, trimmed crimson and a black velvet cap. In April 1773 'Tom', or Thomas Diddy, who was presumed to be making for London, was described as richly dressed with silver buckles, which his master, John Alston of Glasgow, reckoned he would attempt to convert into cash for the journey.[13]

The majority of slaves were brought to Scotland by masters who had spent time in the West Indies, the American colonies, or in the slave trade. In John Galt's *Annals of the Parish*, a former planter Mr Cayenne (possibly a convenient pseudonym for a hot-tempered and peppery character) had a slave stereotypically named Sambo on whom he would vent his wrath. Most publically visible today is an unnamed young black boy who finds a place in a family portrait around 1760 of the Glassford family, which hangs in the People's Palace in Glasgow. John Glassford was a 'tobacco lord' and the largest ship-owner in the city, with a street in the former commercial district named after him. The slave is barely discernable and it is believed that attempts were made to remove him from the picture when it became not only socially unacceptable but illegal to own slaves in Scotland, though not of course in the colonies.[14]

The eight recorded slave sales in Scotland show the popularity of young black servants. Clearly many households saw these youngsters as fashionable accessories. An advertisement in 1769 commends 'a handsome black boy, about 13' and 'very well qualified', though his skills are not specified.[15] Two in 1766 are for eleven-year-old boys described respectively as 'smart' and 'of healthy constitution', and in the same year the only recorded sale of a woman slave, 'Peggy', in Edinburgh, along with her one-year-old child, described her as 'about 19, a good house wench and washer and dresser'.[16] Glasgow's Mitchell Library has a number of letters from William Colquhoun, an Atlantic slave trader, to his family in the city. In 1775 he wrote to his sister from Sierra Leone commending 'a very fine girl about twelve years of age', who had been with him as a servant for eighteen months and whom he offered to his sister Betty in the Trongate rather than selling her as he had done to so many others.[17]

Although the great majority of slaves in Scotland whose details are recorded in the eighteenth century were in personal service, some were apprenticed to a trade. 'Sylvester', a mulatto who ran away from Greenock in 1773, was serving his time a joiner, and 'Cupid', living in the same town, was a cooper. The advertisement for the recovery of 'Caesar' from Ross-shire indicates that he was employed as a cook.[18] In September 1776 an unnamed 'black boy, with long hair, stout made' was advertised as someone who 'takes care of a horse'.[19]

However, the fullest account of a slave in Scottish employment beyond personal service comes from the documents surrounding the case in which Robert Sheddan sought legal redress over his slave Jamie Montgomery. Sheddan purchased Jamie in Virginia from Captain Joseph Hawkins in March 1750 and brought him to Scotland to be apprenticed to Robert Morrice, a joiner in Beith. Jamie worked with Morrice for eighteen months before returning to personal service. Sheddan had arranged to have him repurchased by Hawkins for the original price of £56 plus 1,000 lb of tobacco, representing his increased value as a tradesman. It was reported that on 12 April 1756, having failed to persuade Jamie to return voluntarily to Virginia, Sheddan, Morrice and Gavin Montgomery of Baroger 'drove and dragged him' the ten miles to Port Glasgow where a ship was leaving for the Americas. Montgomery-Sheddan, as he was now designated on his certificate of baptism, escaped from a flesher's house in the port where he was held under guard and fled to Edinburgh. He was finally caught and imprisoned in the Tolbooth by the City Guard. Memorials were then presented before Lord Bankton and a date in January 1757 was set for the hearing before the Court of Session, although Jamie died in prison before the case could be concluded.[20]

TREATMENT, CONDITIONS AND THE LURE OF FREEDOM

What kind of treatment could slaves in Scotland expect in the eighteenth century? Clearly the violence with which Jamie was taken from Beith to Port Glasgow does not reflect well and he was bound and fettered for the journey.[21] In the portraits of the Duke of Perth and the Duchess of Buccleuch, the accompanying slaves have silver collars and the newspaper advertisement in 1721 for the apprehension of eighteen-year-old 'Ann' described her as having 'a brass collar about her neck', on which is engraved 'Gustavus Brown in Dalkeith, his negro'.[22] These collars were not merely decorative and were perhaps seen as a more sophisticated and acceptable form of branding than the crude markings inflicted on the bodies of plantation slaves in the colonies. In the same year that 'Ann' ran away, another notice appeared regarding 'a Negro man about 22 years' who absconded from the Royal Infirmary in Edinburgh and is described as 'branded', but this would probably have been done on his sale abroad. Some would argue that the conditions of colliers and salters was no better and indeed the preamble to the Emancipation Act for them in 1774 stated 'many colliers and coal-bearers and salters are in a state of slavery and bondage'.[23] A collar worn in 1701 by Alexander Steuart, a collier in Sir John Erskine's mines in Alva, is displayed in the Museum of Scotland. However, the legend surrounding it indicates that Steuart had been found guilty of a crime for which he was bound to perpetual service. The accompanying text claims that collars were worn only by 'serfs' in these circumstances and as an alternative to the death penalty,[24] clearly differentiating their status from those worn by black slaves.

With the exception of the cases that went to court, we know little about the treatment given to captured runaway slaves in Scotland, or indeed of the success rate of the advertisements which offered rewards of between one and seven guineas for their apprehension. Ned Johnston, who was purchased by Archibald Buchanan of Glasgow in 1763, claimed to be 'subjected to severe and cruel usage', being 'suspended from the joists of a byre and beaten with rods 'till the blood ran from many wounds in his body' in retribution for a minor offence. Local people helped him to escape and he gained his freedom from the Magistrates in Glasgow.[25] In 1744 John Kincaid of Edinburgh, writing to his friend James Watson of Sauchton, confessed that in response to complaints about a prank with some market women selling fruit, he severely horsewhipped his slave 'Cato' and he added, 'I must own I was a little too severe for him.' The result, understandably, was that Cato expressed a wish to serve a different master and Kincaid proposed to hire or sell him to Watson, adding that 'he will not be exposed to bad company in the country as in town'.[26]

Of course in the context of our modern awareness of the potential for child abuse, any preference for ornamental servants of a young age might indicate a sinister fate for many. For all of those whom we would now regard as unprotected minors, the horrors of being separated from parents, transported thousands of miles and being daily subjected to the caprices of strange adults who held absolute power over their lives was hardly a fate to be envied even in adults. Yet, within the restriction of liberty imposed by domestic slavery, many masters provided not only fine clothes but other advantages as well. Scipio Kennedy's statement at Culzean indicated that he had been offered his freedom at 'twenty eight or thirty years' of age but that he 'maturely and deliberately, without any coercion', chose to remain in Sir John's service, from whom he had 'received clothing, maintenance and education with more than ordinary kindness'.[27] In Dr David Dalrymple's petition to recover David Spens from John Henderson, the farmer who was sheltering the slave, he affirmed that he had given him the best of medical attention when he fell ill and 'had always been indulgent to him' and made his life as comfortable as possible.[28] The estate accounts of the Duke of Gordon show £5-8-0 paid between 1761 and 1762 to James Mackenzie, the schoolmaster at Huntly, for 'teaching the Black Boy Harry'.[29]

In the *Knight* v *Wedderburn* case, Sir John Wedderburn's advocate James Ferguson outlined how much his client had done for the slave since his arrival in Scotland from Jamaica – not only meeting the costs of his marriage to Annie Thomson from Dundee, as well as the laying-in and baptism of their child and his burial after death, but also enabling Joseph Knight to become literate. Some claimed that Knight's bid for freedom was fired by reading reports of the Somerset case in 1772, when Lord Mansfield (himself a Scot, but Chief Justice of England) refused to allow another exiled Scot in London to take his slave back to the colonies. Ferguson even claimed that it was unfair to describe Joseph Knight's situation as 'slavery' – Sir John, he said, simply wished to have his service for life.[30] In answering Jamie Mongomery's Bill of Advocation in May 1756, Robert Sheddan's lawyer claimed that the inconvenience and heavy costs incurred by his client in training the slave as a joiner showed that it was 'by no means intended to put him to the common and usual employment of a slave'. He also argued that 'the respondent has all along treated him as a son than his servant' and he never ill used Jamie, 'even though he has oftener than once eloped from him, which puts him under the necessity of using means to prevent it'.[31]

Many slaves had an understandable terror of returning to the colonies, especially to the Caribbean, where conditions were the harshest and where there would be no chance of proper protection under the islands' laws. Such a fear was explicitly described in the writings of Olaudah Equiano and in the cases taken up in England by the veteran campaigner Granville Sharp. There were poor communities of escaped slaves in London who scraped a living in the shadows, constantly fearing exposure and apprehension, or depended on eking out a living by begging – anything to avoid a return to the plantations. It is impossible to estimate how many of those runaways who feature in Scottish newspapers were under the threat of being taken out of the country. According to Robert Sheddan, Jamie Montgomery had escaped from him several times. The last time, argued Montgomery's lawyer, was a direct result of being threatened with being returned to Virginia.[32] Robert Gray, Procurator Fiscal of the Baillie Court, told the court that Montgomery had been a faithful servant until the petitioners plotted to carry him forcibly out of the country, adding significantly that they planned 'to make a penny of him, reducing him again to slavery', thus clearly differentiating his situation in Beith from that in the colonies.[33]

In the case of Joseph Knight it was not the prospect of returning to Jamaica that caused him to seek his freedom, although in 1773 he related to magistrates at Wedderburn's house a conversation less than twelve months previously in which Sir John, according to Knight, 'said that he would not give him his freedom here because he would starve as no body would employ him but that he would give him his freedom in Jamaica and a house and some ground'. In fact, Knight claimed that a promise had been made on the occasion of his baptism, to the effect that he would be given his freedom seven years hence, 'if he behaved well'. In all probability there were two motives behind Knight's bid for freedom. Despite his financial generosity, Wedderburn had dismissed Knight's wife Annie Thomson when he discovered that she was pregnant. He then refused Knight's request for her to be taken back, or for a house nearby in which they could live together. Knight, it seems, simply wanted to live with his wife and slavery, in contrast to serfdom, did not carry such a right.[34] In addition the Somerset decision in the south, despite its legal limitations and Mansfield's constant claim that he did not rule for freedom, encouraged the impression that no one could any longer be held in slavery in Britain. Joseph Knight had clearly thought this from his reading the details of the case in the Scottish newspapers.[35]

Wedderburn met this bid for freedom by securing a judgement by local magistrates known to him who, meeting in his house, not surprisingly upheld his claim to Knight's service. Knight appealed to the Sheriff Substitute of Perth, William Mercer, and both he and the Sheriff Depute of Perth, John Swinton, in February 1774 dismissed Wedderburn's claim. Just under four years later, after numerous legal wrangles, the Court of Session, by an eight-to-four majority of the judges, confirmed Swinton's judgement, which had been stated in the following terms:

> That the state of slavery is not recognised by the laws of this Kingdom, and is inconsistent with the principles thereof, and finds that the regulations in Jamaica concerning slaves, do not extend to this Kingdom, and repels the master's claim for perpetual service.

The report in the Edinburgh *Caledonian Mercury* of 17 January 1778 was positively ecstatic. It observed that 'the rights of humanity were weighed in the scales of justice' and continued that 'it must give a very high satisfaction to the inhabitants of the United Kingdom, that the freedom of Negroes has obtained its first *general determination* in the Supreme Civil Court of Scotland'.[36]

BAPTISED SLAVES IN CHRISTIAN SCOTLAND

When James Boswell and Samuel Johnson were leaving Monboddo House in 1773 they were escorted to the road by Lord Monboddo's black slave 'Gory'. 'When Gory was going to leave us,' records Boswell, 'Mr. Johnson called to him. "Mr. Gory, give me leave to ask you a question. Are you baptised?" Gory told him he was and confirmed by the Bishop of Durham.'[37] This may have been no more than a pious enquiry by Johnson, a devout Anglican churchman. However, it could well have been much more, for Johnson was passionately opposed to slavery and had made constant enquiries from London about the progress of the Knight case, even directing Boswell to subscribe on his behalf to the slave's legal costs.[38] The veteran man of letters may have seen that in the issue of baptism there was a potential Achilles heel for the whole institution.

Not that this was immediately evident in his own land. For whilst a slave baptism was a great social occasion, a feather in the cap of any missionary and widely understood to confer automatic freedom, no magistrate would allow it.[39] In fact, Christianity when absorbed by London's black community could be a brake on black unrest. Religion provided comfort and hope to many slaves and was also seen to have a socially pacifying effect. But even so, the fears of the master class about the dangers of Christianity were as real in England as in the West Indies. Sir John Fielding wrote in 1768 about the increasing numbers of black men and women who band together in societies 'to corrupt and dissatisfy the mind of every black servant that comes to England; first by getting themselves christened or married, which they inform them, makes them free, though it has been decided otherwise by the judges'.[40]

Yet the law of England appeared to be unclear, even confused. In the case of *Smith* v *Gould* in 1706, Chief Justice Holt held that 'no man can have property in another' and Sir William Blackstone, in his well-known legal commentary, declared 'that a slave or Negro, the instant he lands in England, becomes a freeman'. Paradoxically, several paragraphs later on he also declared that, although 'the slave is entitled to the same protection in England before as after baptism', whatever service 'the heathen negro' owed to his master in the colonies, 'the same (whatever it be) is he bound to render when brought to England and made a Christian'.[41] A crucial view was that given in 1729 by Attorney General Philip Yorke and Solicitor General Charles Talbot in response to enquiries by a West Indian delegation. The opinion was given, as stated in the preamble, 'in order to rectify a vulgar error, that slaves became free by their being in England and Ireland, or from being baptised', that a master's property or right in his slave is not 'determined or varied' by the slave coming to Great Britain or Ireland, 'and that baptism doth not bestow freedom on him, or make any alteration in his temporary condition in these kingdoms'.[42] In 1741 the Bishop of London, Richard Terrick, declared with respect to slaves that 'the freedom which Christianity gives is a freedom from the bondage of sin and satan – but as to their outward condition, whatever that was before, whether bond or free, their being baptized and becoming Christians, makes no manner of change in it'.[43]

Yet the Yorke and Talbot judgement of 1729 did not provide the final clarification that the West Indians had hoped for. In the forty-three years between 1729 and 1772 further decisions added even more confusion. Lord Mansfield's verdict left the relationship between slaves and masters unclear. The wily old London Scot, who had a young black girl, 'Dido', in his own household, wanted to avoid any determination and said as an aside that he would rather that all masters in England would believe their slaves to be free and all slaves hold the opposite view. David Brion Davis claimed that, by this era, 'the growing consensus on baptism effectively eliminated the plea of religion as an excuse for enslavement', but that was perhaps somewhat optimistic for the English situation at that time.[44]

Yorke and Talbot's opinion may have been noted in Scotland, but their writ did not extend beyond the border and they had no authority in this land. The Sheriff Substitute of Perth, William Mercer, to whom Knight had first appealed the magistrates' decision, ruled that 'the petitioner has as good right to the protection of the law as any other subject, being a Christian and married in this country'. David Spens had earlier made the sharp distinction between his former status and the baptised state, which he had recently entered, but Sir John Wedderburn recognised in a submission to Mercer that this was a Pandora's box. He referred to Joseph Knight's baptism shortly after his arrival in Scotland and to 'the infamous and unchristian practice of withholding baptism from Negro servants lest they should gain their liberty', but then immediately cited Blackstone in support of the view that the sacrament left a slave's civil status unaltered.[45] Likewise, David Dalrymple in his 1760 Petition declared that he 'readily agreed' to his slave's request for baptism, 'having no imagination that it would afford him any handle for claiming his liberty'.[46] Robert Sheddan, however, was far less sure of this, as is shown in a written statement to Lord Bankton in June 1756:

> My reasons for opposing [Jamie's baptism] were I was sensible his desirte [sic] of the sacrament of Baptizm did not proceed from any good disposition in him or desire to get free from the bondage of sin and death but that he wanted to make a handle of it to do me an injustice by attempting to free himself of my lawful service being mine lawfully bought of Mr. Joseph Hawkins in Virginia. Also I suspected he would be worse which has really happened. Our minister and elders when instructing him often informed him that his duty as a Christian was to be faithful to his master how far he has observed their instructions his conduct has already determined.[47]

The minister of Beith at the time was John Witherspoon, later to become President of Princeton University and subsequently a signatory to the American Declaration of Independence in 1776. He instructed Montgomery in Christianity and publicly baptised him 'in prefence [sic] of the congregation' of Beith. Sheddan's Declaration and the Memorial for him on 9 July 1756 both confirm his strong opposition to Jamie's baptism, adding that his opposition came 'not so much from any fear of the civil effects thereof, as for the fancies of freedom which it might instil into his slave'. Sheddan further claimed that the baptism took place 'at the pressing instances of the Negro', and that perhaps indicates the way in which the imperatives of Christianity in a nation such as Scotland took precedence over the expressed wishes of a master.

Sheddan reported to Lord Bankton that Jamie Montgomery-Sheddan, as he now was, had been given caveats about obedience to his master and that Jamie had been told 'again and again' by Witherspoon 'that his baptism by no means freed him from his servitude'.[48] But there is no evidence to show that the minister drummed this into him and it may well have been wishful thinking by the master. Curiously his baptism is not recorded in the Beith parish records of that year. Yet it was on 19 April 1756, the day before he was due, against his will, to be taken to Port Glasgow, that Jamie obtained a certificate from Witherspoon stating 'that James Montgomery, since his baptism, has behaved in an orderly manner, free from public scandal, or ground of church censure, so that he may be received as a member of any Christian society where Providence shall order his lot'.[49] Nothing in that text challenged Montgomery's status as a slave. However, if Jamie had persuaded the minister to baptise him against his master's will, he clearly had Witherspoon's confidence. It would have been strange if Witherspoon had not known of Sheddan's intention to transport Jamie back to Virginia, since the latter claimed to have refused to go on two occasions. This being so, and despite Sheddan's assertion about the minister's warnings to the slave regarding his duty, it is hard to see that this certificate, issued as it was the day before the slave was dragged to Port Glasgow, was not something of a *laissez passé* to assist his freedom.

A Kirk elder and local farmer, John Henderson, provided the main support to David Spens in his bid for freedom. Dr David Dalrymple claimed that the farmer 'thought it proper to put into the negro's head that Baptism by the law of this country would emancipate him from his servitude' and he claimed damages and expenses from Henderson.[50] Spens, in the protest served on Dalrymple the day after he had left his house, had threatened his master with the recovery of any damages or expenses for any of his Christian friends who might have to take legal action to assist and protect him from being re-enslaved. Such was the popular support for Spens locally that Henderson's statement that if he was returned to slavery 'the whole country would be inflamed', may not have been a wild assertion. The slave's counsel and agent agreed to act for him without fee and two Writers to the Signet, Walter Ferguson and William Chalmers, undertook to find caution (bail) of £30 for his release.[51] It was reported that the salters and miners in that part of Fife also contributed to his costs.[52] The Kirk Session records of Wemyss Parish Church for 1771 contain a reference to 'a collection having been made in this and some neighbouring parishes for the Negro lad publicly baptised in this parish Church in September 1769 by the name of David Spens'. The minister, Dr Harry Spens, after whom David was named, requested the Kirk Session to receive the balance of the collection from Henderson and William Cornfoot of Balfour, and use it for the benefit of the now free David.[53] Once again there is no evidence that the parish minister directedly assisted a slave to escape, but the speed with which certification of baptism was followed by a bid for freedom, and the minister's key role within a community so supportive of David's liberty, leads to more than a suspicion of collusion.

CHRISTIANITY, FREEDOM AND THE COURTS

The crucial issue was not how did individuals, ministers or Kirk Sessions view slavery in the light of Christian baptism, but how did the civil courts. In his Petition of 3 March 1770 for the recovery of David Spens, David Dalrymple claimed that he had no idea that baptism would make any difference to 'Black Tom's situation, 'as it is established by law and practice of England and the West Indies that baptism has no effect and there is no reason why it should'.[54] Dalrymple's death ended the case before this argument could be properly tested, but in 1775 Robert Cullen, in acting for Sir John Wedderburn, relied heavily on the Yorke and Talbot opinion and quoted Blackstone extensively to show that baptism brought no alteration in Joseph Knight's situation. Cullen went on to cite Lord Mansfield's judgement in the Somerset case, in which the judge

Figure 2 *A house in old Saltpans, near Wemyss, Fife built in the 1760s. David Spens, who was supported by the saltworkers, would have almost certainly have passed that way.*

concurred with the reaffirmation by Yorke (now Lord Hardwicke) in 1749 that 'there was no foundation' for supposing that baptism conferred freedom.[55] Several months earlier Cullen's colleague James Ferguson had spoken of 'a fancy, which enters into the heads of Negroes themselves when brought to this country', that baptism 'gives them a title to their freedom'. Ferguson may have remembered the certificate that featured in the Sheddan case, or he may have realised that this would be a key argument for the pursuer's counsel, for all that he tried to dismiss it as hardly deserving refutation and claimed that the pursuer did not trouble to make much of it in the initial pleading, so obvious was the point of law.[56] Joseph Knight's advocate,[57] Alan McConnochie, claimed that Wedderburn's counsel misinterpreted Blackstone and that 'many have thought that Baptism alone in a Christian country liberates from slavery'.[58] Certainly Scipio Kennedy did so half a century previously when he wrote, in 1725: 'I might have of freedom by the law, on account of embracing the religion of the country.'[59] That was of course four years before the Talbot and Yorke opinion.

Although those advocating freedom seemed unwilling to labour the obvious point that Talbot and Yorke and all that followed from their opinion was applicable only in English law, the defenders of slavery were anxious to show that in continental Europe, particularly in France, embracing Christianity through baptism made no change in the slave's situation. Robert Sheddan's counsel in 1756 stated 'and what puts the Weakness in Practice of this Claim of Freedom, as arising from the mere Ceremony of Baptism, in its true light is, that even where the *Turkish* Captives change their Religion among the *Spaniards* and are baptised, yet they do not thereby recover their Freedom'.

The lawyer continued to assert that although the *Code Noir* of Louis XIV, through which slavery was regulated in France, stated in Article 2 that '*tous les esclaves qui seront dans les isles seront baptisez et instruits dans la religion Catholique, Apostolique et Romane*', ('all the slaves who will be in the islands are to be baptised and instructed in the Catholic, Apostolic and Roman religion') yet in other articles provision is made for the presence of slaves, not just in the islands, but in France itself. It concluded that 'our own slaves are every day baptised in America; and indeed if the effects of Baptism were such as is contended for, it is believed that there would be very few Infidels in that part of the world'.[60]

In 1775 James Ferguson acting for Wedderburn used the same

sources when he stated that 'it never entered into the head of any of the nations of Europe that baptism was to convert a slave into a freeman'.[61] Nor was it in the minds of the Romans when Christianity became accepted in the Empire. So argued Sheddan's counsel, concluding that 'if it had been thought so, the Roman Empire would never have embraced Christianity, for it had in a great measure been a forfeiture of men of any substance in these days by withdrawing from them their property in slaves'.[62] Montgomery's advocate quoted a number of sources from the early Church to demonstrate that 'the manumissions of those days were usually performed in the Church, attended with considerable privileges'.[63] However, Sheddan's lawyers cited part of early Canon Law which had to be specially formulated to enforce the freedom of a slave 'who being neglected by his master had become a Bishop'. If that were needed, they concluded, it was obvious that manumission of ordinary baptised converts was hardly the norm in the early Church.[64]

Earlier Jamie Montgomery had claimed in the Bill of Advocation to Lord Bankton that being 'instructed in the Christian religion and baptized I am entitled to the rights and privileges of his Majesty's other subjects'.[65] In reality, did being under the protection of law negate the state of slavery and was this achieved by baptism? That was a point exercising the Lords of Session in 1778 and it clearly was not absolutely determined for Lord Bankton in 1756, as his note of 27 May indicates: 'the Lord Ordinary having considered the bill and answer it is not clear whether the Complainer after his receiv[ing] Babtism [sic] in this country still remained in a state of Slav[ery] declares that he will report th[is] case to the Lord[s] wit[hout] prejudice'.[66]

Obviously the issue of baptism was central to the claims of Spens, Montgomery and Knight, but it must be seen in the context of the general discussion of the compatibility of Christianity and slavery. Biblical references seemed to be overwhelmingly in favour of the institution, or at least of acceptance of the status quo. Not surprisingly the Old Testament featured strongly in the submissions made on behalf of Sheddan and Wedderburn.

The Memorial for Sheddan claimed that 'the strongest authority that can be adduced in support of this general proposition [the acceptability of slavery] arises from the Law of God'. It cited the particular verses from Exodus, Leviticus and Deuteronomy that dealt with the enslavement of Hebrews, commenting:

From these Authorities it is clear, that even among the *Hebrews*, who were GOD's peculiar People under his immediate Government, separated and set apart from other Nations, Slavery or Bondage was allowed; that they were not only permitted to have Slaves amongst the Heathen Nations, but even among themselves; that liberty was held to be a subject saleable; and that though the seventh Year was appointed as a Year of Jubilee, when such of the Hebrews as had sold themselves for Bond-men were to recover their Liberty, that Privilege was not granted to the Slaves or Bond-men of the Heathens; and that even a *Hebrew* Bond-man might renounce that Privilege and agree to remain his Master's Bondman during life.[67]

There is no doubt that the Old Testament provided plenty of ammunition for the defenders of black slavery. As Cullen noted, the law of Moses held no restrictions for those outside the community of faith that comprised the Hebrew people and terms such as 'heathen' and 'strangers' could easily refer to African slaves. Manumission of Hebrews who become slaves through debt or voluntary contract was, however, a much more sacred obligation than was implied by Cullen's statement. Perhaps the most significant injunction was the protection of all slaves, which provided for immediate manumission following the loss of a tooth or an eye through the violence of the master,[68] a point made much of in the emancipation campaign of the early nineteenth century.

The seventh-year release for those within the community of faith might seem to be a hostage to fortune in the hands of those who argued that permanent slavery was compatible with biblical teaching. Strangely, however, opponents of slavery did not attempt to exploit this. Although Joseph Knight, when examined by the magistrates at Ballandean, affirmed that 'Sir John about the time that he was baptized said he would give him his freedom seven years hence if he behaved well',[69] his counsel did not pursue the point. But Alan McConnochie in 1776 responded in these terms to Ferguson's Memorial for Wedderburn, in which Exodus and Leviticus had been cited as divine sanctions for slavery:[70] 'as to the law of Moses, it permitted many things to the Jews, on account of the hardness of their hearts, which are not to be held up as examples to other nations; but it is plain that their Lawgiver was sensible of the injustice of slavery and that he did all to soften it that he could venture to do, considering the nature of the people with whom he had to deal'.[71]

It was, however, over the writings of the New Testament and especially the Pauline epistles that the keenest disputes arose. James

Ferguson for Wedderburn stated that 'it is evident that our Saviour gave no authority for change and neither the Apostles nor the first Christians ever thought of making any alteration but left matters entirely on the old footing'.[72] This echoed the assertion from Sheddan's lawyers that 'the whole doctrine of the New Testament is not [to] invent new conditions for men, nor to throw down the rights that there were, but to inculcate in men contentment [for] their conditions'.[73]

The lawyers in the Sheddan case used the texts from Paul's letters to the Colossians and the Ephesians, where the apostle exhorted the obedience of slaves to earthly masters; from the letter to Timothy urging the honouring of a master; and from the letter to Titus advising submission to him. For them, the Pauline injunction to the Colossian Church for slaves to obey their masters was matched by the practical act of returning the runaway slave Onesimus to his master Philemon. The letter to the Ephesians compared the obedience of slaves to masters as to Christ. The letter to Timothy encouraged Christian slaves to honour their masters and so honour God and to Titus instructed him to bid slaves give honest submission to their master. The first letter of Peter instructed slaves to be obedient not just to good and gentle masters but to cruel ones as well, comparing this to the suffering of Christ. The letters to the Corinthians, Colossians and Galatians contain strong affirmations of common unity in Christ between slave and free. The latter elevated Christians from the status of slaves to sons of God and the apostle urged the Church in Rome not to fall from the 'spirit of adoption' to the 'spirit of bondage'.[74]

Not surprisingly, the Memorial for Montgomery turned to different texts. The first and only citing of a gospel passage within it contained the words from St John's gospel, 'and ye shall hear the truth and the truth shall make you free'. A more general quotation was taken from 2 Corinthians: 'where the spirit of the Lord is, there is liberty'. More tellingly, the lawyers moved to an early part of 1 Corinthians in which Paul advised Christians not to be 'servants of men'. They continued by quoting from the letter to the Galatians, with its ringing call to 'stand fast therefore in the liberty wherewith Christ has made us free and be not entangled again with the yoke of bondage'.[75]

One text that led to some dispute was the passage in 1 Corinthians in which Paul seemed to be ambivalent: 'Let every man abide in the same calling wherein he was called. Art thou called being a servant? Care not for it: but if thou mayest be made free, use it rather'.[76] Sheddan's counsel expressed the hope that the defence would not take refuge in the word 'Servant' in place of 'Slave'.[77] Montgomery's

counsel did not, even admitting that this seemed to support acceptance of slavery. But he argued that it in no way overturned the other
texts about freedom: 'much less', he said, it 'gives handle to the late
interpretation that has prevailed and to the distinction adopted by
some doctors and divines, betwixt the spiritual and personal slavery',
maintaining that the manumissions in the early Church showed that
these could not be separated.[78] This may have been in response to a
margin note by Sheddan in his Petition to the Edinburgh Baillies that
read – 'whereas by the freedom purchased for us by Christ is plainly
understood, a freedom, of a spiritual sense viz. from the slavery and
bondage of sin, as is observed by Mr. Le Clerc and other commentators'.[79] Robert Gray, the Procurator Fiscal to the Baillie Court, in
representing Montgomery dismissed this as 'having no connection
with the cause', and turned the division between spiritual and social
the other way, arguing that Ephesians 6:5 had no effect on civil or
municipal laws.[80] Freedom as a spiritual or civic state was to become
a key issue in the debates on slavery for most of the next century and
beyond. It arose again in 1775, when James Ferguson quoted the
verse in 1 Corinthians in full, including the words 'for he that is called
in the Lord being a servant is the Lord's freeman',[81] and adding:

> After this it is surely impossible to say that any change was made by the
> introduction of Christianity with regard to this in particular and indeed it
> was never the doctrine of our holy religion to encroach on any particular
> upon order or government, or to change the condition of men, but on the
> contrary to make them contented with their lott [sic] and to act their parts
> with propriety and che[a]rfulness in that situation where providence has
> placed them.[82]

ENLIGHTENMENT THINKING IN COURT AND STIRRINGS AGAINST THE SLAVE TRADE

A curious defence of the ethical foundation for present conditions was
offered by Robert Sheddan's lawyers, who said 'men may talk of
abstract Rights or Wrongs as they please; but what Mankind in general
concur in, is generally right: and therefore according to those
Principles, we find that slavery has at one time or another been adopted
by almost every nation under the sun'.[83] In the same way, Robert
Ferguson argued two decades later that slavery was neither contrary to
the law of nature or nations and that it was supported by the laws and
practices of almost all nations, 'which are the best commentary upon
the Law of Nature'.[84]

As we have seen, the opponents of slavery in these cases did not attempt to use scriptural texts for their case and admitted the acceptance, in part at least, of the institution of slavery in the ancient world. What they did was to claim that the spirit of Christianity weakened and would eventually destroy slavery and that where its influence spread in Europe, civilised practice prevailed. In this they depended much on Scottish legal commentators who in turn had been influenced by the ideas of Moderate churchmen. The most specific expression of this was by Alan McConnochie, when he summed up that part of the case in April 1776:

> As to Christianity, it is indisputable that slavery is inconsistent with the principles and spirit of it. It is extremely true that Jesus Christ and the Apostles, did not, in express terms, declare against it and the reason is obvious: The propagation of Christianity was to be accompanied not by means sudden and violent, but gradual and gentle. Christ and his Apostles therefore, did not arraign the injustice of slavery in direct terms, but as the very purpose of the gospel was to procure *peace on earth and goodwill to men, of every nation, kindred, tongue and people* and as it required the practice of the purest morality in this world, as an indispensible [sic] condition of obtaining happiness in the next; its doctrines sapped the very foundations of slavery, so that wherever the one was perfectly established, the other could not but fall of course. Accordingly, in fact, we learn from history, that it was the influence of Christianity that banished it from the several countries of Europe; but soon after, the western world was, unhappily for mankind, discovered by an adventurous Genoese and the avarice of men being whetted by the prospect of gain, became too strong for the restraints of religion; the consequence of which was, that a new species of slavery was established in the continent of America and the adjacent islands.[85]

The last part of that paragraph owes, as McConnochie freely acknowledges, a debt to the eminent historian and churchman William Robertson, who in a sermon in 1755, claimed that it was not the authority of 'any single precept in the gospel, but the spirit and genius of Christian religion, more powerfully laying a particular command, which hath abolished the practice of slavery throughout the world'. Robertson admitted that the continued existence of slavery in the colonies seemed to contradict this, but he further argued that the revival of an institution 'which Christianity had utterly abolished' indicated an unchristian devotion to avarice and 'must be charged upon the corruption of the human heart, not upon the religion that testifies against it'.[86] McConnochie further cited Robertson to support the contention that the equality of all men under God was inconsistent with servitude. He noted that the historian also recognised the strength of the institution. In the first volume of his *History of the Reign of the Emperor Charles V*, Robertson spoke of the humane spirit of the Christian religion as it 'struggled with the maxims and manners of the world – and contributed more than any other circumstances to introduce the practice of manumission'.[87] McConnochie underlined the last sentence of the quotation and went on to argue that that if Christianity was so opposed to the system of servitude known in Europe as villeinage, it would hardly be less so to the harsher system endured by negroes. And he asked:

> Will the common law of this country, which supposing villeinage did exist, adopted every method to put an end to it and which has embraced the purest form and doctrines of Christianity as its greatest honour and support, will our common law, I say, admit of a new institution so adverse to its former practice and to the spirit of our religion?[88]

Those who argued for liberty were not slow to distance themselves from ancient or English legal practice and to cite Scottish legal authorities to affirm the unique nature of the nation's law. Montgomery's counsel argued that 'it will be a vain and fruitless attempt to maintain slavery upon the ancient laws of nations which never were received unto the law of Scotland'.[89] Knight's lawyer not only stated that English law was irrelevant to the case, but cited Mackenzie's claim that Roman law on slavery had no relevance to Scotland. Sheddan's counsel claimed that the seventeenth-century lawyer Fletcher of Saltoun 'held it [slavery] not inconsistent with the rights of a free government'.[90] Ferguson, for Wedderburn, bracketed Fletcher with Plato, Cicero and Thomas More, stating that these 'have all considered the institution of slavery as a proper ingredient in a perfect government',[91] but no other Scottish jurist was quoted by the slave-owners' lawyers. The most that was claimed by them was that the citing of Lord Stair, Sir George Mackenzie and Lord Bankton on whether slavery existed in Scotland was not relevant to the case of *Sheddan* v *Sheddan*.[92]

For Robert Gray, however, it was highly relevant. 'There is no such thing as slavery in this country,' he said and claimed Lord Bankton in support of this. On the margin of the documents he added 'Stair' and 'Mackenzie', and continued: 'and slavery has been so much discountenanced by the Court of Session that in a case where one by action became bound to serve another for life or three [times] nineteen years

(Decr. 1728 Alan Skene) the same was found to be *pactum illicitum*, contrary to natural law, void and null'.[93]

Alan McConnochie in his various representations for Knight claimed that Lord Stair clearly saw the law of Scotland to be averse to slavery, that only traces of absolute slavery remain in most Christian countries and that in Scotland there was no such thing. Again he repeated Mackenzie's dismissal of the very possibility of slavery in Scotland because it was contrary to Christian liberty to make slaves of men in a Christian country.[94]

From all this it might be assumed that an unassailable case had been made. However, the sanctity of property and trade were not to be dismissed so easily. Dr David Dalrymple claimed that he had 'the sole and undoubted rights to the said Negro's service and slavery and may order and dispose of him as his own property'.[95] He was far from alone in Scotland, as the advertisements for runaway slaves indicate. Robert Sheddan, in his submission to Lord Bankton to be permitted to send Montgomery to Virginia, argued that 'slavery or bondage has been received and practiced where the public good requires it and such is the case your Lordship knows with our American plantations where it is absolutely necessary'.[96] Ferguson echoed this by detailing the necessity of slave labour in the colonies, without which the vital sugar trade would collapse.[97]

If James Ferguson attempted to win over the Court towards accepting slavery by showing the damaging effects of its abolition on trade, Alan McConnochie by contrast brought before the judges extensive descriptions from various European sources of the cruel and illegitimate methods involved in the slave trade. The justification of this on commercial grounds implies, he claimed, that 'justice and morality are empty sounds', and continued:

> If one nation can enslave another, in order to get sugar and tobacco; surely one individual may rob another in order to get these commodities, or the money with which they are purchased. Every argument that justifies slavery subverts the first principles of morality: and it would be well for the nations who engage in the slave trade, that they had considered this before they began it, for the experience of past ages has demonstrated the truth of this maxim, that honesty is the best policy; and that it is as applicable to nations as to individuals, if a healthful political longevity and not a short feverish existence be their object and aim.[98]

Some of these same arguments would be part of the campaign against the slave trade a decade further on. Henry Dundas, the

Lord Advocate, at the hearing before the judges in 1776, declined to
make a value judgement on the African slave trade, though he admitted to 'very great improprieties and even villanies' within it. He dismissed the validity of taking authority from the practice of ancient
nations and even if there had been slavery in Scotland in the past, he
declared that it had nothing to do with the present, claiming that
'there was not now a slave in Britain, nor could possible be from its
constitution'.[99]

THE JUDGES DECIDE

In 1778 the Court of Session finally made its decision in the case of
Joseph Knight, confirming the Sheriff of Perthshire's judgement that
in Scotland there was no such thing as slavery and that Sir John
Wedderburn of Ballandean had no right to force Knight to remain in
his service. The result had been eagerly anticipated by many. The
Caledonian Mercury commented that 'on no such occasion . . . did
our Bench display more learning and ability', no doubt seeking to
please its readers by such a commendation. However, it was by a
majority of eight to four and, as the legal historian John Cairns
observed, not quite 'so resoundingly in favour of freedom as one
might expect'.[100] Yet the four judges who voted for Wedderburn's
right to Knight's perpetual service did so with a determination that
the newspaper described as 'softened and guarded'. Three of them –
Lords Monboddo, Elliock and Covington – specifically stressed that
in his treatment of a slave, a master was bound to abide by the laws
of Scotland and that Wedderburn could not exercise his right over
Knight contrary to these. Others regarded the fact that the harsh laws
of Jamaica held no validity in Scotland as a conclusive argument for
Knight's emancipation. Lord Braxfield observed that Wedderburn's
right to property under Jamaican law depended on violence, since the
young Knight did not become a slave by consent, crime or war. Lord
Westhall, who declared himself 'for liberty in the fullest extent',
would not even consider that a non-native of Jamaica should be
subject to the laws of that island, let alone those of Scotland. Lord
Kennet stated that 'there is no equity in that law concerning Negroes',
and Lord Kames claimed that 'slavery is a forced state – for we are all
naturally equal'. Lord Auchinleck, the father of James Boswell, went
further and declared that slavery was consistent with neither humanity nor Christianity.

Hailes agreed with Yorke and Talbot's opinion on baptism and he was the only judge to mention it. He declared himself reluctant to introduce scripture in a court of law, but quoted a Christian slave Euelpistus on trial in the second century who asserted that he was *servus et liberte donatus*. Hailes regarded this as what he called 'orthodox theology', but it was the injustice of the possible return to the colonies and separation of the family that convinced the judge to vote for freedom. Monboddo was the only one to quote St Paul – 'servants obey your masters' – and declared that 'religion says nothing against slavery'. Braxfield mentioned Jewish law when he weighed up the question, but dismissed it as inapplicable to the present day. The Lord Justice Clerk observed that slavery was 'contrary to the spirit, although not to the enactments of our religion', but his main reason for voting against Wedderburn was that Scottish law did not allow for service without wages and in this he was joined by Gardenstone.[101]

When the *Caledonian Mercury* reported the verdict, it paid tribute to the man who had made the first moves to give Knight freedom:

> To the honour of John Swinton Esquire; Sheriff-Depute of Perthshire, it must be observed, that the vote which carried by the ten judges [in fact it was eight to four], was *remit simplicitur* to him, or in other words to *affirm* his interlocutor, which was in the following clear and comprehensive terms: 'Finds that the state of slavery is not recognised by the laws of this Kingdom and is inconsistent with the principles thereof and finds that the regulations in Jamaica concerning slaves, do not extend to this Kingdom and repels the master's claim for perpetual service'.[102]

THEOLOGY, HUMANITY AND LEGAL INDEPENDENCE

The use of scriptural passages was not a major weapon in the argument over slavery in Scotland, but this did not mean that religious ideas and concepts were insignificant in the three cases before the Court of Session in the eighteenth century. In England, courts may have been able to separate religion and the law in relation to property rights, but Scotland was a land where religion and theological discussion were far more deeply embedded in the mainstream of educated thinking. It would therefore have been surprising if some discussion of Christian teaching did not play a prominent part in its courts. When this was allied to Enlightenment thinking, it may well have been one of the most important influences in the 1778 decision. The 1707 Union settlement had preserved the distinctiveness of the Scottish legal system and Scotland's judges were very sensitive to this and to their own position within it. Even the most ardent defender of the British constitution would be found vigorously resisting any implication that the law of another land would determine the decisions of a Scottish court. Above all, there was a general feeling that slavery was simply wrong. It was a perception that was not limited to any class or social group. Despite the commercial pressures on the profitability of slavery, there was a substantial degree of support for the idea that a black man had the same rights in Scotland as any other, and this view was reflected in the highest court of the land.

In the final stages of the Knight case an interesting theological division was to be seen amongst the judges. More than half of the speeches from the Lords of Session included references to the concepts of liberty, natural equality, humanity, brotherhood and the spirit of contemporary religion, and these were offered in support of Knight. Those whose summaries made literal use of scripture were defenders of Wedderburn's claim. Monboddo, a pedantic and dogmatic debater, quoted Paul on the duties of slaves to their masters, of which he of course was one. Covington declared that the argument about slavery being contrary to the state of nature was not just erroneous, but a blasphemous attack on God's law, which clearly taught otherwise, and it challenged, in his view, the scriptures of both the Old and New Testaments.

In the later stages of the campaign against slavery it was evangelical churchmen who turned unashamedly to a detailed biblical analysis and used it to mount an attack on the very foundations of the institution in the British Empire. Yet even at this time, to allow slavery to continue in Scotland, especially on the grounds of biblical literalism, would have been to fly in the face of the spirit of the times. It was an age that rated benevolence as a prime virtue and which was influenced strongly by ideas such as Robertson's 'gentle spirit of Christianity'. Such property in human beings, especially in those who had embraced the Christian religion and its association with the human traffic from Africa to the colonies, stood in sharp contrast to all this. It was a blot on the landscape of a society which saw itself as enlightened and, in contrast to its self-deprecating past, its intellectuals believed now in the progress of humanity and the development of civilisation.

The judges were strongly influenced by the national pride in their nation's law. Even Hailes, who took what he called 'the famous opinion of Talbot and Yorke' as his 'text' and was ambiguous over the status of a black person in Britain, concluded that there was enough in Scottish law to bar slavery.[103] We have already noted

Viscount Stair's observation on this. Sir George Mackenzie, Stair's contemporary, had stated clearly that 'we have little use in Scotland of what the Roman law teaches concerning slavery; for we as Christians, allow no men to be made slaves, that being contrary to Christian liberty'.[104] In the mid-eighteenth century, Lord Bankton, then the advocate James McDowall, claimed that although slavery 'was anciently our law', it had for a long time been banished throughout Christendom 'as inconsistent with Christian liberty'.[105] There were no ringing declarations of support for the views of Stair or Mackenzie in 1778, but in many of the comments there was a jealous concern to judge by the precepts of Scottish law and not to allow the laws of other countries, and in particular that of Jamaica, to play a determining role in the final judgement.

Some of the judges were concerned about property rights and service without wages. But they were also concerned about what Sheriff Swinton described as 'the regulations in Jamaica, concerning slaves' and by association the conditions attending the slave trade that supplied so much of its human cargo to that island. Alan McConnochie had done his research well and the intense interest in the case guaranteed that there would be a wide audience amongst Scotland's intelligentsia who would absorb the horror stories which he unfolded for them. Nothing like that had featured in the Somerset case in England. Parliament had not yet set up a committee to investigate the trade and the published works of Ramsay and Clarkson did not appear until the next decade. The full implications of the 'middle passage' would not make an impact on the Scottish public for another ten years, but the ground was being laid.

Baptism in the Church of Scotland is a public act. When Mr Gory was baptised by the Bishop of Durham in the Anglican tradition it might well have been at Lord Monboddo's home. However, Scipio Kennedy and Joseph Knight would most probably have made a profession of faith in the face of a congregation and in the context of a community, as we know for certain that Jamie Montgomery and David Spens had done. It was, for them and other baptised slaves, a significant rite of passage within the local community. The support from the local Kirk Session has already been noted in the Spens case. Montgomery's Certificate of Christian Conduct reflected some measure of involvement in the congregation of Beith, even if simply by regular attendance at worship, and would have provided him with an entry to congregations elsewhere. There is not enough evidence to claim that baptism in Scotland provided automatic immunity to re-enslavement; but the public involvement in such an act, over against the more private English practices, meant an exposure to local communities wherein the assumption of fundamental freedoms were growing and against which black slavery jarred.

Baptism apart, there are several recorded instances of local people rallying in support of a slave or a former slave who had become part of community and little evidence that race acted as a brake to this humanity. In the graphic account of the cruelties suffered by Ned Johnston, it was the neighbouring community who rescued him and helped him to escape to Glasgow. Peter Burnett, a runaway slave from Virginia, became in the 1780s a weaver in Paisley, with great acceptability amongst that radical community, and was a close friend of the local poet Robert Tannahill's family.[106] When Thomas Jenkins, another ex-slave, was debarred by a cautious Kirk Session from being offered a teaching post in the Borders, it was the local people who expressed their solidarity by paying his salary.[107] Nowhere was this phenomenon perhaps more dramatically demonstrated, however, than by the report of the miners and salters of Wemyss collecting from their meagre resources to subscribe to David Spens' cause.

The reality, as we have seen from advertisements in the press prior to 1778, was often somewhat different from the theory, as it was with the involvement in the slave trade and plantation slavery of those who were living within an enlightened culture. There is no doubt about the leading role that Scots played in the establishment of slavery in the British Empire. But the Knight judgement and the thinking surrounding it was to make a strong impact on a nation that would, ten years later, begin to play an equally significant part in the campaign to rid that same Empire of its worst legacy.

Notes

1 Dr David Dalymple of Lindifferen and William Aytoun Writer to the Signet, Petition to the Court of Session, 3 Mar 1770. NAS CS 236/D/4/3.
2 Wemyss Parish Church, Baptismal Records, 10 Sep 1769. NAS OPR 459/3.
3 Dalrymple, Petition.
4 A. S. Cunningham, *Rambles in the Parishes of Scoonie and Wemyss* (Leven, 1905), pp. 154–6.
5 At this time, the ministers of the national church of Scotland tended to belong to one of two unofficial, yet divided, groups, ensuring there was often a power struggle for key university posts and for the office of

Moderator of the Kirk's General Assembly. It is difficult to describe them without caricature, although there was plenty of that on both sides. The 'Moderates' tended to emphasise the 1690 settlement guaranteeing state support for Presbyterianism, whereby ministers were appointed by the crown through a system of patronage. Many Moderates, however, embraced a more liberal theological position in common with the ideas of the Enlightenment and resisted the fervour or 'enthusiasm' for revival that often characterised the 'Popular' or 'Evangelical' party. The latter were keen on mission and evangelism, took a more literal view of the Bible, and were increasingly restless over patronage and aspects of the state connection. See John R. McIntosh, *Church and Theology in Enlightenment Scotland: The Popular Party 1740–1800* (East Lothian, 1998) and R. Sher, *Church and University in the Scottish Enlightenment: The Moderate Literati in Edinburgh* (Edinburgh, 1985)

6 James Walvin, *The Black Presence: A Documentary History of the Negro in England, 1555–1860* (London, 1971). Professor Walvin cautions against taking this figure as more than a guide – no census returns are available.

7 Ailsa Muniments. NAS GD 25/9/72/9.

8 James Dalrymple, Viscount Stair, *Institutions of the Law of Scotland*, ed. D. M. Walker (Edinburgh, [1681] 1981), Book 1, Title 3, pp. 98–9.

9 John Kincaid to James Watson, 28 Aug 1744. NAS GD 150/3526/25.

10 W. Orr, 'Slave Labours' *The Scotsman*, weekend 30 Jun 1982, p. 2.

11 James Boswell, *Journal of a Tour to the Hebrides with Samuel Johnson*, F. Bottle and C. Bunet, eds (New York, [1785] 1961), p. 58.

12 Discharge Accounts of the Estate of the Duke of Gordon, 1762. NAS GD 44/51/80/2.

13 *EEC*, 6 Sep 1760, 31 Mar 1764, 8 Jun 1768, 5 Apr 1773.

14 Mary Edwards, *Who Belongs to Glasgow?* (Glasgow, 1993), p. 17.

15 *EA*, 20 Jan 1769.

16 *EEC*, 27 Sep 1766, 6 Dec 1766, 30 Aug 1766.

17 Elspeth King, *The Hidden History of Glasgow's Women* (Edinburgh, 1993).

18 *EEC*, 9 Jan 1773, 22 Jun 1771.

19 *EEC*, 3 Sep 1776.

20 George Wallace, *A System of the Principles of the Law of Scotland* (Edinburgh, 1760), p. 67.

21 Answers for Montgomery, 19 May 1756. NAS CS 234/S3/12.

22 *EEC*, 7 Mar 1721.

23 Cunningham, *Rambles in the Parishes of Scoonie and Wemyss*, p. 156.

24 Museum of Scotland. Exhibit P28/H.MR 3.

25 Orr, 'Slave Labours', p. 2.

26 Kincaid to Watson.

27 'Contract betwixt Sir John Kennedy & Scipio Kennedy his Servant for 19 years', Ailsa Muniments. NAS GD 25/9/72/9.
28 Dalymple, Petition.
29 Discharge Accounts, 27 Jul 1762.
30 Sir John Wedderburn's Memorial (Defender against Joseph Knight, a Negro, Pursuer), Feb 1775. NAS CS 235/K/2/2, p. 9.
31 Robert Sheddan, Petition to the Baillies, 19 May 1756. NAS CS 234/53/12.
32 Answers for Sheddan on Bill of Advocation, May 1756. NAS CS 234/S3/12, Box 165.6.
33 Answers for Montgomery, Box 165.6.
34 Memorial for Joseph Knight, late Servant to Sir John Wedderburn of Ballandean, Bart. in the Process of Advocation against him at Sir John's instance. NAS CS 235/K/2/2.
35 Memorial for Wedderburn.
36 CM, 17 Jan 1778.
37 Boswell, Journal of a Tour to the Hebrides, p. 58.
38 James Boswell, Life of Johnson, ed. R.W. Chapman (Oxford, [1791]1953).
39 Walvin, The Black Presence, p. 14.
40 J. Fielding, Penal Laws (London, 1768), pp. 144–5.
41 Sir William Blackstone, Commentaries on the Laws of England (Oxford, 1786), Book. 1, p. 424.
42 Walvin, The Black Presence, pp. 94–5.
43 Quoted in 'A letter from one of the Windward Islands', 24 Dec 1740, Gentleman's Magazine, Vol. 11 (1741), p. 147.
44 David Brion Davis, The Problem of Slavery in the Age of Revolution, 1773–1823 (Ithaca, NY, 1975), p. 479.
45 Extract Process, 22 Dec 1773. NAS CS 235/K/2/2, pp. 16, 23, 24.
46 Dalrymple, Petition.
47 Robert Sheddan, Declaration, 22 Jun 1756. NAS CS 234/S3/12.
48 Bill of Advocation on behalf of James Montgomery, 22 May 1756. NAS CS 234/S3/12.1.
49 Memorial for James Montgomery-Sheddan, 23 Jul 1756. Session Papers, Campbell's Collection, Vol. 5.
50 Dalrymple, Petition.
51 Bond of Caution, 6 Mar 1770. NAS CS 236/D/4/3.
52 Cunningham, Rambles in the Parishes of Scoonie and Wemyss, p. 56.
53 Wemyss Parish Church, Register of Discipline, 21 Dec 1771. NAS CH 2/365/6 256.
54 Dalrymple, Petition.
55 Information for John Wedderburn, Esq; of Ballandean, Defender; against Joseph Knight, a Negro, Pursuer, 4 Jul 1775. Advocates Library, Edinburgh, pp. 18, 32, 33.

56 Memorial for Wedderburn, p. 26.
57 In Scots law, an 'advocate' pleads a case in court. In England the term is 'barrister'.
58 Memorial for Knight, p. 30.
59 'Contract betwixt Sir John Kennedy & Scipio Kennedy'.
60 Memorial for Robert Sheddan of Morricehill, late Merchant in Glasgow, 9 Jul 1756. Session Papers, Campbell's Collection, Vol. 5, 9.
61 Memorial for Wedderburn, p. 26.
62 Answers for Sheddan, NAS CS 234/S3/12.3.
63 Memorial for Montgomery-Sheddan, p. 8.
64 Memorial for Sheddan, p. 9.
65 Bill of Advocation on behalf of Montgomery.
66 Note by Lord Bankton, 22 May 1756. NAS WRH CS 234/S3/12.
67 Memorial for Sheddan, p. 6.
68 Leviticus 25:44–6, Exodus 21:2, 26–7.
69 Extract of Process, 15 Nov 1773. NAS CS 235/K/2/2, p. 9.
70 Memorial for Wedderburn, p. 26.
71 Additional Information for Joseph Knight, p. 20.
72 Memorial for Wedderburn, p. 26.
73 Memorial for Sheddan, p. 9.
74 Colossians 3:22; Ephesians 6:5; Titus 2:9; Philemon 10–19. Ephesians 6:5; 1 Timothy 6:1–2; 1 Peter 2:18–21. 1 Corinthians 12:13; Colossians 3:11; Galatians 3:28; Romans 8:15.
75 John 8:32; 2 Corinthians 3:17; 1 Corinthians 7:23; Galatians 5:1.
76 1 Corinthians 7:21–2.
77 Memorial for Sheddan, p. 9.
78 Memorial for Montgomery-Sheddan, p. 7.
79 Sheddan, Petition, p. 5.
80 Answers for Bill of Admonition, p. 4.
81 1 Corinthians 7:2.
82 Wedderburn, Court of Session Process, p. 28.
83 Memorial for Sheddan, p. 6.
84 Memorial for Wedderburn, p. 11.
85 Additional Information for Joseph Knight, 20 Apr 1776.
86 William Robertson, *The Situation of the World at the Time of Christ's Appearance and its Connection with the Success of His Religion Considered* (Edinburgh, 1755), pp. 41, 44.
87 William Robertson, *The History of the Reign of the Emperor Charles V*, 2 vols (Dublin, 1762), Vol. 1, note 20.
88 Memorial for Knight, p. 29.
89 Memorial for Montgomery-Sheddan, p. 6.
90 Memorial for Sheddan, p. 6.
91 Memorial for Wedderburn, p. 14.
92 Answers for Sheddan, p. 3.

93 Answers for Montgomery, p. 5.
94 Argument before Lord Kennet, 7 Feb 1775; Memorial for Knight, p. 30.
95 Dalrymple, Petition.
96 Answers for Sheddan, p. 3.
97 Memorial for Wedderburn, p. 16.
98 Additional Information for Joseph Knight, p. 20.
99 *CM*, 21 Feb 1776.
100 John Cairns, 'The Scottish Law of Slavery', unpublished lecture, University of Edinburgh, 6 Dec 2000.
101 M. P. Brown, ed., *Decisions of the Lords of Council and Session from 1766 to 1791*, collected by Lord Hailes (Edinburgh, 1826), pp. 777–9.
102 *CM*, 17 Jan 1778.
103 Brown, *Decisions*, pp. 776–8.
104 Sir George Mackenzie, *Institutions of the Law of Slavery*, second edition (Edinburgh, 1688), p. 20.
105 Quoted by Cairns, Lord Bankton, *An Institute of the Law of Scotland*, 3 vols (Edinburgh, 1751–4), Vol. 2, p. 68.
106 Angus Calder, 'Picture of a Hidden Past', *The Herald*, 18 Mar 2004.
107 Mark Duffil, 'Black Blood, White Skin', Radio Scotland, 12 Oct 2003.

2

THE LORDS AND THE PROFITS – WEST INDIAN COMMERCE AND THE SCOTTISH ENLIGHTENMENT

∾

> Jamaica indeed, is greatly indebted to North Britain, as a near one third of the inhabitants are either natives of that country, or descendants of those who were . . . such is their industry and address, that few of them have been disappointed.
>
> Edward Long, Jamaican planter, politician, historian,
> *History of Jamaica*, 1774

'Eighteenth century Scotland is an extraordinary case of a small society that developed a heavy economic commitment to slavery at the very time when its intelligentsia were vehemently criticising it.' So wrote Duncan Rice in the opening chapter of his book on the contribution of Scots to the abolitionist movement in the United States.[1] There certainly was extensive involvement of Scots in the slave trade and on the slave plantations of the Caribbean, from the great merchant houses of Glasgow and Scots entrepreneurs in London, through professionals in medicine, law, the army and government administration, to the managers and overseers of Scots estates whose owners were often at home. In contrast to that was the philosophical challenge to slavery amongst some of the leading thinkers of the Scottish Enlightenment, grounded on natural law, theories of human happiness and benevolence. Slavery was also critiqued from the standpoint of efficiency and profitability and this period saw the beginnings of a solid theological challenge on moral depravity and the perception that the enslavement of others contradicted Christianity.

Nonetheless there were those who proved to be significant exceptions. Though the majority of Scots in the West Indies remained uncritical of slavery, a few became leading opponents of the system. There were also variations amongst the attitudes of philosophers and some of their ideas were open to be taken and used by supporters of slavery. The economic needs and temptations amongst so many Scots to make a living and some to make a fortune, albeit in a very unhealthy physical and social environment, was almost bound to override other considerations. Loyalty to the values of their society was essential for employment, promotion or even survival, and this made it well-nigh impossible to think of challenging the system on which Caribbean prosperity and much else seemed to depend. Those who broke ranks did so almost always when they returned from the West Indies, which few of them regarded as a permanent home.

The tension between the commercial advantages of slavery, with its impact on the home economy, and the growing unease about its continuation in a 'civilised' society was, of course, a British and not simply a Scottish phenomenon. However, it was probably increased by the concentration of both commercial interests and intellectual thought in a small nation. And that, as we will see, resulted in disproportionate amounts of energy being expended in attacking and defending the question of slavery.

PLANTERS AND OPPORTUNISTS – QUICK MONEY AND NEW CAREERS

Edward Long's enthusiasm for the contribution of Scots to the development of Jamaica came at a time when Scottish involvement with the slave trade and Caribbean slavery was reaching unprecedented levels. In the last quarter of the eighteenth century, the number of estates on Jamaica that were owned and in many cases managed by Scots rose from less than 20 to nearly 30 per cent of the total. In a survey of residents in six northern Jamaican parishes compiled in 1804, Scots accounted for more than 29 per cent of the total population. These were spread through nine parishes on the island and in two, Hannover and St Thomas in the east, the percentage exceeded forty.[2] In the same year that Long published his history, Jamaica's wealth was estimated at over £28,000,000 out of just under £50,000,000 in the entire British Caribbean. The island accounted for 40 per cent of the slaves in the British West Indies and one historian has claimed that the island, 'during its heyday of stench and elegance, brought the Empire, in 1774, a clear profit of over £1.5 million and provided a more attractive outlet for capital than Britain itself could easily offer'.[3]

Scots sought their fortunes and contributed to the ownership and management of estates throughout the whole of the British West Indies during the eighteenth century. One-third of the land grants in St Kitts were made to Scotsmen, the majority of the white population of Tobago was of Scottish origin and of those who acquired estates in St Vincent in 1765, 26 per cent gave their place of residence as Glasgow.[4] An Edinburgh banker in the 1770s drew attention to 'the extensive speculations that were entered into by some Scotchmen for the purchase and cultivation of newly acquired West Indian islands'.[5] Not only did a number of Scots own estates in Grenada and St Lucia, but these islands were for a time governed by Scots, and when Janet Schaw, the 'Lady of Quality', visited Antigua in 1795, she dined with a fellow Scot who owned five plantations.[6] This was perhaps hardly surprising, as the more lucrative offices on the island in the 1770s were reportedly held by Scots, through the influence of the Scottish-born Lord Chief Justice of England, Lord Mansfield.

Imports to Scotland from the West Indies more than doubled in the years after the American War of Independence, rising to £371,656 in 1790. Over the same period exports from Scotland to the Caribbean rose by 60 per cent to £318,805. The number of ships leaving the Clyde ports of Port Glasgow and Greenock bound for Jamaica reached a peak in 1797 of twenty-seven, with a similar number going to the rest of the Caribbean. This compared to only three sailings that year to the colonists on the Chesapeake, which, a quarter of a century beforehand, had one year seen forty-one. In 1779 as many as seventeen ships left Edinburgh's Port of Leith bound for Jamaica and a further sixteen in 1790, with an average of twelve going to other West Indian islands, whilst for eight years in this period not a single journey was made to New England. Dundee and Aberdeen contributed in a lesser way to this trade and Peterhead has a Jamaica Street, inhabited in the nineteenth century by local sea captains.

Few ships left Scottish ports bound for the Guinea coast to transport slaves, though Glasgow did send some out in the early part of the eighteenth century. In the 1750s merchants in Montrose owned four slave ships which made a number of journeys via English and continental ports.[7] Merchants from the Solway ports of Dumfries and Kirkcudbright were involved in the same way, probably in connection with the nearby English Port of Whitehaven, a major trader in slaves.

Yet these occasional sailings represented only a small part of the role that Scots played in the trade. The Glasgow West Indian merchants invested large amounts of capital to facilitate plantation settlement, with the replacement of slaves being amongst the heaviest of calls on finance. A consortium of London merchants, led by two Scots, undertook fifty-nine slave-trading voyages between 1748 and 1784 at a total profit of £30,841. Scots were also prominent in the Bristol trade, notably Evan Baillie from Dochfour, Inverness, who returned from his family plantations in Grenada to form an alliance with the powerful Pinney family there through the marriage of his son and to become a Member of Parliament for the city in 1802.[8] John Law, a Scottish fugitive from justice, built up an empire in France that included the Guinea Company, which had a monopoly of the French trade through Nantes and a contract for 30,000 slaves every year.[9] A merchant from Kirkliston, Archibald Dalzel, after six years of slave trading in West Africa, was confident that by the following year he would have enough money to enable him 'to spend the remainder of life in ease'.[10]

Who were the Scots involved in slavery at this time? Some were businessmen, many of whom had no experience of the West Indies, still less of Africa. Some were merchant adventurers, with a few of them building up consortia and contracts that made fortunes. Others owned estates and staffed them with kinsmen or relatives of their friends, and some of these sought quick profits from sugar and rum in order to reinvest in land or industry at home. For doctors, lawyers and bookkeepers there were greater prospects of financial reward in their profession abroad than could be offered at home, and for some artisans the employment situation in Scotland forced them, as it would later generations in colonial Africa, to accept a post in the Caribbean as an alternative to destitution in Scotland.

From the mid-eighteenth century until the end of the Napoleonic Wars, more than seventy Glasgow merchants were members of firms whose major involvement was the importation of sugar, cotton and rum from the West Indies, raw and processed materials that were labour intensive in their farming and, of course, dependent on slave labour. The largest and most prominent of these was Alexander Houston, with assets by the end of the century of £630,000, six business enterprises in Grenada and a large estate in Renfrew.

In earlier years a small group of merchants in the city had dominated the importation of tobacco from America. This multiplied a factor of six between 1740 and 1770 and accounted for half of Britain's total tobacco trade. After the American War, the end of British monopoly over trade with her former colonies meant that exports to Europe replaced many of those to Britain and the power and wealth of the Glasgow 'tobacco lords' began to decline. An analysis of the backgrounds of the seventy-three partners in Glasgow West Indian companies in the last quarter of the eighteenth century revealed that a high ratio of them were sons of 'tobacco lords'[11]

The Union with England in 1707 had removed the restrictions on Scottish entrepreneurs trading with the colonies. It had also led to an exodus of Scots seeking fame and fortune in London. Richard Oswald was born in 1705 in a Caithness manse. After his father's death, he joined his cousins in business in Glasgow and then moved to London where he formed a partnership with five others, including two fellow Scots, Alexander Grant and Augustus Boyd. Grant had been an itinerent country doctor in Jamaica, treating Scots in the western parishes and finally acquiring land and trading contracts. In 1739 he too moved to London, marketing supplies for the plantations and acting as the agent and banker for the commercial enterprises of the Grant clan. Augustus Boyd went to St Kitts in 1700, built up extensive land and trading interests and married the daughter of the Speaker of the island's Assembly. However, because he was not English he was frustrated in his ambition for a seat on the island's Council and at the age of fifty-eight he also moved to London, seeking to expand his trading opportunities from there.

Early in 1748 Oswald negotiated the sale of Bance Island, a 'trade castle' on the Sierra Leone River. This was formerly owned by the Royal African Company but had become derelict. The partners completely rebuilt the fort, extended the buildings to form what they termed a 'slave factory' or holding station, stocked it with provisions and ran a business that, at its height, had thirty-five white staff and loaded an average of a thousand slaves a year onto ships from many countries. Despite the mortality rate (a young Scottish accountant estimated that eighty to ninety slaves died each year on Bance Island),[12] the proprietors succeeded in creating a very successful enterprise in financial terms and in the third quarter of the eighteenth century exported even more slaves, especially through Oswald's friend Henry Laurens of Charleston, to the Carolinas. In the peak year of 1762, when 2,000 slaves were exported through Bance Island, Alexander Grant wrote to his kinsman that the place was 'a territory where my Dominion is most absolute'.[13]

Oswald himself has been described as representing those on the 'commanding heights' of the triangular trade, amassing £500,000 for himself, a massive fortune in the eighteenth century.[14] Although most of his financial success was achieved from London and he never visited Africa, his Scottish roots (to which he was to return in retirement) were important to him, yet expressed sometimes in the most bizarre way. Tartan had been suppressed after the Jacobite rebellions and was yet to enjoy an early nineteenth-century revival following

George IV's visit to Scotland. But Oswald saw to it that a two-hole golf course was built on Bance Island for the diversion of sea captains and others awaiting the completion of their business, and kitted out the African caddies in tartan loincloths.[15] It held the same irony as the dinner jacketed Jewish musicians taken from the concentration camps in the 1940s to give cultural evenings to Nazi officials. But Oswald was not unique in this. A Jamaican planter named Macpherson was accustomed to order tartan from the same supplier as Oswald, William Wilson of Bannockburn, believing that dressing his slaves in this way would make them more conspicuous.[16]

Bance Island served as a place of employment for young Scots who were kinsmen of the partners, or of their friends, often those who were fleeing a past life at home and others for whom there were no alternative prospects. Between 1751 and 1773, 25 per cent of the whites on the island were born in Scotland or had Scots parents, and between 1748 and 1776 nine out of thirteen agents were Scots. Later we will see something of the tensions between this flourishing slave station and the newly formed free colony of Sierra Leone downriver, whose governor was a Scot, but over this period Bance Island served almost as a tiny Scottish colony.

With their wealth from slavery the London Scottish associates bought, built or remodelled houses and estates in their native land: Oswald at Auchincruive in Ayrshire, Grant at Dalvey in Forres on his clan's lands, and John Mill and Michael Herries at Old Montrose and Haugh of Urr near Castle Douglas. Some Scots used income from their estates at home to invest in land in the Caribbean, some set up their families on Caribbean estates, others ploughed money earned by trade into land in the West Indies. James Stirling of Keir in Perthshire fathered no fewer than twenty-two children until his death in 1749, but even his substantial estate (worth £130,000 by the end of the century) could not adequately finance that number of dependents. One son, Robert, went to Jamaica, buying Frontier estate in St Mary's parish in 1748 and Friendship estate in Westmoreland parish shortly afterwards, with money provided by his brother Archibald, the heritor of Keir. Another brother, James, joined him in 1757 and together they purchased Hampden estate in Trelawny parish. The ventures were not successful, however, and debts outweighed profits.

Other Scots fared better. In Jamaica there was an area known as an 'Argyll Colony', where Highlanders had an interest in large plantations in Hannover, Westmoreland and St Elizabeth parishes. By 1770 the

Malcolms of Poltalloch, overlooking Jura, were owners of five plantations, giving them an annual profit of over £40,000.[17] The history of
the Grant family from Glasgow illustrates the intricate net of finance,
ownership, employment and management that made up Scots involvement in Jamaica. John Grant, who became the island's Chief Justice in
1784, after managing sugar estates, made enough money to buy the
Perthshire estate of Kilgraston, to which he retired in 1791. His brother
Francis purchased Georgia plantation in Trelawny Parish in 1778, but
soon afterwards sold it to John's friend Charles Gordon, who had
recently arrived in Jamaica. Gordon returned to Scotland in 1781 and
never visited Jamaica again. He left Georgia under Francis Grant's
management and made no attempt to interfere. Despite the debts accu-
mulated on the plantation, Grant built up an extensive business for
himself, becoming involved in the management of the Stirlings' three
plantations and in John Gordon's Glasgow estate in St James' parish.
Alexander Grant, Oswald's business partner, acquired six estates
spread over four parishes on the island between 1752 and 1768. In
total these had 7,803 slaves and were valued at £61,345. Other Grants
found a different way of acquiring riches in Jamaica. Sir Archibald
Grant, Alexander's cousin, whose Aberdeenshire estate of Monymusk
was renowned as a model for pioneering improvement, was enabled to
achieve wealth not by any profits made whilst in Jamaica in the 1740s,
but through marriage to a rich widow, Elizabeth Callender.

If Grant was a familiar name in Jamaica, the same could be said of
Wedderburn. We have already encountered the master of Joseph
Knight who retired from Jamaica to Perthshire. Another John
Wedderburn managed 300 slaves for the Glasgow merchant William
Cunninghame on the latter's 3,500-acre Grandvale plantation in
Westmoreland. In a contemporary planter's diary there are also ref-
erences to a James Wedderburn, the overseer at Mount Pleasant in
Hannover.[18] Sir James Wedderburn owned Bluecastle Estate in
Westmoreland along with his younger brother, a doctor. James's story
is extensively related in the writings of Robert Wedderburn, his son
by a slave woman, who became a radical Methodist preacher in
London in the early nineteenth century. Robert visited Scotland in
1795 to lay claim to some of his heritage, but he was never allowed
over the threshold at Inveresk Lodge at Musselburgh and was sent
away with a draught of 'small beer' from the cook and 'a cracked six-
pence' from the footman.[19]

The acquisition of estates in Jamaica was paralleled, on a different
scale, in other islands, especially those acquired by military conquest

Figure 3   Inveresk Lodge, Musselburgh, built by the Wedderburn family.
Professor Geoff Palmer demonstrates how the lay-out of the estate was modelled
on a Jamaican sugar plantation.

or secession. In 1765 John Aitcheson of Rochsolloch in Airdrie bought
the Belmont estate in Grenada along with its 170 slaves. For fifteen
years no member of his family visited the island, but in 1780, when
his sister Bethia made the journey to sell Belmont, she brought
£21,183 with her back to Scotland.[20] An analysis of Waltham, an
estate on the same island owned by Ninian and George, the Home
brothers from Berwickshire, one of whom became Lieutenant
Governor whilst the other stayed in Scotland, reveals it to be a
'medium sized' plantation of 752 acres with 210 slaves. The manager
was another Scot, John Fairbairn.[21] Janet Schaw noted in 1775 that
there were many Scots on Antigua. One of them was Walter Tullideph
from Perthshire, who arrived in 1726 to assist in his brother's business
on the island and to practise medicine, having learnt it at Edinburgh
University. Whilst on his rounds he began trading and lending to
planters, and by 1763 he owned 500 acres with 270 slaves and bought
an estate in Scotland.[22] Between 1741 and 1767, Tullideph, like many
other merchants of the time, bypassed the London sugar market by
using agents in the north and west of England, in Ireland and in

Scotland selling direct to Glasgow, Leith and Dundee, creating a demand which helped to raise the price.

Of the seventy-two doctors listed for Jamaica in the *Medical Register for 1780*, two-thirds were Scots. Edinburgh produced a much larger number of medical graduates than could find employment in Britain, still less in Scotland, and doctors in the colonies were able to make a good living if they had the right connections amongst the wealthier planters. They were, however, only paid a flat rate for treating slaves on the plantations and the charge of neglect was a familiar one. Many were prepared to combine commercial enterprises with medicine. William Stephen in St Kitts bought sick slaves, treated them and resold them at a profit, whilst Dr Alexander Johnston from Aberdeen invested money made from his wealthy clients in cattle-ranching and slave trading.[23]

In Jamaica, as in other British Caribbean islands, the court system was based on English law. For Scots, this presented the obstacle of having to serve apprenticeships before being able to practise. There is little evidence that Scottish solicitors or advocates had long-term or profitable careers in Jamaica, yet they kept going there. The West Indian islands were highly litigious societies and there were many opportunities for lawyers to be involved. Bookkeeping and accountancy were also valued, especially when the owners of plantations were in Scotland. The confidence of the planters would be greatly increased if their financial affairs, including the management of slaves, who formed a large part of their 'assets', were in the hands of relatives or close friends.

Those with fewer professional skills formed a substantial part of the Scottish community in the Caribbean. Newspapers in Scotland frequently had included in them advertisements for carpenters, plumbers and other trades. Those who had the basic educational background became administrative secretaries, clerks or bookkeepers on the sugar estates, the latter post often deceptively named and frequently entailing the oversight of slave labour. It was this that Robert Burns sought to do before the commercial success of his Kilmarnock Edition enabled him to stay in Scotland. One who was later to be a leading abolitionist, Zachary Macaulay, as a young man became a bookkeeper in Jamaica, and the English poet Samuel Taylor Coleridge observed that three out of four overseers in the West Indies were Scots.

The cases of Ninian Home in Grenada and John Grant in Jamaica demonstrate how Scots were involved in the government of the colonies. Most major political offices in the West Indies were held by

Scots and Alexander Lindsay, the Governor of Jamaica in the 1790s, has been described as 'one of the most powerful figures in the Empire'.[24] The heavy commitment of troops to defend the West Indian islands, especially at the time of war with France, exposed many military men to the reality of slavery and quite a few were repulsed by it. One who went from military to civilian command was David Stewart of Garth in Perthshire

Stewart was a career soldier who first saw service in the West Indies, fighting the French in St Lucia, St Vincent and Trinidad. In the meantime, his brother John had left Perthshire to become part-owner of the Parkhill plantation in St Vincent. David's biographer justified his ownership of slaves on Parkhill by his paying for their food and shelter when 'the islands were at war, their economies had ceased to function and the Negroes were being slaughtered, starved, or caught up in the fighting'. After military service in Barbados and Trinidad, the end of the Napoleonic wars left him unemployed, but he finally achieved a colonial appointment in the last year of his life, becoming governor of St Lucia in 1829.

Stewart took little interest in being a part-owner of a plantation, but when in Trinidad he busied himself with plans and suggestions to the planters for 'better treatment of slaves and more profitable plantations'. It was this mixture of humanity and concern for efficiency on the plantations that occupied much of his time for the few months he had in St Lucia. His report to the colonial office on the condition of slaves followed a detailed inspection of the island and he sought far greater legal protection for slaves' rights. Uniquely in the West Indies at the time, he turned around a slave rebellion by instituting an inquiry and without any subsequent killing or floggings. Stewart was no abolitionist, but when in London in 1814 he responded to a request from James Stephen and William Wilberforce for details about improvements to the condition of the slaves, and he noted about Stephen: 'I believe I may assure myself of his cordial support.'[25]

SLAVERY EXAMINED BY SCOTTISH PHILOSOPHERS AND THEOLOGIANS

Classical civilisation had a strong influence on the Scottish Enlightenment. In the universities the teaching of Latin and Greek was well established, but there was a new enthusiasm for the culture out of which the language sprang. This spilled into the intellectual circles in which academics, writers and men of letters moved. Edinburgh New Town's architecture owed much in its inspiration to classical form. Rome became a magnet for the intelligentsia as well as the aristocracy on the 'grand tour'. Contemporary painters such as Gavin Hamilton, Alexander Runciman and Alexander Naysmyth frequently portrayed classical scenes in their works, and the frontispiece of the *Encyclopaedia Britannica*'s third edition in 1788 showed arts, science and technology in a classical setting. Of course these same classical civilisations of Greece and Rome that the new Scottish denizens of culture so much admired had the institution of slavery built into their foundations.

Slavery and the natural right of any person to freedom occupied a great deal of attention amongst the Enlightenment philosophers, who were generally critical of this aspect of the ancient world. Francis Hutcheson, Professor of Moral Philosophy at the University of Glasgow, argued that despite Aristotle's contention that some by nature are destined to work for others, 'no endowments, natural or acquired, can give a perfect right to assume power over others without their consent'. Hutcheson was amazed that 'wise and civilized nations [Greece and Rome] should ever have introduced such a cruel action.'[26]

Adam Ferguson, who held a similar chair at Edinburgh, was similarly sceptical about a 'natural' justification of slavery through appeals made to the philosophy of the ancient world. Ferguson was influenced, as were many of his contemporaries, by the French thinker Montesquieu on issues of political reform and the abolition of slavery, and in his *Essay on Civil Society* in 1767 he challenged the notion that slavery was an acceptable state. He contrasted the justification of slavery for political expediency with liberty and argued that since by nature man is a member of a community and the happiness of individuals is the great end of civil society, then there could be no public good if certain members are unhappy. 'Liberty', wrote Ferguson, 'is a right which every individual must be ready to vindicate for himself and which he who pretends to bestow as a favour, has by that very act in reality denied.'[27] Two years later he underlined this rejection of Aristotelian thought in his statement that no person can be 'a thing or subject of property', and that 'the supposed property of the master in the slave, therefore, is a matter of usurpation, not of right'.[28]

In Aberdeen's Marischal College, James Beattie claimed that he had consistently taken an anti-slavery position in his lectures, and in his *Elements of Moral Science* he wrote that slavery was inconsistent with the 'dearest and most essential rights of man's nature', because it degraded into brutes those 'with rational souls and created for immortality'. For him to treat someone 'on the same footing with a beast or a piece of wood' meant that it was 'vain to talk any longer of the eternal distinction of right and wrong'. He found it difficult to 'preserve that lenity of language and coolness of argument which philosophy recommends' when confronted with slavery. 'In a word,' said Beattie, 'it is repugnant to every principle of reason, religion, humanity and conscience.'[29]

Yet the argument over natural slavery was by no means confined to university professors. In 1755 Charles Stewart, Minister of Cramond, introduced the subject to the Edinburgh Speculative Society and slavery was discussed annually in that body. Votes were only recorded from 1782 and five years later, when the question debated was 'Is slavery justified by the law of nature?', the members voted against this idea by ten votes to four.[30] A young lawyer, George Wallace, whose treatise on the laws of Scotland was published in 1760 and became a remarkable early abolitionist document, asserted that liberty was 'a natural faculty', that slavery was 'contrary to nature' and that this practice of the ancient world, though sanctioned by Roman law, 'appears so horrid and so contrary to the feelings of humanity, that it cannot be agreeable to the law of Scotland'.[31]

Hardly anyone was prepared to argue that slavery was a natural state for others, but there were three circumstances held to justify it – for prisoners taken in time of war; as a result of crime; or as a deliverance from the perceived miseries of African 'savagery', this last being a key argument in favour of the slave trade made by a prominent Scottish slave trader. Hutcheson challenged the justification of enslaving prisoners in war on the grounds that most subjects have no part in the decisions of their leaders to make war. For him, even in a democracy, women and servants have no say in the matter and it was totally unjust to 'punish' them at all. He summed it up in a torturous but telling statement: 'the violent possessor must in all cases show his title especially where the old proprietor is known. Each man is the original proprietor of his own liberty. The proof of his losing it must be incumbent on those who deprive him of it by force.'[32] Wallace went even further than this, disputing even the right of free men to become slaves by their own consent. 'A man', he argued, 'is not the proprietor of himself: can he therefore be a proprietor of others?'[33]

Adam Ferguson was totally opposed to any form of property in human beings and felt strongly enough to resist making any exception to this, even in the case of crime. In his *Essay on the History of Civil Society*, he explored the roots of despotism and the danger of allowing anyone unlimited power over others, conscious of what he termed 'the passions and follies of men'.[34] In his later *Institutes of Moral Philosophy*, Ferguson admitted that 'a right to command is sometimes acquired by forfeiture, when a person who has done a wrong becomes bound to repair it by his services', but he was adamant that 'no contact or forfeiture can deprive a man of all his rights or render him the property of others'.[35] At first sight this seemed to echo Hutcheson's assertion that the laws of God and nature prohibited the great and strong from depriving 'the meanest'. However, Hutcheson added a reservation in the words 'where no public interest require it', and it was this that separated the two philosophers.[36]

The question then arose as to the circumstances of 'public interest' that might justify slavery. At the end of the seventeenth century, Andrew Fletcher of Saltoun, concerned about the number of beggars and vagabonds without work, had proposed a legalised enslavement to maintain social order and ensure productivity.[37] Hutcheson recommended 'making perpetual slavery of this sort the ordinary punishment of idle vagrants, as after proper admonitions and trials of temporary servitude, cannot be engaged to support themselves or their families in useful labour'. He did, however, temper this with a recommendation of a seven years trial 'to see if diligence be learnt'. If that did not work, 'they should be adjudged to slavery for life'. [38] 'Armed with the crosscut teeth of benevolence and utility, Hutcheson easily sawed through the conventional rationalisations for slavery' – so wrote David Brion Davis, but he qualified this by stating that the 'doctrine of utility', the same reservation that led to his plans for slavery, 'leaves a somewhat jagged edge'.

The question of the profitability of slavery was addressed by two key figures of the Enlightenment – Adam Smith, Hutcheson's pupil and successor, and the Edinburgh philosopher David Hume. Davis described Hume as 'anything but an abolitionist', but conceded that 'he helped to put the slavery controversy in a new perspective by demolishing the traditional belief that, owing to the great fertility of slaves, Europe's population had been vastly larger in antiquity than in modern times'.[39] In his essay *Of the Populousness of Ancient Nations*, Hume argued that population growth depended on certain economic and social factors and that slavery in ancient Rome was not only extremely wasteful, but highly expensive. Although admitting a 'shocking' comparison between the management of people and cattle, he demonstrated that in rich and productive areas, and in great cities where costs were high, few cattle were bred, since it was cheaper to acquire them from remote areas. In the same way, the Romans relied on a constant supply of slaves from the provinces. Hume continued to argue that severe treatment retarded the growth of the population and that few saw the breeding of slaves as economically viable. 'All I pretend to infer from these reasonings', he said, 'is that slavery is in general disadvantageous both to the happiness and populousness of mankind and that its place is much better supplied by the practice of hired servants.'[40]

Adam Smith, in *The Wealth of Nations*, argued that the free and competitive nature of labour, on which much of his economic theory was founded, was, by definition, excluded in slave societies. The slaves of the rich in the ancient world occupied trades and free men were excluded from employment. Furthermore, he maintained that slaves were rarely inventive. 'Should a slave propose any improvement of this kind', wrote Smith, 'his master would be apt to consider the proposal as the suggestion of laziness. The poor slave, instead of reward, would probably meet with much abuse, perhaps with some punishment.' Slaves, for Smith, gain no advantage for themselves by good husbandry and it was this that explained the decline in villeinage in Europe. For this reason, in order to make the tobacco and sugar plantations profitable there have to be a very large number of slaves.

Yet it is by no means clear that Adam Smith was making out a case for emancipation. In his chapter on 'The Colonies', he simply argued for better management in the West Indies, maintaining that slavery was more efficient and the rights of the slave better protected under an arbitrary government such as that of pre-Revolutionary France, than under the 'free' government of Britain, where a magistrate attempting to regulate slavery would be deemed to interfere with private property.[41]

Some philosophers employed biblical and theological arguments on the issue of slavery. Hutcheson cited Mosaic law, contrasting with it the arbitrariness of modern slavery. Even when slavery was justified in the Old Testament, for crime or by consent, he pointed out that there were time limits on it, as evidenced from the biblical rules about the jubilee year of release. There were other limits, too. The laws dealing with foreign slaves had merciful provisions against undue severity. However, under Christianity, Hutcheson argued, whatever lenity was due from a Hebrew towards his fellow countryman must be due toward all. Distinctions of nations were removed on issues of justice, mercy and right. Even rights over foreign slaves were to be only seen as indulgencies, as in the case of polygamy and divorce, and did not, for him, provide justification for the general principle. [42]

James Beattie argued that scripture asserted that 'all the nations of men on earth are of one blood' and he then considered the soul of a slave. This was no academic theological question, since one of the traditional justifications for slavery was that Africans were 'savages' without souls and by definition not full human beings. He concluded, 'as to his soul, it is certain that he has reason and a capacity for improvement. Either his soul is human or ours is not human.'[43] In correspondence with the Bishop of London, Beattie described Rev. Raymond Harris, an apologist for the slave trade, as 'labouring to pervert scripture in order to vindicate one of the most impious and inhuman practices that ever disgraced the sublunary creation'.[44]

William Robertson's attack on slavery is best seen in his 1775 sermon, which Alan McConnochie used effectively in the Knight case. 'No inequality of condition,' Robertson maintained, 'no superiority in power, no pretext of consent, can justify this ignominious depression of human nature, or can confer upon one man the right of domination over the person of another.' The only check on the cruelty and degenerate nature of slavery was, according to Robertson, the onward march of Christianity. Curiously glossing over the flourishing of slavery in many Christian lands and the acceptance of the trade within Britain, he stated: 'it is not the authority of any single detached precept in the gospel, but the spirit and genius of the Christian religion, more powerful than any particular command, which hath abolished the practice of slavery through the world'.[45]

A further argument against slavery related to the moral depravity resulting from unlimited power wielded over others. Ferguson was convinced of it and Hume spelt out the practice in the colonies when he wrote in his essay *Of the Populousness of Ancient Nations*: 'the little humanity, commonly observed in persons, accustomed from their infancy, to exercise so great authority over their fellow creatures and to trample upon human nature, were sufficient alone to disgust us with that unbounded dominion'. The 'barbarous manners of ancient times', for Hume, were a direct result of slavery by which, 'every man of rank was rendered a petty tyrant and educated amidst the flattery, submission and low debasement of his slaves'.[46] Adam Smith, in his *Theory of Modern Sentiments*, expressed this even more strongly when he asserted that 'there is not a negro from the coast of Africa who does not, in this respect, possess a degree of magnanimity which the soul of his sordid master is too often scarce capable of conceiving'. For him, it was a cruel trick of fate that subjected the negroes to the 'refuse of the gaols of Europe, to wretches who possess the virtues neither of the countries which they come from, nor of those whom they go to and whose levity, brutality and baseness, so justly expose them to the contempt of the vanquished'.[47]

Robertson had claimed that the 'spirit' of Christianity stood in opposition to slavery. For Wallace, the institution was 'so contrary to the feelings of humanity, that it cannot be agreeable to the law of Scotland'. That language reflected a society that at one level was being deeply influenced by the importance of benevolent feelings to others, both as natural attributes for civilised men and an essential ingredient in the march of progress in civilised societies. Hutcheson argued that the innate moral sense encourages us to do disinterested good to others, whilst at the same time approving of the same actions for others. This natural inclination to utility and the public good meant that delight in benevolence was an instinctive reflex. From 'the most extensive benevolence', claimed Hutcheson, we derive our 'most distinct notion' of God.[48]

The elevation of benevolence found literary expression in 1771 when Henry Mackenzie, who was once described as 'the arch-priest of Scottish sentimentality', published *The Man of Feeling*. There is in this, and in the same author's *Julia de Roubigne*, a mixture of romantic tragedy which has been compared both to *Othello* and to the seventeenth-century play *Oroonoko*, with its tale of betrayal, suffering and slavery. It is not hard to see how attractive this was to the intelligentsia in late eighteenth-century Scotland, reflecting as it does the tussle of emotions in which benevolence, sympathy, progress and sensibility were to triumph in the end.

A recent survey identified no fewer than nineteen eighteenth-century Scottish poets who touch on the theme of slavery. These included the advocate John Maclaurin and Francis Gardenstone, the Court of Session judge, both of whom were involved in the Joseph Knight case. Robert Tannahill was the radical champion of the weavers in Paisley.[49] Another poet, James Thomson, as early as 1744 made reference to the 'direful shark' who 'dyes the purple seas with gore' as he 'from the Partners of that cruel Trade, which spoils unhappy Guinea of her Sons, demands his share of Prey, demands themselves'.[50] Captain Marjoriebanks' long study of slavery in verse took its inspiration from his experience of military service in Jamaica, which made an indelible impression on him. It began by reflecting on the betrayal for commercial gain of British freedoms won by the likes of himself, continued by providing graphic details on the cruelty of slavery and concluded in searing terms: 'Let Afric's children tread their native shore/And British ruffians ravage them no more!/ The galling chains of Servitude remove/And leave them all to liberty and love'.[51] Most poets were content to write in general terms, but Marjoriebanks' polemic was addressed to Campbell Haliburton, Secretary to the Edinburgh Society for Promoting the Abolition of the Slave Trade. In 1789 John Jamieson, United Secession minister of Forfar, had claimed in his poem *The Sorrows of Slavery* to provide 'a faithful statement of facts respecting the African slave trade.'[52]

By contrast James Boswell published anonymously in 1791 a poem entitled *No Abolition of Slavery or the Universal Empire of Love*. He obviously regarded it as a contribution to the debate surrounding Wilberforce's forthcoming bill, since he wrote to a friend, 'I am think-ing to curtail my poem on the slave trade and throw it into the world just before the great question comes on next Wednesday.'[53] Boswell observed on the natural state of slavery: 'slavery, subjection, what you will, /have ever been and will be still', and in an extraordinary biblical interpretation continued: 'each bear his own, th' Apostle spoke:/And chiefly they who bear the yoke./From wise subordina-tion's plan/Springs the chief happiness of man.'[54] Robert Burns had a whimsical short poem entitled 'The Slave's Lament', with the lines: 'It was in sweet Senegal that my foes did me enthrall,/For the lands of Virginia, ginia O;/Torn from that lovely shore/And must never see it more.'[55] Boswell and Burns illustrate two aspects of the phenomenon of Scottish involvement in slavery – the first demonstrating that Enlightenment thought was no automatic ally in the anti-slavery cause, and the second that despite educated and enlightened Scots having a philosophical distaste for slavery, social and economic factors could outweigh this and enable many of them to accept a living through its fruits.

ENLIGHTENMENT JUDGEMENT ON SLAVERY – A DOUBLE-EDGED SWORD

'Many of the key ideas of the Enlightenment', wrote David Brion Davis, 'could easily be turned against pleas for the abolition of slavery.' There was, he argued, a perpetual tension between 'the two polar extremes of the divided mind of the Enlightenment' – on the one hand the need to regulate society by laws that were as unalterable as the laws of physics and on the other the absolute gulf between present society and the transcendent laws of nature. 'Neither position', said Davis, 'provided the basis for perceiving a single institution as an unmitigated evil.'[56]

An important example of this was the interest generated over the biological differences between the races and its consequences. Lord Monboddo, Court of Session judge and a leading figure in social and literary circles, had long taken an interest in orang-utans, believed that men originally had tails and held to the idea that apes were a variety of the human species. Although he has been seen as anticipating the evolutionary ideas of Darwin, the rigidity of his grouping of peoples and the closeness of apes to 'primitive people' in his theories held other possibilities as well. Given this gradation, it was a short step to the kind of theory of racial inferiority that is based on a scale in which environmental differences hold little weight.

Two philosophers who appeared to give emphasis this position were David Hume and Henry Home, Lord Kames. James Beattie attacked Hume for his claim of a 'uniform and constant difference' between peoples, which had no regard for the crimes and vices of Europe and for the potential of African improvement. He warned that the doctrine of the inferiority of negroes was the first step towards attacking the authority of scripture, which taught the unity of the whole human stock.[57] Beattie's friend and university contemporary James Ramsay, priest and surgeon in St Kitts, maintained that Hume's opinions were eagerly seized on in the West Indies to justify slavery. William Dickson from Moffat, in his reports from Barbados and Jamaica, claimed similarly that Voltaire, Kames and Hume put negroes only a little higher than apes. Kames had argued in his *Sketches of the History of Man* that there were a number of distinct species within the human race and that negroes were in many respects inferior to Europeans.[58]

Hume went even further. In his footnote on *National Characters* in the 1754 edition of his *Essays*, he claimed that there 'never was a polished society but of the white race, to which all others are naturally inferior'. He admitted that there were reports of a negro of learning in Jamaica, but Hume judged him simply to have the capabilities of a parrot.[59] These views notwithstanding, William Dickson wrote optimistically: 'if the humane Voltaire and the good-natured, benevolent Hume', in expressing doubts about Africans being men co-ordinate with ourselves, 'had dreamt that their conjectures would have been magnified into arguments by the apologists for slavery', they would have immediately repudiated them.[60]

It was an easy transition from this racial distinction to argue that Africans were better off in the West Indies than in their native land, that they had a greater toleration of the conditions there and that the harshness of plantation slavery was not felt so strongly by them. It was a theme enthusiastically taken up by planters and defenders of the trade. In a letter to a Glasgow newspaper in 1792, a correspondent 'Hanway', himself engaged in West Indian commerce, wrote that the Scottish opponents of the slave trade 'will find in their near neighbourhood many a sober, industrious Christian, who is neither so well fed, so well clothed, nor so well attended to in sickness, as the Negroes of our colonies are'.[61]

Even if cruelty was admitted, the perception of Africans as a breed apart from humanity who lacked the same human emotions as the inhabitants of 'civilised' nations was a convenient barrier to feelings of pity. When Janet Schaw arrived in St Kitts in 1775, she commented on the use of the cart-whip on half-naked men and women. 'However dreadful this must appear to the humane European,' she wrote, 'when one comes to be better acquainted with the nature of the Negroes, the horror of it must wear off. It is the suffering of the human mind that constitutes the greatest misery of punishment, but with them it is merely corporeal.' Schaw described a slave market where 'they stood up to be looked at with perfect unconcern – the husband was to be divided from his wife, the infant from his mother, but the most perfect indifference ran through the whole.'[62] Such a naïve and seemingly callous view from 'a lady of quality' was possible within the mixed messages of Enlightenment thinking on slavery.

COMPLACENCY AT HOME AND COMPLICITY OVERSEAS

John Millar, Professor of Law at Glasgow University, whose lectures contained a strong critique of slavery, hailed the Joseph Knight decision in 1778 as 'an authentic testimony of the liberal sentiments entertained in the latter part of the eighteenth century'. Millar expressed his surprise at the strange paradox that those who talked of political liberty and the inalienable rights of mankind 'should make no scruple of reducing a great proportion of their fellow creatures into circumstances by which they are not only deprived of property but almost of every species of right'.[63]

The contrast has been interpreted in various ways. The shortest contemporary explanation was that given by Michael Fry – 'Presbyterian hypocrisy'. Duncan Rice argued more gently that Scots who were most exposed to the enlightened critique were not yet influenced by the evangelical imperatives that had driven the Clapham Sect into action. This reflected James Beattie's comment that the 'Moderate' party in the

Church of Scotland talked of 'eternal concerns with a frigidity and languor, which a good economist would be ashamed of, in bargaining for half a dozen haddocks'.[64] Most recently T. M. Devine has claimed that the influence of Presbyterianism on generations of Scots made them uniquely qualified to run the Empire 'with an inbred instinct for harrying the unregenerate poor, or negroes or natives, for their own good as well as for their employer's'.[65] None of these adequately explain the phenomenon, though. For such double standards were made possible by the detached and at times unrealistic way in which the issue was discussed. Although the leading philosophers of the Scottish Enlightenment were overwhelmingly opposed to slavery, they rarely focused on its practice in the British colonies and even less on involvement in it by Scots. Even William Robertson and John Millar centered mainly on the Americas, which incidentally drew some extra-ordinary comments in the first edition of the *Encyclopaedia Britannica* in 1771, edited by William Smellie, the antiquary and biographer. Under the entry for 'Negroes' was a strong condemnation of the commerce 'which is scarce defensible on the foot of either religion or humanity'. However, under 'Slavery' appeared a claim that 'slavery is absolutely abolished in Britain and France as to personal servitude'.[66] This was seven years before Scotland's judges were to end it by a majority, and there was no comment at all in the entry for the colonies.

Another indicator of this detachment is to be found in how few figures of the Scottish Enlightenment became identified with the anti-slavery movement. It is true that many of them were writing long before the campaign against the slave trade was launched in 1787. However, only William Robertson and James Beattie, whose major work preceded this date by many years, had contact with William Wilberforce and the British movement. Wilberforce wrote to Robertson in 1788 testifying to the value of information provided by him for the parliamentary campaign.[67] Beattie drafted a petition from Marischal College to Parliament on the trade in 1788 and persuaded Aberdeen City Council to do likewise in 1792. He greatly assisted a tour made by William Dickson that year on behalf of the London Committee for the Abolition of the Slave Trade, through giving Dickson a number of introductions in the north-east. But perhaps Beattie's most significant influence was on a young Marischal student, James Stephen, who many years later would return from the West Indies to become one of the giants of the abolitionist cause.

It was probably Stephen above all who was in Beattie's mind when he wrote to his friend Lady Montagu – 'many of my pupils have gone to the West Indies and I trust have carried my principles with them and exemplified those principles in their conduct to their unfortunate brethren'.[68] Yet there is little evidence to support this hopeful claim. Beattie's friend James Ramsay wrote that overseers from these shores were 'universally more cruel and morose towards slaves' than other taskmasters and the wife of a Scottish planter in St Vincent claimed that the slaves disliked Scots overseers more than their English counterparts for their 'proverbial' obsession with hard work and economical measures.[69]

Yet the work ethic and the stereotypical image of the mean Scot is only part of the explanation for the complicity of Scots in slavery. A more reasonable starting point lies in the disastrous immediate past history of the nation. Scotland in the early part of the eighteenth century had entered a union with England born of financial desperation. The nation's economy had been ruined by the disastrous colonisation project in Panama – a huge amount had been sunk in the Darien Scheme. The trade barriers which had been partly responsible for the bankrupting of the nation were now removed and the early eighteenth century provided new opportunities for commercial enterprise and for investment in the colonies from those who had the capital to do so. However, the very precariousness of past commercial ventures made any Scots on the make reluctant to question the morality of an enterprise that at last seemed to bring such a potential windfall in profits. Dr Alexander Johnston wrote to his brother in 1784 that he was considering trading several hundred slaves a year, but with an eye to possible reaction at home instructed him to 'keep these matters . . . entirely to yourself' and not even to speak about them to relatives.[70]

For those without capital, the West Indies provided job opportunities. Professional men and those with education and skills found opportunities Scotland lacked. For those without specific qualifications, the management needs of the plantations were an outlet, often a raft, on which to cling within the sea of unemployment in Scotland's cities, or higher rents and the destruction of traditional subsistence farming in the rural areas. They sought their fortune abroad through the increasingly developing patronage webs of Scots in places such as Jamaica, at a time when the patronage of a clan system at home could no longer be relied on to protect their welfare. This network, which provided the chance of employment and even advancement, alongside social intercourse with those who shared a common culture in a land that was difficult, where disease and death always threatened and where whites were in a substantial minority on the estates, exerted pressures for unquestioning complicity in the slave system that would be well-nigh impossible to resist. Those who were so dependent on other Scots were unlikely to bite the hand that fed them by breaking ranks in what was a very defensive planter society. Zachary Macaulay kept his head down when working on a Jamaican estate, William Dickson's *Letters on Slavery* from Barbados were written from the secure bastion of the Governor's office where he was Secretary, and James Ramsay's demonstration of concern for the slaves under his medical care in St Kitts forced his departure from the island. As in many tightly knit societies that experience economic or political insecurity, those who did raise any serious questions or even demonstrated some humanity towards the ruled found themselves under suspicion and in danger of ostracism, or worse.

A large number of the colonists in the West Indies saw themselves as temporary sojourners who intended to return home when they had made their fortunes. Permanent emigrants tended to come from the lower echelons of society and were much more numerous in the American colonies than in the Caribbean. However, the fortunes dreamed of on the voyage from Scotland turned out to be limited to the few. For the time being, many were effectively imprisoned in the inhospitable nature of the West Indies, having almost as little hope of any change in their situation as the slaves whom they supervised. That, and the struggle to preserve some kind of status, was accompanied in many cases by a kind of desperate frustration and bitter resentment, qualities that did not commend themselves to humane treatment of slaves.

SOCIAL CONTROL AND COMMERCE

Many Scots on the plantations were under intense pressure to maximise sugar production. The jobs of those managing and supervising estates, often in the absence of the proprietor, depended on a healthy profit being shown. Given the universal belief that only the harshest physical punishment, or fear of it, would induce slaves to work, this seemed to be the only way to operate a plantation. Throughout most of the eighteenth century there was little challenge, let alone threat, to the slave trade. Enthusiasm for breeding slaves in the Caribbean was only significant in the last two decades and up to then it was thought to be more economical to simply replenish stock. The sensible option would appear to be to work slaves to, and if necessary beyond, their human capacity, after which they would be replaced. It is hardly surprising that the Scottish traditions of work ethic and prudent economy were adapted to this and it would have been strange if many had baulked at its implications.

Inducing fear amongst the slaves by violent punishment or its ever-present threat was seen as vital for their control, but fear was a prevalent force amongst the white population, too. As James Walvin has pointed out, 'planters lived in more or less permanent fear of slave violence and revolt', talking constantly about it and forever imagining plots against them.[71] The correspondence in the West Indian newspapers and the talk at dinner time in the presence of the slaves had frequent references to the fear of revolts. After the success of the uprising on the French island of St Domingue in 1791, this was to grow out of all proportion. The disparity in numbers between slaves and white staff led to permanent vigilance and frequently to paranoia. In the American colonies many planters owned a handful of slaves and knew them all, but in the Caribbean the average was 240.

In his observations made to a parliamentary investigation of the slave trade, James Ramsay claimed that the system required slaves to be treated worse than animals. 'A master', he wrote, 'considers not his horse or his mule as ever opposed in point of interest to him; but this is the constant light in which the slave is viewed.' For Ramsay, the slave was 'suspected and hated and treated as a rival and an enemy', therefore 'all must be forced out of him without feeling'. This, for him, arose 'not for any particular depravity in the master, but from the very nature of slavery'.[72]

Yet depravity there certainly was. Visitors to the West Indian plantations were struck by the orgies of drink and sexual exploitation. Once again the slaves were at the sharp end of this 'recreation'. In later years the lifestyle on the plantations became one of the most effective arguments employed by abolitionist writers and speakers to demonstrate the evils of slavery. There were examples of planters and others having something approximating a marriage relationship with a negro woman in an age when a large proportion of marriages in Scotland involved at least the threat, if not the substance, of sexual abuse and violence. Lady Nugent's diary speaks of a Scottish overseer living with his 'Cher amie', described as 'the favourite Sultana of this vulgar, ugly, Scotch Sultan'.[73] The majority of female slaves were under at least the threat of casual use at will by whites. This not only established domination over them, but at the same time disempowered any male slaves who might be their brothers, fathers, husbands or lovers.

When Scots were transported to the West Indies as forced labourers in the seventeenth century, they found themselves working alongside the slaves and sharing their deprivation and oppression. By the middle of the next century, the hierarchy was much more structured and even the poorest whites on the plantations had some authority over the slaves. Their physical separation made it easier to accept all the racial myths of black 'savages' and of slaves being creatures who did not share the same needs and emotions as themselves. The indispensability of the whip as the badge of authority, and its use as a necessary tool of social control, was accepted by planters and overseers alike.

BANALITY AND PROPERTY

Billy Kay, journalist and producer of a radio series *A Black History of Scotland*, has spoken of the sheer 'banality' of the slave trade. This may appear to underplay the horror of what many Africans regard as their Holocaust. But for Scots who made their money from the trade, that is how it seemed. Starved of commercial success for so long, the nation welcomed this economic miracle in which trade associated with slaves and slavery played an important role. The confidence of commercial growth dovetailed in with the new freedom to trade. This was partly generated by the ideas of the Enlightenment and partly reflected in them. Its visible effects are seen in the New Town of Edinburgh and the Georgian areas of Glasgow. Trade became a religion in the new Scotland to the extent that some of the most telling arguments made against the slave trade were those pointing out that human beings and capital could be more profitably employed elsewhere. For this reason, men such as Oswald and Grant had no hesitation in including on their coats of arms a black slave, thus openly acknowledging the source of their wealth.

The sanctity of property was an almost unassailable concept and any challenge to it seemed to threaten the whole fabric of society. The result of such property overseas, out of sight and out of mind even for educated Scots, was the visible evidence of progress reflected in the mansions at Auchincruive or Inveresk. In the late 1820s, when the pressure on slavery became intense throughout Britain, this sanctity of property became a key argument in the petitions against abolition sent by Scottish merchants and owners of plantations. The abolitionists had to work hard to bring the Enlightenment views of Hutcheson, Wallace or Beattie to bear on the assumption that slaves were property and in the end it took strong theological arguments to win the argument that there could be no property in human beings.

SLAVERY AND ENLIGHTENMENT – THE STRANGE PARADOX

All these factors help us to explain the complex nature of the seeming dichotomy between enlightened thinking in Scotland and the intense Scottish involvement in the slave trade and slavery. The lack of a focused critique by all but a few Enlightenment leaders, and action by even fewer, seemed to pose little threat to the established order of trade and settlement in the West Indies. The lure of commercial success in a nation hitherto starved of it, and the struggle for survival by ordinary Scots in the Caribbean, were to eclipse any specific concern for the sufferings of other races. Indeed, these sufferings were both profitable for many and perceived as a necessary means of security for others. It was a very depressing picture and seen from one angle would expose the progressive ideas of the Enlightenment as useless cant.

Yet Enlightenment ideas were employed not just in the courts but in pulpits and in pamphlets by those who challenged slavery. When Scotland led Britain in the last decade of the century in challenging the slave trade through petitions to Parliament, many of the petitioners from church and civic bodies were influenced by the ideas expressed by Scottish philosophers earlier in the century. They witnessed clearly to the common humanity of slaves and those who sought to enslave them and posed fundamental questions about who were the 'civilised' and who the 'savages'. The themes of benevolence and universal happiness are to be found throughout many of them, as is a concern to bring the benefits of Christianity to those who have been brought forcibly from Africa.

All this was not only alongside a trade on which the livelihoods of many Scots were dependant, but also in the face of a well-organised West India Association in Glasgow and its leading organ, *The Glasgow Courier*. The correspondence in the *Courier* in 1792, the same year that was to see so many petitions sent from Scotland, showed how easily the reports from St Domingue could sway the thinking of some of those who saw themselves as urban enlightened Scots and who believed that any tampering with the system would not only be disastrous for Scottish interests but even for the African slaves. The abolitionist campaign during the eighteenth century was entirely limited to getting rid of the trade and it was only in the early 1820s that slavery itself became the target. Just as the theological arguments about common humanity and individual worth could not be limited to the issues of capture and transatlantic passage, neither could the broad sweep of Enlightenment teaching on civilisation, society and benevolence be similarly restricted. Ironically, it was the same broad principles whose generality blunted the short-term effects on national policy and attitudes to the West Indies that in the end helped to ensure that Scots would not stop short at limited abolition. Even in 1833, when the last push took place to close the door on imperial slavery, speeches and petitions of the abolitionists reflected Enlightenment thinking.

The best of Enlightenment ideas on slavery were planted in a nation whose people had long experienced examples of other races living among them, but had not yet succumbed to the racist ideas in England expressed by Queen Elizabeth's proclamation in 1601 ordering blacks to be shipped out of the country because they caused annoyance to 'her own liege people' and consumed scarce foodstuffs. Many of those black slaves who were taken to Scotland from Virginia and the West Indies received support from ordinary Scots when they sought their freedom. Those who worked alongside slaves in the joiner's shop, met them in the street or sat with them in the kirk, discovered a common humanity and at the same time a nagging sense of wrong. However, this was not limited to ordinary folk. Lord Kames has been described as the 'hard cold edge' of the Scottish Enlightenment. His treatment of relationships was crude and blunt and he seemed to take a ruthless delight in pronouncing the death sentence. But in giving his judgement on the Knight case he had no doubt that to hold a black man in slavery in Scotland against his will was fundamentally wrong. 'We sit here', he told his fellow judges, 'to enforce right, not to enforce wrong.'[74] An obvious statement in a society that claimed to be ruled by justice, but one which was to mark a watershed in Scotland's relationship with slavery.

Notes

1 C. Duncan Rice, *The Scots Abolitionists 1833–1861* (Baton Rouge, LA, 1981), p. 19.
2 Alan Karras, *Sojourners in the Sun: Scottish Migrants in Jamaica and the Chesapeake 1740–1800* (New York, 1992), pp. 175, 178.
3 Angus Calder, *Revolutionary Empire* (London, 1981), p. 632.
4 T. M. Devine, 'An Eighteenth-Century Business Elite: Glasgow–West India Merchants', *Scottish Historical Review*, Vol. 57 (1978), pp. 51–2.
5 Sir William Forbes, *Memoirs of a Banking House by the late Sir William Forbes of Pitsligo* (Edinburgh, 1860), pp. 51–2.
6 Janet Schaw, *Journal of a Lady of Quality: Being the Narration of a Journey from Scotland to the West Indies, North Carolina and Portugal in the years 1774–1776*, ed. Evangeline Walker Andrews (New Haven, CT, [1776] 1939), p. 95.

7 David G. Adams, *Montrose – A History of its Harbour, Trade and Shipping* (Tayport, 1993).

8 Douglas Hamilton, *Scotland, the Caribbean and the Atlantic World 1750–1820* (Manchester, 2005), pp. 92–3.

9 Hugh Thomas, *The Slave Trade* (London, 1997), p. 243.

10 Archibald Dalzel to Andrew Dalzel, London, 13 Apr 1771. EU Special Collections, Dk.7.52.

11 Devine, 'An Eighteenth-Century Business Elite', Appendix 1, pp. 54–65.

12 James Low to Archibald Grant, 10 May 1762. NAS GD 345/1180.

13 Sir Alexander Grant to Sir Ludovick Grant, 27 Apr 1765. NAS GD 248/350/3/25.

14 Adam Hochschild, *Bury the Chains: The British Struggle to Abolish Slavery* (London, 2005), pp. 26–7.

15 David Hancock, *Citizens of the World* (Cambridge, 1995), pp. 2, 48, 50–3, 54–65, 175.

16 Research Report, Scottish Tartans Society, Dunkeld. I am grateful to Mrs Gudrun Joyce, former Museum Curator of the STS, for this information.

17 Allan I. McInnes, *Clanship, Commerce and the House of Stuart 1603–1788* (East Linton, 1996), p. 229.

18 Douglas Hall, ed., *In Miserable Slavery: Thomas Thistlewood in Jamaica 1750–1786* (London, 1989), p. 208.

19 Robert Wedderburn, *The Horrors of Slavery and Other Writings*, ed. Iain McCalman (Edinburgh, [1824] 1991). I am indebted to my friend Professor Geoff Palmer of Heriot Watt University, who has made a study of the Wedderburn Jamaican/Scottish connection and showed me over the grounds of Inveresk Lodge.

20 David Watson, 'Monklands and the Slave Trade', *The Journal of Monklands Heritage Society*, Vol. 5 (Sep 2000), p. 32.

21 Sonia Baker, 'Paradox in Grenada – Ninian and George Home, a Study of Slave-Owning Scots of the Enlightened Age', unpublished MA (Hons) dissertation, University of Edinburgh, 1999.

22 Michael Fry, *The Scottish Empire* (East Linton, 2001), p. 72.

23 T. M. Devine, *Scotland's Empire* (London, 2003), p. 234.

24 Fry, *The Scottish Empire*, pp. 245, 234–5.

25 James Irvine Robertson, *The First Highlander-Major-General David Stewart of Garth CB, 1768–1829* (East Linton, 1998), pp. 34, 69, 179–81, 71.

26 Francis Hutcheson, *A System of Moral Philosophy* (Glasgow, 1755), Book 3, p. 204.

27 Adam Ferguson, *Essay on the History of Civil Society*, ed. D. Forbes (Edinburgh, [1767]1966), pp. 270, 266.

28 Adam Ferguson, *Institutes of Moral Philosophy* (Edinburgh, 1769), Part 5, pp. 10, 165.

29 James Beattie, *Elements of Moral Science* (Edinburgh, 1817), Book 3, 24; 'On the Lawfulness and Expediency of Slavery particularly that of Negroes 1788', AUL, Safe 3, Box B49.
30 *History of the Speculative Society* (Edinburgh, 1845), 27 Nov 1787, p. 375.
31 George Wallace, *A System of the Principles of the Law of Scotland*, (Edinburgh, 1760), Book 3.2, p. 89.
32 Hutcheson, *A System of Moral Philosophy*, pp. 204–11.
33 Wallace, *Principles of the Law of Scotland*, p. 94.
34 Ferguson, *Essay on the History of Civil Society*, p. 264.
35 Ferguson, *Institutes of Moral Philosophy*, p. 166.
36 Hutcheson, *A System of Moral Philosophy*, p. 299.
37 Alexander Fletcher, 'The Second Discourse Concerning the Affairs of Scotland: Written in the Year 1698', in *Selected Political Writings and Speeches*, ed. David Daiches (Edinburgh, [1698] 1979).
38 Hutcheson, *A System of Moral Philosophy*, p. 201.
39 David Brion Davis, *The Problem of Slavery in Western Culture* (Ithaca, NY, 1966), pp. 377, 426.
40 David Hume, *Political Discourses* (Edinburgh, 1752), pp. 167, 177.
41 Adam Smith, *An Inquiry into the Nature and Causes of the Wealth of Nations* (London, [1776] 1884), pp. 289, 159, 241.
42 Hutcheson, *A System of Moral Philosophy*, p. 211.
43 Beattie, *Elements of Moral Science*, Book 3, pp. 56–7.
44 James Beattie, *The Letters of James Beattie to Sir William Forbes* (London, 1820), Vol. 2, p. 166.
45 William Robertson, *The Situation of the World at the time of Christ's Appearance and its Connection with the Success of His Religion Considered* (Edinburgh, 1755), pp. 33, 35.
46 David Hume, *Essays Moral, Political and Literary, including 'Essays Moral and Political', 'An Enquiry into the Principles of Morality' and 'Dialogues concerning Natural Religion'*, T. H. Green and T. H. Grose, eds (London, 1889) p. 161.
47 Adam Smith, *The Theory of Moral Sentiments* (New York, [1759] 1966), p. 299.
48 Hutcheson quoted in Davis, *The Problem of Slavery in Western Culture*, pp. 375–6.
49 James Basker, ed., *Amazing Grace: An Anthology of Poems about Slavery 1600–1810* (New Haven, CT, 2003).
50 James Thomson, *The Seasons*, ed. James Sambrook (Oxford, 1981), p. 106.
51 J. Marjoriebanks, *Slavery, an Essay in Verse* (Edinburgh, 1792), pp. 1, 28.
52 J. Jamieson, *The Sorrows of Slavery, a Poem containing a Faithful Statement of Facts respecting the African Slave Trade* (London, 1789).
53 James Boswell to Rev. W. J. Temple, in *Letters of James Boswell* (London, 1857), p. 337.

54 Thomas Crawford, *Boswell, Burns and the French Revolution* (Edinburgh, 1990), p. 37.

55 Robert Burns, *Poetical Works*, ed. W. Wallace (Edinburgh, 1902), p. 535.

56 Davis, *The Problem of Slavery in Western Culture*, pp. 392, 424.

57 James Beattie, *An Essay on the Nature and Immutability of Truth, in Opposition to Sophistry and Scepticism* (London, 1807), pp. 56–7.

58 Henry Home, Lord Kames, *Sketches of the History of Man* (Edinburgh, 1813), Vol. 1, pp. 3–65.

59 Hume, *Essays Moral, Political and Literary*, Vol. 2. pp. 244–52.

60 William Dickson, *Letters on Slavery* (London, 1789), p. 60.

61 *GC*, 23 Feb 1792.

62 Schaw, *Journal of a Lady of Quality*, pp. 127, 128.

63 John Millar, *The Origin of the Distinction of Ranks* (Edinburgh, 1806), p. 293.

64 James Beattie to T. Blacklock, 1 Aug 1768. NLS Fettercairn Papers, Box 1, Acc. 4796.

65 Devine, *Scotland's Empire*, p. 249.

66 W. Smellie, ed., *Encyclopaedia Britannica*, first edition, 4 vols (Edinburgh, 1771), Vol. 3, pp. 396, 605–6.

67 William Wilberforce to William Robertson, 20 Feb 1788. NLS MS 3943 ff. 230–4.

68 James Beattie to Mrs Montagu, 25 May 1789. NLS Fettercairn Papers, Box 92, Acc. 4796.

69 Quoted in Devine, *Scotland's Empire*, p. 245.

70 Karras, *Sojourners in the Sun*, p. 7.

71 James Walvin, *Questioning Slavery* (London, 1996), pp. 121, 122.

72 James Ramsay, Evidence to the House of Lords Committee of Council 1798. RHO, MS 1787, p. 33.

73 Lady Maria Nugent, *Journal of a Resident in Jamaica*, ed. P. Wright (Kingston, [c. 1804] 1966), p. 29.

74 M. P. Brown, *Decisions of the Lords of Council and Session from 1766 to 1791*, collected by Lord Hailes (Edinburgh, 1826), p. 779.

3

PULPITS, PRESBYTERIES AND PETITIONS ON THE TRADE

∾

It is somewhat surprising, that neither the established clergy in Scotland, in their corporate capacities of Presbyteries or Synods, nor the Royal Burghs, have taken any steps in this humane business. The Manager of the Theatre Royal, to his credit let it be said, has not been so inattentive. Southern's excellent tragedy of Oroonoko is well calculated to rouse the spirit of liberty in every feeling breast.

Caledonian Mercury, 7 February 1788

In January 1788 the author of an anonymous letter to James Beattie in Aberdeen expressed surprise that 'no body of men' in Scotland had taken up the campaign against the slave trade. 'Africanus' said that he could not give his name. Not only had he spent twenty years in the West Indies and the Southern States, but he still had extensive business interests there. However, he was anxious to see the matter brought before Parliament and urged Beattie and 'some other eminent men in your church and universities' to take a lead in this matter, suggesting that petitions might be sought from Edinburgh, Glasgow and Paisley in addition to Aberdeen. 'Petitioners from Scotland will be the more necessary', he claimed, 'as counter petitions in favour of the slave trade are hatching at Liverpool, Lancaster, Bristol and Pool[e].'[1]

It was not entirely surprising that by the beginning of 1788 there had been very little activity in Scotland. Although the Society of Friends petitioned Parliament against the trade in 1783, it was to be the founding of the London-based Society for the Abolition of the Slave Trade in May 1787 that marked the start of an organised mobilisation of public opinion throughout Britain. 'Africanus' was, however, not to be disappointed for long. By the end of June 1788, the Universities of Glasgow and Aberdeen, the Town Councils of Paisley and Dundee, and the Chamber of Commerce in Edinburgh, had all sent petitions to Parliament. Not only had the Presbyteries of Edinburgh, Glasgow and Aberdeen also done so, but Kirkwall and Kirkcudbright at the extreme ends of the country joined them and the Synods of Glasgow and Ayr,

Merse and Teviotdale, Ross, Moray, Galloway and Dumfries had added their voices, frequently prompted by deliverances from several presbyteries within their bounds.

Pulpits, gatherings in churches and ministers of the Kirk fulfilled a key role in mobilising public support against the slave trade between 1788 and 1792. The courts of the church, civic bodies and public gatherings produced petitions to Parliament at this time and these were often initiated through Scottish committees specifically formed to campaign against the trade. For a small country a large number of people were involved in producing varied arguments and providing a wide range of reasons for their action. Together they made a very significant contribution towards the first round of what was, to date, to be by far and away the most extensive popular campaign in British history.

THE PULPIT AGAINST THE SLAVE TRADE

Moderate Church of Scotland leaders William Robertson and Hugh Blair of Edinburgh both used the pulpit to take issue with slavery as an institution. However, they painted with a broad brush and did not specify the West Indian connection, still less the slave trade itself. In Robertson's correspondence with William Wilberforce, the latter expressed his gratitude for receiving a copy of a Robertson sermon, but clearly felt that Robertson's more specific depictions of slavery in his *History of America* were important in providing evidence for the campaign.[2] Clearly the slave trade was a subject frequently aired from the pulpit in the early 1790s. Yet the only published sermons in these years came from Glasgow and Jedburgh ministers, the former expressing opposition to the slave trade within the context of an appeal for overseas mission and the latter giving thanks to God for the prospect of the end of the trade.

Dr John Erskine, the acknowledged leader of the Evangelical party and Robertson's colleague in Edinburgh's Greyfriars Church, was strongly in favour of foreign mission. In 1796 he made a passionate though unsuccessful plea for the national church to give practical support for evangelism overseas. 'Rax [pass] me that Bible, Moderator,' he demanded, and then read the biblical commission in Matthew's gospel. The missionary impulse was a constant element in the anti-slavery movement, though it is too simplistic to characterise anti-slavery activity simply as a tool for evangelism. Erskine was described by an abolitionist as 'zealous, well informed and inquisitive' on the slave trade and he was keen to explore the possibility of 'certain black missionaries' being sent to the new colony of ex-slaves in Sierra Leone.[3] He was the founder of the Edinburgh Missionary Society and a subscriber to the Edinburgh Society for the Abolition of the Slave Trade. Erskine in 1788 pressed the Presbytery of Edinburgh to request from the Moderator a special meeting of the Commission of Assembly in order to debate the issue of the slave trade.

At the foundation of the Glasgow Missionary Society in 1796, Dr Robert Balfour preached a sermon that linked the issues of foreign mission and slavery. Balfour, born and educated in Edinburgh, was minister of the East Parish, connected to Glasgow Cathedral. His central theme was an appeal for evangelists to go to the ends of the earth 'to convey to the simple sons the knowledge of the true God, to convert the barbarous cannibal to humanity, to Christian gentleness and goodness'. This was a curious combination of the racial stereotyping that was so often used to justify the slave trade and the language of the Enlightenment. He continued with an appeal for missionaries to challenge the institution of slavery. 'Hasten to the shores of long-injured Africa, not to seize and sell the bodies of men, but to save their perishing souls,' he pled and continued to urge Christian ministers to 'follow the miserable captives to their several sad destinations of slavery, with the inviting proclamation of spiritual liberty, while you inculcate the strictest duty to their masters'.[4]

That might seem a somewhat muted cry for abolition, despite the passion with which it must have been delivered. However, Balfour's motion to the Glasgow Presbytery in early March 1792 left no doubt about where he stood. At his instigation the Presbytery declared 'that the African slave trade is founded in cruelty and injustice and is carried on by methods inconsistent with the first principles of morality and religion'. It went on to remind all who enjoyed the blessings of freedom and Christianity to exert themselves 'by every prudent and constitutional measure to break the yoke of oppression and abolish a traffic shocking to humanity' and a hindrance to the propagation of the gospel.[5]

Thomas Somerville's sermon in April 1792 was much more specific in its focus of giving thanks for the prospect of the abolition of the slave trade. As minister of Jedburgh, Somerville had persuaded his Presbytery to send an overture to the Synod of Merse and Teviotdale and it petitioned Parliament on 5 May for abolition. He began his sermon by recommending the proposed abolition as 'a transcendent mercy and a singular cause of rejoicing and of gratitude to the author of all goodness'. A nation ripe for destruction, he claimed, is one 'which has adopted a systematic plan for oppressing and persecuting their fellow creatures, without limitation of time or regulations of control, without any provocation or complaint or injury sustained'. If war was used as a justification for the slave trade, he continued, it was clear that this argument did not apply to Britain's relations with Africa. Africans, he claimed, never invaded British territories, made war against Britain or assisted her enemies. In his prayers that day Somerville offered thanksgiving 'for the prospect of an approaching abolition of that ungodly traffic in slaves, which has brought reproach and guilt upon our nation' and adoration for God's long suffering 'in suspending those judgements which our sins have deserved'. 'From what vengeance', he asked, 'has not this country escaped?'

Somerville's sermon echoed that of Balfour in its concern for the evangelisation of Africa. The abolition of the trade, he claimed, would enable Britain to reverse a process whereby the cruelty and bloodshed offered by those who boasted of Christianity and civilisation provided an impenetrable barrier. 'Ethiopia', he said, 'shall stretch forth her hand to God. They who have hitherto been foreigners and strangers shall be made fellow citizens with the saints and the household of God.' He continued by commending the recently launched scheme to settle free slaves in Sierra Leone, which he believed would serve as a model for different relationships with Africa by approaching 'the heathen nations under the alluring address of friends and brothers', with just dealings towards them. Only then, he claimed, would the Christian religion be viewed 'in its genuine purity and simplicity, then and not till then, may the Christian expect the triumph of his faith'. The sermon made frequent reference to the principle of benevolence, 'that noble principle of our nature', and it echoed Robertson in asserting that it was this principle 'calculated by the genius and precepts of our religion' that has been 'productive of real, substantial and extensive good. It has wrought the deliverance of oppressed nations.'[6]

Somerville encountered opposition from 'some gentlemen in the country' and his enthusiasm for the agreement in 1792 to abolish the trade seems a little premature.[7] Wilberforce's parliamentary motion that year was severely trimmed through an amendment from the Government's leading Scottish member, Henry Dundas, who proposed simply that 'the slave trade ought to be *gradually* abolished'. Somerville anticipated this reservation when he admitted that some might think that the final determination 'is yet distant and uncertain'.

He told his congregation that even though he would have preferred immediate abolition, he was persuaded that the Government had no intention of eluding or postponing it, 'nor if they had any such intention, do I believe it possible for them to succeed in it.'[8]

A substantial contribution was made by ministers to the campaign for abolition, and pulpit and church meetings were mobilised for its purpose. In March 1792 it was reported from Peebles that 'in consequence of an intimation from the pulpit, the greatest part of this town and parish met in the Church for considering a petition on the abolition of the African slave trade', and Newlands in Tweeddale made a similar pulpit advertisement.[9] The Magistrates of Stirling drew up their petition in the East Church and the inhabitants of Falkirk at a meeting presided over by their veteran minister, John Muir, formed one of the many gatherings that resolved to send money to the Edinburgh campaign against the trade. The inhabitants of Largo in Fife, meeting in their parish church, resolved to boycott sugar and rum, denying themselves 'the indulgence of delicacies that are prepared by cruel stripes' and to join in any 'constitutional measure to get rid of the African slave trade'.[10] Most of the key figures in the 1792 campaign were Church of Scotland ministers and the meetings and petitions depended very heavily on the facilities and support of the Kirk at various levels.

WILLIAM DICKSON'S 1792 TOUR

After the 1788 petitioning campaign, William Wilberforce persuaded William Pitt to support an investigation into the slave trade by the House of Commons, and Sir William Dolben, MP for Oxford, brought in a bill to regulate conditions on slave ships. In 1789 Wilberforce introduced twelve resolutions on the trade, but the Commons insisted on hearing further evidence. The following year the Dolben Bill became law but in 1791 Wilberforce again failed to carry the question of abolition by 163 votes to 88. That year was described as 'a good one' for the English slave trade, with new inroads being made into the Cuban market.[11] Despite the strenuous efforts of the London Committee, and especially of Thomas Clarkson, who toured various parts of Britain in 1788, 1790 and 1791 covering a prodigious 35,000 miles to promote the cause, it seemed an endless and uphill task. A contemporary diarist reported that Clarkson 'was received in Scotland with that attention his philanthropy entitles him' and received a dinner in his honour in Glasgow.[12] However, his own estimate of the tour was that it was 'the most vexatious' of any he had undertaken and the unwillingness of people to come forward and provide evidence 'disgusted' him.[13] By his own admission, he was exhausted and he persuaded the Committee to send someone else to Scotland next time.

In January 1792, the Scottish anti-slavery writer William Dickson left London for Edinburgh. The mandate given to him was to encourage the widespread distribution of the *Abstract of Evidence* against the trade as a spur to producing a large number of petitions. The Committee was confident that these would follow from the appreciation of such horrifying facts. Yet Clarkson's instructions to Dickson were to avoid making direct requests for petitioning, allowing this to come from local people. This was in response to the charge made by the West Indian lobby that all petitions were fomented by the London abolitionist committee. Large towns were to be selected and used as centres from which to carry the campaign to smaller communities. 'All appearance of unnecessary petitions from the same place is to be avoided', ran the instructions. Dickson was urged to emphasise that prominent parliamentarians such as Charles James Fox, Edmund Burke and William Pitt had all voted for abolition. He was instructed to contact key people in every community and work on their 'vanity or interest'.[14]

Dickson took with him not only copies of the *Abstract*, but also a number of cameos produced by the pottery firm of Wedgwood and featuring the symbol adopted by the campaign of a kneeling slave in chains. In Paisley he gave a token to a ten-year-old boy who had vowed to abstain from sugar, and after convincing a man in Fochabers who had been in the West Indies that 'our evidence is quite just', he presented the man's wife with a cameo.

Most of the contacts that Dickson made were ministers of the Church of Scotland, though some were from the secession churches. Amongst those who took an active part in the campaign were five who were to be Moderators of the General Assembly, one who went on to become the leader of the Evangelical party in the Church during the late eighteenth century, and two who were to hold the distinction of being 'Father of the Kirk' in length of service at the time of their death.

Shortly after his arrival, William Dickson met the minister of St Giles and Professor of Rhetoric, William Greenfield. In their discussion, Greenfield expressed his disapproval of devoting any sermon to the subject of slavery, but agreed with Dickson over 'occasional but

Figure 4   *'Am I Not a Man and a Brother?' The motif of the kneeling slave became a central emblem of the campaign. It was designed by Josiah Wedgwood and reproduced on pottery, jade cameos, and lead, copper and silver tokens. In later years it would be criticised for its portrayal of a slave begging on his knees for freedom. It could alternatively be seen as depicting a slave rising from his knees and breaking the chains.*

forceful reference to it in prayer and sermon'. Towards the end of his visit, Dickson attended an evening service in Edinburgh. He noted with approval that the preacher, James Hall of Broughton Place, in his sermon on the text 'add to your faith, virtue' from 2 Peter, had 'introduced the topic of the slave trade 'in a most apposite, forcible manner', and concluded it by announcing that the anti-slave trade petition was available for signing at Gordon's Coffee House.

William Greenfield was a leading figure in the Moderate party in the courts of the Church and in the University of Edinburgh. He was to be Moderator of the General Assembly in 1796. Greenfield was by no means inactive in his support for the campaign, for all his caution over sermons on the subject, and Dickson described him as 'zealous and well informed'. He was elected to the Committee of the Edinburgh Society for the Abolition of the Slave Trade in October 1789 and is listed amongst subscribers to meet its expenses. It is therefore not surprising that he was appointed in 1788 and 1792 as one of the committee charged by the Presbytery of Edinburgh to prepare petitions to the House of Commons on the abolition of the slave trade. Greenfield was among a number of leading churchmen and academics in Edinburgh who were active in the campaign. William Robertson's son William, who for over twenty years was the Procurator of the General Assembly, became a member of the Society for Abolition after reading the *Abstract* in 1792. In his enthusiasm for petitioning he urged Dickson to 'give us time, Scotland will not be outdone by England in this glorious rivalry'.

The role of parish ministers, particularly in rural areas, was a vital one and it is reflected not just in the petitions from church courts, but also in popular support within the whole community. John Muir of Falkirk assured Dickson that the town and parish were 'almost certain' to petition, the two ministers in Queensferry guaranteed a petition 'along with the townspeople', and Paisley's Anti-Burgher minister, James Alice, with whom Dickson stayed, was one of the most active in the town. Dickson noted that, largely due to his efforts, 'a petition for Paisley [was] certain'. The spectacular number of petitions from those in the north-east and between Dundee and Aberdeen partly reflected Dickson's efforts early in the year. In Inverurie, George Adam assured him: 'The Presbytery of Garrioch shall petition. I can answer for them.' Alexander Mollison told him that Brechin Presbytery was certain. In Cullen, Robert Grant gave encouraging news about the probability of a petition from Fordyce Presbytery. The Moderator of Turriff Presbytery, William Stuart, after taking a bottle of wine with Dickson, told him that the Presbytery was 'always unanimous' and that he was totally confident about their commitment.

At the other end of the country, two Ayrshire ministers who were both associated with Robert Burns played their part. John Russel, a Popular party minister of Kilmarnock – 'black Russel' in Burns' poem 'Twa Herds' – played a key role in Irvine Presbytery's detailed deliverance and petition. Dickson dined with him, found him an enthusiastic ally and left twenty copies of the *Abstract* with him. William Dalrymple, a leading Moderate in Ayr, had in 1759 baptised Burns, who termed him 'Dalrymple mild' in 'The Kirk's Alarms'. Dickson thought him 'cold but polite' and full of reservations about the campaign on account of a letter he had received from the West Indies.[15] Yet Dalrymple, who had been Moderator of the General Assembly in 1781, showed his support for abolition in 1789 by subscribing two guineas to the newly founded Edinburgh Committee.[16] In 1792 he was Moderator of Ayr Presbytery. The Presbytery did not itself send a petition, which no doubt disappointed Dickson, but it published strong opinions in the Glasgow and Edinburgh newspapers, associated with other petitioners and offered financial assistance to their efforts.[17]

There is no record of the leading Glasgow ministers being involved in the Society there. When Thomas Clarkson made a visit to the city in 1791, his contacts were laymen and included Professors Millar, Wilson and Young at the university. Dickson also found more encouragement in academic circles, where these three 'hearty friends' assured him of the certainty of a petition from the university, whilst the Presbytery was only 'probable' and anything from the Magistrates was most unlikely. However, he also described Robert Balfour as 'very hearty'. Balfour was possibly unsure that Glasgow Presbytery could deliver and pressed Dickson strongly to work with Edinburgh Presbytery to petition 'for examples sake'.[18] In the end, Glasgow followed Edinburgh by petitioning shortly afterwards. The Presbytery sent it to William Wilberforce, stating that they considered the slave trade 'as subversive of every principle of justice, humanity and religion'. They requested the Commons 'that the most expedient measures will then be immediately taken for bringing to an end this species of commerce which is inconsistent with the most valuable rights of man, with the honour of a country distinguished by its love of liberty and with the gentle spirit of Christianity'.[19]

THE COURTS OF THE CHURCH – PRESBYTERY, SYNOD AND GENERAL ASSEMBLY

Edinburgh Presbytery was first introduced to the slave trade through a speech delivered in February 1788 by Robert Walker of Canongate, best-known for his portrait as the skating minister on Duddingston Loch. Walker expressed the hope that his brethren, who had shown such concern about Lord's Day observance, would 'not now be less zealous in the great and generous cause of humanity'.[20] His motion to petition was accepted by Presbytery, who also, at the suggestion of Dr Erskine, agreed to request the Moderator of the General Assembly to call a special Commission of Assembly to consider the matter. Dickson met Walker four years later and found him 'cordial' and interested in the Sierra Leone colonisation scheme for freed slaves.

The Presbytery appointed a committee to prepare and transmit the petition. Walker and Greenfield were nominated, as were William Moodie of St Andrews Church (also the university's Professor of

Hebrew) and Andrew Hunter of New Greyfriars (the Professor of Divinity). Hunter was to be Moderator of the General Assembly in 1792, as was Moodie seven years later. In 1788, though, he was free to speak as a commissioner at the Assembly and made a powerful refutation of the idea of slavery being sanctioned by scripture. He claimed to have considered it a natural infringement of liberty from the earliest of his days and looked for the Assembly's support in alleviating the suffering of the African people and bringing to them 'the blessings of the Christian religion'. Hunter joined the committee of the Society at Edinburgh for the Purpose of Effecting the Abolition of the African Slave Trade and in his moderatorial year became its Chairman. Dickson described him as 'very zealous', and he carefully steered the Society through its efforts in securing from the city a petition that would attract nearly eleven thousand signatures.[21]

Yet there was considerable caution in 1788 from bodies as yet unused to petitioning Parliament and a general reluctance to be seen to tell the legislature what to do. Following the traditional format of petitions to the General Assembly, the Presbyteries of Glasgow, Edinburgh and Aberdeen made it clear that they had full confidence in the legislature to take the measures that it would judge best. Glasgow specifically stated that it did not presume to know what these measures might be. Some synods, such as Angus and Mearns, called for the 'total and speedy abolition of the practice of making traffick of the human species'. However, Moray's petition confined itself to a call 'to devise such measures that may mitigate if not entirely remove that evil', and that of Dumfries urged that measures should be taken to 'mitigate and in the end relieve, the sufferings of their fellow creatures'.[22]

In 1792 special meetings of Stirling, Paisley and Dumfries Presbyteries were held, called by the Moderators in response to members who urged action. There is no doubt that this was in part as a result of Dickson's groundwork, but it also gave the lie to those who accused abolitionists of simply responding to control from the centre. The Presbytery of Hamilton at its March meeting formally approved the Moderator's action of circulating a letter to various ministers and elders to alert them to the issue. It then turned itself into a committee to draft and unanimously approve a petition.[23] Perth Presbytery did not petition, but 'a number of ministers' were reported to form a committee under the Moderator, which proposed to seek confirmation and publication of their resolutions at the next Presbytery.[24] Most presbyteries appreciated the urgency of the situation and set up special committees to draft petitions that were agreed the same day. Others, such as Kirkcaldy, were either more cautious or more democratic. At their meeting in February, a member moved for petitioning. All members were sympathetic in their 'abhorrence of the trade', but agreed that any decision should be postponed until the March meeting, recommending that members should 'use their diligence to obtain and bring forward the opinions of their parishioners on the subject'. At the next meeting, the members declared that 'almost all the people under their charge were of the same sentiment' and, armed with that mandate, the Presbytery resolved to petition, not, as some did, for Parliament to end the trade in their own good time, but for 'immediate' abolition.[25]

The 1788 General Assembly received three overtures on the slave trade from the Synods of Lothian and Tweeddale, Angus and Mearns, and Merse and Teviotdale. The latter, very largely as a result of Thomas Somerville's work, was the only one of the three to petition Parliament. The *Scots Magazine* reported that 'a debate ensued, not on the general measure, on which the assembly appeared unanimous, but as to the mode in which they ought to interfere'. Yet not all commissioners taking part in the debate appeared to support abolition. Professor Walker of Edinburgh, in what was described as 'a sensible speech', feared the loss of property and the probable murder of Europeans by negroes, if the trade were abolished. Dr Grieve from Dalkeith declared his belief that when the investigation by the House of Commons was completed, it would be demonstrated that the cruelties and abuses of the trade were seen to be greatly exaggerated. On the other side, Professor Hunter was careful to limit his remarks to the slave trade, although from early days he said that he had considered slavery as an infringement of natural rights and hoped that one day it would be 'politic or possible' to abolish it. By contrast, in what was reported as a 'very pathetic speech', Dr Johnston of Leith had no such reservations. After detailing 'the shocking barbarities' of the planters and shipmasters, he declared his total support for the abolition of African slavery. The Moderate leader, Dr Alexander Carlyle, represented those who wanted to include the subject in a loyal address to the King. He believed that for the General Assembly, the supreme court of the national church, to petition the House of Commons would be beneath its dignity and that the Address to the Throne would be a more vehicle for such an august body. Although the motion to petition Parliament was lost by thirty-four votes, there was unanimous support for the declaration that: 'The General Assembly think themselves called upon as men, as Christians and as members of the national church, to declare their abhorrence of a traffic contrary to the rights of mankind and the feelings of humanity.' It expressed the earnest wish of the Assembly 'that the wisdom and mercy of the legislature may be speedily exerted for the relief of that unhappy portion of their fellow creatures'.[26]

Similar sentiments were expressed by two subsequent General Assemblies. In 1791 the deliverance of 1788 was reaffirmed. The Assembly added that they judged 'it not necessary to proceed further in this business', but contented themselves with trusting the 'wisdom and mercy of the legislature' in taking 'such steps as they shall think proper for the relief of this unhappy race of men'.[27] The 1792 Assembly produced a somewhat stronger deliverance. The trade was described as 'incompatible with the great principles of religion and morality', attended 'with circumstances of injustice and cruelty' and 'shocking to the feelings of virtuous minds'. It acknowledged with satisfaction the widespread public concern 'entertained by people of every rank and distinction' and declared that abolition would be 'an example of humanity and enlightened policy given by Great Britain to the other countries of Europe'. The Assembly expressed 'ardent wishes and earnest prayers' that Parliament should speedily act to bring the trade to an end.[28] The celebrated ex-slave Olaudah Equiano, now an activist in the London campaign, observed that debate and offered in a subsequent letter to the *Edinburgh Evening Courant* 'the warmest effusions of a heart overflowing with hope from your pious efforts'. The Assembly still resisted petitioning, but its sentiments were echoed in many a petition from lower church courts.

The only church petition in 1792 which came from outside the Church of Scotland was from the Dissenting Congregation of Morebattle on 29 February. Episcopalians were small in number and suffered from the after-effects of being on the losing side in the Jacobite uprisings. Methodists, destined to be very active in the next round of popular pressure, were similarly absent from the campaign, despite John Wesley's enthusiasm for abolition and his visits to Scotland. Baptists were to play a significant part in the later years of the campaign.

There were, however, expressions of opinion on the slave trade that year from those who had seceded from the national church. The Associated Presbyteries of Perth and Edinburgh were amongst those who issued statements in the newspapers and the Relief Congregation of Pittenweem produced a seven-point statement and took a special collection to contribute to the cause.[29] Some of the strongest views on the subject came from non-petitioners. The Gaelic Congregation of Edinburgh expressed its 'detestation of the oppressions of every kind by which the coasts of Africa have been harassed and desolated . . . by this traffic in human flesh'. Those in Pittenweem spoke of being 'involved in a guilt of the most atrocious nature'. The Associate Presbytery of Edinburgh prayed that there would be an immediate end to a trade which 'commencing in injustice, is conducted with fraud and violence and terminated in the full and unabated misery of its unfortunate victims'.[30]

There is no doubt from this of the strength of feeling amongst many dissenting church communities. Many of them shared in the petitions of others, which became co-operative ventures and involved different churches. The March meetings in Alloa and Paisley included the ministers of different denominations. The report of Comrie's meeting specifically mentioned 'the inhabitants of the parish of all denominations', and that of Bothkenner in Stirlingshire stated that it was from 'the inhabitants of various congregations'.[31] Given all this, it seems strange that there was, with one exception, a total absence of actual petitions from dissenting congregations and Presbyteries. The reason was probably a reflection less of the strength of the national church in the eighteenth century than of the reluctance of those churches who had broken away from the state connection to be seen to approach the high court of Parliament with a separate request on their behalf. By 1823 and thereafter, when the petitions against slavery itself started to flow into the Commons and the Lords, that situation was to change dramatically.

CIVIC BODIES

In 1788 there were five Scottish petitions from non-ecclesiastical bodies – Edinburgh's Chamber of Commerce, the Universities of Aberdeen and Glasgow, and the Provost, Town Council and Magistrates of both Dundee and Paisley.[32] The first to be presented to the Commons was that of the Edinburgh Chamber of Commerce, whose Chairman, Sir William Forbes, and Secretary, William Creech, were both to be elected to the Edinburgh Abolition Society in the following year. Creech, a bookseller and publisher, was Lord Provost of Edinburgh from 1811 to 1813. Forbes was a banker and close friend of James Beattie. Beattie himself, as Secretary of Marischal College, was very much involved in the college's petition. The Chamber of

Commerce took on board one of the key arguments put forward by defenders of the trade, that it was a commercial necessity. They declared their strong conviction that the slave trade was less profitable than had been claimed. 'But even if this were not so much the case as the Chamber is inclined to believe it', they continued, 'the feelings of your petitioners as men, would overbear their opinions as merchants and lead them to sacrifice somewhat of the convenience and profit of commerce to the rights and principles of humanity.'[33]

In 1792 synods, presbyteries and congregations were still well represented, but the majority of petitions came from 'the inhabitants' of various towns and burghs, some in association with the magistrates and town councillors. Others came from trades associations and corporations. In a letter to the *Caledonian Mercury* in February, 'Humanitas' expressed his pleasure that there were so many associations expressing their abhorrence of the slave trade, but asked 'why do not the Counties call meetings to take the opinion of the gentlemen of landed property on the subject?'. A lengthy response to this question by 'Freeholder' pointed to the difficulty landed gentry faced in being involved in any issue that 'would have a tendency to disturb the public peace', but it argued that the slave trade was an issue where the overwhelming need of justice and humanity made it necessary to have the voice of landed interest ranged against it. The same correspondent followed up some days later with the information that the heritors of Stirlingshire and Kirkcudbright had recently met to consider petitioning.[34] In fact, freeholders and landed proprietors either petitioned or associated with others in petitioning in Banff, Leith, Dumfries and Kippen, in addition to the two mentioned.

At the same time a large number of civic groups who never sent in petitions followed the seceding churches in making their opposition to the slave trade known publicly in the newspapers, many at great length. Once again the largest number of public declarations came from smaller towns and villages. Many individual guilds, whilst being part of associations that petitioned, chose to publicise their individual resolutions, often with vehemence. The Brewers of Paisley declared the slave trade to be 'attended with the greatest enormities of fraud, cruelty and oppression'. The Journeymen Shoemakers testified to their abhorrence of the 'unjust, inhuman and barbarous measures' which they judged to be 'contrary to the law of God and every well regulated country'. The Candlemakers of Edinburgh 'blushed' that such terrible things existed and 'regretted that a sense of right should have lain so long unawakened'.[35]

The petitions and public statements were sometimes accompanied by encouragement to boycott sugar and rum, the products of slavery. In support of this action, Edinburgh dealers were offering 'free sugar' from the East Indies. Dickson, although more cautious than Clarkson in this regard, noted with pleasure when individuals whom he met on his travels decided to abstain from West Indian goods. Largo's Kirk Session and its Inhabitants, although not actually petitioning, resolved to boycott West Indian products and agreed to join in 'every constitutional measure' to get rid of the slave trade. A meeting of Leslie's 'respectable inhabitants' saw the refusal to buy sugar and rum produced by slave labour as a means of 'putting an end to the African slave trade in case the legislature refuse to abolish that infamous commerce'. An enthusiast even wrote to the *Glasgow Courier* in January of that year declaring that eating West Indian sugar was equivalent to whipping a slave,[36] but most groups couched their intentions in less dramatic language.

Although the civic authorities in most of the ports that had been involved in the trade were silent, Montrose was an exception. The Provost, Magistrates and Town Council resolved to petition Parliament to abolish 'a commerce so disgraceful to a free and enlightened nation' and agreed to contribute to the costs of the campaign and undertake 'any lawful action' until abolition was secured.[37] In 1788, the Town Council had received a letter from the Manchester Committee requesting support, but although they instructed their MP to vote for abolition, there was no petition to the Commons.[38] In 1792 they made sure that their views were communicated to Parliament.

There were, however, some unusual aspects to the campaign. 'Africanus' had urged Beattie to use his influence in the Church and universities in Scotland. Although the Universities of Aberdeen and Glasgow petitioned, those of St Andrews and Edinburgh did not. The former's reluctance was mentioned by William Dickson when he described the Principal and some other academics as 'indifferent', and there was academic resistance to the Presbytery's petitioning. What is extraordinary is the absence of any petition from the University of Edinburgh, given the number of academics enthusiastically and actively involved in the campaign. It may be simply that it followed the pattern of Oxford in that it did not regard itself a suitable body to petition, to the embarrassment of the MP for the city, Sir William Dolben.

Of the 101 petitions to the House of Commons on the slave trade in 1788, 16 came from Scotland, the majority of these from the courts of the national church. The most northerly Presbytery to petition was Kirkwall in Orkney.[39] In 1792, the next year when petitioning took place, the Commons received 519 petitions, of which 185 came from Scotland, representing over 35 per cent of the British total. Synods and presbyteries accounted for only 28 petitions, but they included by far the most populous areas. That year Caithness followed Orkney's earlier example and neighbouring Presbyteries of Stranraer, Wigtown, Dumfries and Annan joined Kirkcudbright in its second petition. The impressive contribution of Galloway was matched in the north-east, where six Aberdeenshire presbyteries petitioned; but not surprisingly, the main concentration was around the cities of Glasgow, Ayrshire and Paisley, Edinburgh (including Leith), the Lothians and the central belt, Dundee, Tayside and Fife. The shipping communities of Greenock and Port Glasgow saw no petitions and only the Synod of Ross petitioned from the western Highlands. A number of presbyteries and parishes made their views on the slave trade known through resolutions sent to the newspapers. Petitions from civic bodies and citizens numbered 112, and many included references to ministers and Kirk Sessions that were associated with them.

If the 67 published newspaper statements are added to the 184 petitions, allowing for some overlap, the volume of declarations against the slave trade from Scotland in 1792 number around 250. Although a lively correspondence in the *Glasgow Courier* in the first quarter of 1792 saw a number of arguments in favour of the trade, not a single petition or corporate statement appeared in support of it that year. Despite the friendly warning to James Beattie by 'Africanus', the powerful Glasgow West India Association was not yet formed, and when Dickson first met the Glasgow Committee he was assured that 'there was little or no danger of counter petitioning in Scotland'.[40]

DISSENTING VOICES

For all that there were a large numbers of ministers of the Kirk involved in the 1792 petitioning campaign, others were cautious or reluctant to become involved. Dickson reported that some were persuaded that the slaves were happy. A minister in Perth was apparently 'terrified of insurrections', in Forfar another minister was very exercised about the compensation given to planters if the trade were abolished, and in Keith, Dr Dougal was, according to Dickson, 'an honest man, hearty though full of doubts and crotchets infused into his thinking mind by

West Indian planters'. One minister he encountered in the Presbytery of Fordoun assured Dickson that there was little hope of a petition from that source 'since the Moderator, Mr Walker of Dunnotyr, had been heard to defend slavery from scripture'.[41]

Strong opposition to the action of the majority came in two presbyteries. The language used in Glasgow's petition in April 1792 was to lead to some critical correspondence in the *Glasgow Courier*. One member of the court exercised his right to record a 'dissent and complaint' against the presbytery's decision to petition. James Lapslie, minister of Campsie, was a paid Government informer who became noteworthy for his part in the transportation of the radical advocate Thomas Muir and in obtaining three months' imprisonment for William Dunn, the Moderator of Glasgow Presbytery in 1791, after Dunn preached a sermon sympathetic to electoral reform. Lapslie's first ground for dissent was that the debate was prejudged, since many members had already signed petitions in their personal capacity against the slave trade. Whilst conceding that the Presbytery had been at pains to emphasise its concern with 'the general principles of humanity', he went on to declare the slave trade a political issue and state his view that an ecclesiastical court, in addressing it, had 'stepped out of their sphere'. His third objection was that the Presbytery was seeking to address 'partial abuses' in the slave trade, whilst ignoring 'great flagrant abuses' in this country in which Britons were more interested. Lapslie warned that interference by the Church into questions that concerned the legislature could lead to the Church of Scotland itself suffering from Government interference. Finally, he concluded that it was 'dangerous to foment that spirit of dissatisfaction and licentiousness which is apparently too prevalent in the present day'. The Church, in his opinion, should 'check and moderate the present national phrenzy [sic]' instead of seeking to interfere 'and add to the flames'. He hoped that the legislature would take measures relative to the slave trade that 'shall appear consistent with the interests of the colonies, the safety of private property and the principles of sound policy'.[42] The Presbytery of Glasgow appointed Messrs Balfour and Dunn as a committee to answer the dissent and report. There is no record in the minute book of their findings, but Lapslie was shortly to have his revenge on the latter.

On the same night as the Glasgow debate, the Presbytery of St Andrews decided to petition. Dr George Hill, the Principal of St Mary's College, St Andrews, rose that evening to move a countermotion. Hill proposed that the Presbytery should, instead of petitioning, simply declare in the public newspapers 'their abhorrence of a system of cruelty which pervades the whole conduct of the African slave trade'. He agreed entirely with the spirit of the petition, but argued that it did not fall within the Presbytery's power to challenge the time and manner of abolishing a system which was undoubtedly evil, but 'with which many interests are intertwined' and for whose ending they must 'rely with entire confidence on the instinct, the wisdom and the humanity of the legislature'. When the decision to petition was passed, Dr Hill and Dr Joseph MacCormick, Principal of St Leonard's College, entered their dissent on two grounds. They objected to any appeal to people on an issue which was already before Parliament and in which the petitioners had no 'patrimonial interest', further arguing that those petitioning had only partial information on which they could not competently judge and that this 'abuse of the rights of petitioning' would perhaps overawe the legislature. In addition, it might introduce 'amongst the people a spirit of turbulence and a desire to dictate to the legislature', that, if followed in other situations, might 'be the instrument of unhinging our excellent constitution'.[43]

THE ABOLITIONIST SOCIETIES

By 1792 there were five societies in Scotland dedicated to the abolition of the slave trade – in Aberdeen, Perth, Glasgow, Paisley and Edinburgh. No minute books survive of any of them and their roles in the campaign are varied. No petition was presented from the inhabitants of either Aberdeen or Perth. The Presbytery of Aberdeen and Marischal College both petitioned once again, as they did in 1788, although Dickson commented that the Presbytery's text was simply a copy of the earlier document and the deliverance was strongly opposed by two members. The university petition was only obtained through considerable lobbying of senior academics. A few days later these two bodies were joined in petitioning by the Provost, Magistrates and Town Councillors of the city, though only by seven votes to six, with two Baillies entering a strong protest.[44]

The Edinburgh Committee for the Abolition of the Slave Trade was the oldest and by far the strongest in Scotland. Under the chairmanship of Lord Gardenstone, it published detailed resolutions in the Edinburgh newspapers in February 1789 and in the following year the Society reprinted the 1788 petitions from the Presbytery and the Chamber of Commerce requesting their circulation in each neighbourhood 'as to produce the most general knowledge of this

important subject among men of liberal and enlightened minds'.[45]
The subscribers' list attached to the reprint included many prominent
Edinburgh ministers, as well as Dr Dalrymple of Ayr and the Writer
to the Signet, Mr (later Sir) Walter Scott, Sir William Forbes and
William Creech assisted in taking in the subscriptions and defraying
expenses. The Committee's treasurer was Alexander Alison of the
Excise Office, but a colleague in that department, Campbell
Haliburton, undertook the major work of the committee throughout
this whole period. Haliburton was an enthusiastic correspondent
with the London and Manchester Committees, and as far away as
Shrewsbury, Katherine Plymley wrote: 'the committee at Edinburgh
have been very active, particularly Mr. Houlbrooke [sic] who is doing
great things in Scotland'. Despite Plymley's misnomer, it is from her
diary that we learn of the attempt to supply every parish in Scotland
with a copy of the *Abstract of Evidence* on the slave trade and the
pasting up of the plan of a slave ship in public places, an enterprise
for which Campbell Haliburton was responsible.[46]

The printing and distribution of the *Abstract* was a task that the
Edinburgh Society undertook on behalf of the country, inviting
the Glasgow Society to participate. When it appeared by the end of
the year, the text on the flyleaf indicated that it was printed at the
expense of both committees, but there was no doubting which Society
did the work. The *Abstract* was a 128-page summary of the four-
volume minutes of the House of Commons committee. It contained a
list of those who gave evidence (almost all of whom had experience
of the Caribbean or the Guinea trade); accounts of the methods of
procuring, transporting and selling slaves, including a large folding
plan of a slave ship; and evidence of the conditions of slaves in the
West Indies, with details of their treatment that spared nothing.
Towards the end, a chapter entitled 'A Graveyard for Seamen' paralleled the brutal treatment given to slaves and that given to seamen,
conclusively accompanied by figures of the losses by death of the
crews of slave ships each year from 1784 to 1790.[47]

The following year, in preparation for the city-wide signing of a petition in March, a further 25-page summary of the *Abstract* was made
by the Edinburgh Society to be distributed even more widely. This document was prefaced by *A Short Address to the People of Scotland on
the Subject of the Slave Trade* and ended with instructions about petitioning.[48] The growing influence of the Edinburgh Society was evidenced by the fact that petitions from Tranent, Jedburgh and Falkirk
were specifically channelled through Haliburton, while Kettle, Falkirk

and Bathgate declared willingness to give financial support to the Edinburgh Committee, as did the Beneficial Society of Coldstream, who sent five guineas, and Inverkeithing Town Council, who agreed to subscribe eight. Perth Presbytery resolved to communicate its views to the Secretary of the Edinburgh Society and Ayr Presbytery resolved to help bear the costs of the Societies applying to Parliament for abolition. Edinburgh was not specified, but since the Moderator was a personal subscriber to that Society, it is likely that the presbyters' generosity was directed there. By contrast, the Glasgow Society only rated one mention in petitions outside the city, that of Kirkliston.

The work of the Edinburgh Society culminated in the city's petition in March 1792. A meeting was held in February, with Professor Hunter in the chair, to approve the text of the petition. On 5 March over 3,500 signatures were gathered in the Circus and in subsequent days in various churches and coffee houses. By the end of the month, the petition was closed with 10,885 signatures, a total exceeded in any city outside London only by Manchester.[49] It was transmitted through Secretary of State Dundas, the local MP, ironically the same Henry Dundas who was to be the proposer of the amendment in Parliament that was to effectively delay abolition for nearly two decades.

Perth Presbytery was one of very few in southern Scotland not to petition, although they strongly condemned the trade, commended the efforts of the Glasgow and Edinburgh Societies, offered to 'cheerfully contribute some pecuniary aid' to the cause and urged presbyters to advance 'the same cause of humanity' within their parishes. However, the incorporated trades in the city sent a petition on 7 March and in their resolutions commended 'the benevolent exertions' by 'the Society lately formed in this place for the abolition of this horrid traffic'.[50]

Early in February 1792, at a public meeting in Paisley of 'Magistrates, Town Council, Ministers and Inhabitants', an association was formed and a committee elected to prepare a petition. Although there was no specific petition from that meeting, there was no lack of activity from Paisley. On 16 March a petition was presented to the House, subscribed by the 'Incorporated Trades and twenty-one other Societies', including several weavers' groups and a Soldiers Union.[51] The previous day the Commons received one from the Presbytery of Paisley, arising out of a special meeting called for that purpose on 6 March.[52] In their enthusiasm they had sent it directly to William Wilberforce. At the next meeting, the Moderator reported on a response from Wilberforce thanking the Presbytery for the honour, but going on to say that, in view of an impression by those hostile to the cause that petitions were a result of 'my fomenting and stirring up rather than to the spontaneous impulse of the people', he had asked a friend to present it.[53]

The Glasgow Committee in 1791 printed and distributed *An Address to the Inhabitants of Glasgow, Paisley and the Neighbourhood*. It was read to a meeting on 18 January and reflected Clarkson's research on the means by which slaves were taken from Africa, the conditions on slave ships and the sales in the West Indies 'without regard to ties of blood or friendship where husbands are separated from their wives and children are torn from their parents for ever'. The pamphlet addressed the objection that abolition of the slave trade would ruin West Indian commerce and concluded 'that if the trade be founded in iniquity it ought to be abandoned whatever the consequences'. Care was taken to distance the pamphleteers from any thought of imminent emancipation of West Indian slaves, although they did 'indulge the hope' that the slaves 'along with other advantages, by enjoying the means of religious instruction will gradually rise in the scale of being' to be reckoned to merit more liberty.

The pamphlet was accompanied by the diagram of a slave ship published by the abolitionist printer James Phillips for the London Committee in 1789, along with details of conditions on board. This was between two pages of the text and concluded with a recognition of the identification of 'The flourishing towns of Leeds, Manchester and other parts of Britain' with the work of the London Committee and the hope that the inhabitants of Glasgow, Paisley and the neighbourhood, 'whose manufactures and trade are, by the blessing of God, in so thriving condition, will surely not be averse to join the general voice of the disinterested part of the nation and to add their mite in supporting the cause of justice and humanity'. In recognition of the strength of West Indian commercial interest in the west of Scotland, it expressed the hope that even individuals involved in the West Indian trade 'will not be intimidated from doing their duty by a mere shadow of pecuniary interest' and that those who who were connected to the merchants by friendship would still obey 'the clear and strong dictates of morality and religion'. The pamphlet continued with the somewhat optimistic conviction that those in such commerce might not be swayed by this argument alone and realistically feared that, even in 'this enlightened age', selfish considerations and a 'sordid attention to mere profit and loss' had all too often 'taken such hold of mankind as to deaden their feelings of right and wrong and to render them indifferent to the sufferings of their fellow creatures'.[54]

William Dickson was a little disappointed by his visit in January 1792 to the Glasgow Committee, which he found very disorganised and its Secretary expressing the fear that Thomas Clarkson's appeal to boycott sugar and his keenness for the French Revolution would hurt the cause. This was hardly surprising, considering the strength of the West Indian interest in the city, and when Dickson met with Professors Millar, Young and Wilson the next day he learnt from them that petitions would most likely be obtained from the people and from the university, but not from the magistrates.[55] That prediction was accurate. The university, with Wilson as Clerk of Senate, presented the first petition from Scotland that year on 15 February. A petition drafted by the Glasgow Society on 1 February was lodged in the Session House of the Tron Church and two others and presented to the House of Commons at the end of March. Despite the reluctance of the magistrates as a group, the Trades House, Weavers and Skinners and Glovers all petitioned. David Dale, the noted philanthropist, founder of New Lanark and father-in-law of Robert Owen, was then Chairman of the Glasgow Society, which, at a meeting in February 1792, directed that thanks 'for his unwearied and manly support of views and measures fraught with such humanity' should be published in Glasgow, Edinburgh, London and Manchester newspapers.[56]

THE ARGUMENTS AGAINST THE SLAVE TRADE

A large number of the Scottish petitions in 1788 described 'the present state of the African Slave Trade' as being 'contrary to the principles of justice, humanity, good policy and religion' and stressed that the national prosperity made 'a generous commiseration for the unhappy' imperative. Glasgow Presbytery was 'ambitious to see the national character rescued from every imputation of oppression and cruelty'[57] and Edinburgh Presbytery lamented 'that any of the human race should have cause to complain of oppression from Britain'.[58] The Synod of Glasgow and Ayr declared its conviction 'that the national guilt has been much increased by this unjust and barbarous traffic; that it is displeasing to that God who has made of one blood all nations of men and declared himself the friend and avenger of the oppressed; and that it is at the same time hurtful to the interests and disgraceful to the character of a free and generous nation'. The Synod

Figure 5   *The journeys of William Dickson throughout Scotland, January–March 1792, on behalf of the Society for the Abolition of the Slave Trade.*

of Dumfries in its petition spoke of 'the political interest of the nation and the spirit of liberty and Christianity', and the Synod of Ross claimed that the trade was 'inconsistent with the principles of humanity as well as Christianity'.[59]

Two aspects in 1788 contrast strongly with the petitions to Parliament four years later. The first was the way in which little distinction was made between abolition of the slave trade and of slavery itself. Aberdeen Presbytery resolved that 'every trial for extending liberty to them who are under slavery ought to be supported'. Glasgow Presbytery's petition expressed an ardent wish 'that laws which render them free may extend their benign influence to every person in the British Dominions', and in its overture to the General Assembly the Synod of Angus and Mearns wished to see 'as soon as may be, a total abolition of such slavery and of the traffic whereby it is supported'. The petition from the University of Aberdeen's Marischal College, at James Beattie's instigation, struck a slightly more cautious note, but still looked towards emancipation. It prayed Parliament to 'alleviate the rigours of Negro slavery and prepare the way for its final extirpation in every part of the British Empire'.[60] The pressures from the West Indian lobby and increasing fears of insurrection caused by the French Revolution were to lead to more modest goals being expressed by many petitioners in 1792.

Those who represented the national campaign expressed a concern not to lose the immediate cause by embracing the wider one. Dickson complained of supporters in Perth that he could 'hardly get them to separate emancipation from abolition'. Events in France continued to disturb many over revolutionary excesses, thus the campaign against the slave trade had to be careful it did not become confused with support for revolution, or even for reform of the franchise. When Dickson visited Portsoy, he felt it necessary to note that neither of the local leaders had any connection with the French Revolutionary Club and that he had charged them 'to beware any allusion to it or even to liberty'. At a meeting of the Committee in Edinburgh in March 1792, he became anxious about suggestions that Henry Dundas did not represent the 'people' of the city. Some members were opposed to transmitting their petition through Dundas. 'I prevailed upon them', wrote Dickson, 'to say no more in this way connected with Burgh Reform or any other cause whatever, good or bad.'[61]

What were the main themes that ran through the petitions and resolutions reported in the press? The first was sheer horror at the cruelty of slavery. The graphic details of the trade contained in the *Abstract* clearly had an effect. The Congregation of Rathillet declared their indignation at hearing of their fellow men 'being dragged from their native shores and in a distant clime, under a burning sun, sweating out a miserable existence under the lash of a capricious and barbarous taskmaster'. That of Falkirk posed the question: 'what ear can hear without disgust, of thousands of wretches who, driven or stolen from their homes, are crowded together, oppressed by their miseries, by a foul air, by the vermin that devour them, by despair and by a rancour still more cruel, live in the fermentation of a stifled rage', and it went on to ask 'Why? What evil have they done?'. Undeserved injustice was a theme with which a number of petitioners engaged in response to the justification sometimes offered that enslavement was a result of war, brutality or crime. Dundee's petition described the slave trade as 'productive of extreme misery and degradation to a race of men who never injured us', and the Edinburgh Candlemakers saw 'our countrymen a scourge to an innocent race of people who are no less men than we are'.[62]

This basic affirmation of common humanity found expression in several ways. Glasgow Presbytery's first deliverance began: 'That as God hath made of one blood all the nations of men to dwell on the face of the earth we with pleasure recognise in their common nature our kindred brothers and their equal rights as men.'[63] The Relief Congregation of Pittenweem spoke of 'all nations of men being thus equal by the law of their creator' and Bo'ness Beneficent Society urged 'that Africans being part of the human species, are as justly entitled to the liberties and privileges of mankind as any other people on the globe'. Some petitions recognised the racist ideology underpinning slavery. Falkirk's declared that 'they differ from Europeans by colour – perhaps luxury hath need of them', and the resolution from Bathgate affirmed that it was 'as absurd to think you can make a man a slave because he is black, as to maintain that the height of stature, strength of body and fairness of complexion are moral virtues'.[64]

Pride in the professed British traditions of justice, civilisation and liberty was a familiar feature and it is contrasted with a traffic in human beings that patently denied these values. At a special meeting of Hamilton Presbytery, the method by which slaves were procured and transported in the middle passage was deemed to violate justice, natural rights, the precepts of the gospel and 'the free and happy constitution of government under which Britons live'. Stirling Presbytery considered 'every instance of tyranny and oppression as repugnant to the British Constitution and inconsistent with the liberty and civilisation of a refined people and an enlightened age'. The inhabitants of Anderston, commending the enlightened work of Wilberforce and the societies working for abolition, looked to the time 'when an innocent race of men will be allowed the due possession of their natural and inalienable rights, which are the boast of Britain and of the enlightened nations of the earth'.[65]

In an age that took divine wrath for granted, this aspect found frequent mention and not only in ecclesiastical circles. Cupar Presbytery declared that much guilt had been contracted by the slave trade and that the nation was 'exposed to the judgement of heaven'. Edinburgh Presbytery was 'anxious to avert the vengeance of God who executeth judgement for the oppressed'. However, the strongest statement on divine retribution came from the 'Incorporated Trades of Paisley with twenty-one other Societies'. They pointed to the 'awful consideration in a religious view' of the daily accumulation of guilt from a disgraceful trade and West Indian barbarity, and continued: 'if a timely stop is not put to their oppression there is reason to conclude that such a system of iniquity cannot long escape the righteous judgement of God'.[66]

The slave trade and the profession of Christianity were set against each other. Paisley Presbytery spoke of 'the reproach which it has so long brought upon the Christian name'; Stirling Presbytery observed that the trade, 'when examined by the principles of the Christian religion . . . appears to us unjust and impious'. The petition from St Andrews Presbytery saw it as 'repugnant to the principles of instinct and humanity, derogatory to the honour of the national character and inconsistent with the genius of the Christian religion', and Hamilton Presbytery, after criticising it on grounds of justice, natural rights, cruelty and morality, added that it was 'inconsistent with the spirit and precepts of the gospel'. The Relief Presbytery of Hamilton, although claiming to 'have not freedom to unite with others in petitioning Parliament', having examined the evidence in the *Abstract* declared strongly that they 'consider the African Slave Trade in its present mode of existence and throughout all the stages of it as a direct violation of Jehovah's righteous laws which positively require every man to love his neighbour as himself'. ' "Whatsoever we would that others should do to us to do even so unto them," is altogether consistent with the spirit of Christianity', said the Presbytery, and it considered that all should follow the author of the faith and 'breathe tender pity and compassion into the souls and bodies of men'.[67]

Petitioners would be familiar with the argument that the slave trade was necessary for the continuation of the productive West Indian colonies and for the British economy. The forthright rejection of this argument by Edinburgh's Chamber of Commerce in 1788 has already been noted. In 1792 many petitioners indicated clearly that they had absorbed the arguments offered against this in the *Abstract*. The Burgesses of Dundee were convinced that this argument 'is completely lost since it has been proved that slaves already in our islands, if treated with humanity, would not only support but increase their number'. Irvine Presbytery was convinced that those slaves already imported would, if treated better, be more reconciled to their fate, faithful in their service and 'from whom a more certain supply of honest, industrious and worthy labourers might be expected'. The humanitarian arguments were tempered in this way by an appeal to practical commerce. Conscious too of the widespread fears of slave insurrections, the large gathering in Paisley, after a reasoned resolution contrasting the annual loss of slaves in Jamaica with those West Indian islands that import no slaves, added that abolition would 'preserve our fellow human beings from the alarms and dangers to which they are exposed by introducing amongst them men of warm passions and untutored minds, who must ever regard them with feelings of indignant hatred and resentment'.[68]

Another familiar argument in favour of maintaining the trade was that of providing a necessary training ground for seamen. The statistics for the annual loss of crew members on slave ships and the extreme cruelties suffered by the sailors were well documented in the *Abstract*. Bo'ness Beneficent Society proclaimed that 'the said trade is nothing less than a slaughterhouse for our seamen'. The town of Leith expressed its concern that more seamen were killed in the African trade than any other branch of commerce and declared that its inhabitants, 'many of whom pursue a maritime life, feel themselves particularly interested in the abolition of a Trade, so destructive to seamen, the strength and glory of the British Empire'. The Fife coastal town of Anstruther complained that the trade, far from being a training ground for sailors, 'defeats the end it professes to have in view and destroys thousands of our sailors, a national calamity which we cannot but deplore'. It continued to make the pragmatic argument that in a period of national emergency, when there was an urgent need for personnel in the navy, it would fall on fishing communities to supply every sixth man, to replace the seaman, to the detriment of the community.[69]

Practical arguments apart, many petitioners relied simply on the moral case against the slave trade. Some were dismissive of justification as greed. Comrie's petition saw the opposition to abolition as 'the base struggles of interested persons, who wish to grow rich and fare sumptuously at the expense of their fellow creatures, to be exalted on the ruins of humanity'. Several were careful to distance themselves from commenting on the political expediency of abolition, but immediately followed this, as Falkirk did, by claiming that what was morally wrong could not be politically right. The Masons in Edinburgh stated that no 'commercial advantage or public expediency' justified the trade. An Association of Three Farmers in Renfrewshire admitted that they were not qualified to make political judgements, but added that 'they are capable of knowing what is a violation of the laws of religion, of justice and of humanity'. However, the most spirited contributions on this theme came from Bathgate and the Associate Congregation of St Andrews. 'If profit and advantage,' wrote the former, 'abstract from justice, is a good reason for continuing the slave trade, the pirate and the highwayman may urge the same plea for continuing their equally honest, humane and honourable employment.'[70]

An argument that would become familiar when the campaign for emancipation started in the 1820s was that slaves had happier lives in the plantations than in Africa and that they lived in better and more secure conditions than labourers in Britain. This was strongly advanced in the *Glasgow Courier* by a correspondent 'Hanway', who was connected with the West Indian group in the city and who declared that slaves were 'provided against every want, supplied with accommodations unknown in the greater part of the cottages of Europe'. The declaration from the Benevolent Society of Coldstream anticipated this kind of argument, however, when it stated that it rejected the ideas of those 'who presume to draw a comparison between the situation of the poorest mechanic, who enjoys the blessings of our free constitution and that of a slave, however happy they may paint it to be, while subject to the caprice of any master'.[71]

A constant theme in the correspondence was the implied threat of emancipation. Fear arising from current reports of insurrection in the French colony of St Domingue, with attendant stories of destruction of life and property, led to the argument that this sort of disruption would, as a result of the abolitionists' work, become a reality in the British Caribbean. 'Hanway' proclaimed that it was 'as clear as any of Euclid's demonstrations' that 'the whole mischief which has been lately done in St. Domingue' was the responsibility of the 'officious zealot who is opposed to the slave trade'. Others argued that 'The African slave trade which we want to abolish, is the radical evil, which in the colonies must ever favour revolt and blast every movement of humanity'. Thomas Clarkson joined the debate in a letter from London. He even cited Edward Long to argue that rebellions stem from imported slaves and urged that exertions must be redoubled 'in order that the present proprietors (in the islands) may preserve their estates to themselves and perpetuate them to their posterity'.[72]

The argument that abolition of the trade would preserve the plantations indicates how careful the London Committee was to separate abolition from emancipation. In the same series of letters, 'Gustavus', the pseudonym of the former slave Olaudah Equiano, wrote: 'the known intention of the proposed application to parliament is, not to abolish, but to regulate, the servitude of the West Indies'. Many petitioners in Scotland were careful to make this distinction. Pittenweem Parish was 'convinced that it would not be safe to extend the blessings of civil liberty to those who are already slaves in the British Colonies', but fervently wished 'that their situation was meliorated' and suggested religious education to assist in this. Newlands said that it might wish for immediate emancipation, but was concerned as to 'how far such a measure, if immediately adopted, might prove ruinous both to the master and to the slaves themselves'. Furthermore, those who argued on philosophical or theological grounds found themselves unable to keep to the fine distinctions required by the politics of the campaign. The Medical Society of Edinburgh echoed the ideas of George Wallace in arguing that the laws of war afforded no justification for slavery, just as criminality in parents did not warrant the enslavement of children. They further stated that an implied consent was invalid, since 'even the slave's rights are his masters', and they closed with the warning of divine judgement 'if slavery be not speedily abolished'.[73]

The statement from the inhabitants of Whitburn on 2 March admirably demonstrates the tension between abolition and emancipation. Although they did not petition, 360 citizens signed the statement and a committee of three, including two local ministers, was charged with transmitting it to the Edinburgh Committee. It began with the customary description of the trade as unjust, uncivilised and inhuman, and approved all the efforts made to abolish it. It then expressed 'surprise and grief at the unexpected issue of the question that lay before the House of Commons' through the vote in 1791 'of a majority giving sanction to the illicit trade'. The statement then continued by looking at slavery itself. Whilst recognising that the subject of emancipation might be reckoned 'too delicate for them to touch on', and that the practical difficulties are such as to 'forbid them to hope for its sudden accomplishment', nevertheless 'they are not satisfied that this desirable object should be altogether relinquished, or excluded from the views of those who are contending for the abolition of the trade, upon the general and immutable principles of humanity, equity and religion'. To underpin this declaration, they argued that the power exercised over slaves in the plantations was based on no legitimate right or contract and that it could only be maintained by the same pretexts of policy that were used to justify the slave trade.

'They are of the opinion', read the statement, 'that the condemnation and consequent abolition of the perpetual and hereditary slavery of the transported Africans are necessarily connected with the consistent maintenance of the great principles on which the petitions for abolishing the trade proceed and on which alone they can be effectually prosecuted.' Whitburn's statement then analysed the effects of improving conditions for the slaves and of religious instruction and drew on the French anti-slavery philosopher and historian the Abbé Reynal in appealing for breaking of 'the bonds of so many victims to our mercenary principles . . . The productions of these colonies may be cultivated by the hands of free men and then be reaped without remorse.'[74]

A FOCUSED TASK AND NO DIVERSIONS FOR THE LONG HAUL

In 1792 the last petitions on the slave trade were sent to Parliament. Yet despite Thomas Somerville's optimism, it was not until 1808 that abolition became law. William Wilberforce introduced measures in Parliament year after year and in 1795 attempted to make effective the promises of 1792, only to be defeated by a further amendment by Henry Dundas to postpone abolition until the end of the war. Wilberforce attempted to win over the West Indians on pragmatic grounds, the Irish on humanitarian grounds and to constantly enlist Pitt's support, but it was an uphill struggle. Why was there so little public pressure over these years and why was abolition so long delayed?

The obvious answer to both questions was the war with France, which started early in 1793 and – apart from two brief respites given by the Treaty of Amiens in 1802 and Napoleon's hundred days' exile in 1814 – continued until France's defeat at Waterloo in 1815. Fears of the spread of revolution to Britain led to harsh measures being imposed to prevent any meetings of political nature. The Sedition Act of 1795 and the Combination Act of 1799 were aimed more at any challenge to the suffrage and at gatherings of workers to improve their lot, but they were a catch-all. But the absence of petitions to Parliament over this period was not the whole story. Thomas Clarkson toured England again in 1805, claiming huge enthusiasm for the cause, and there is little doubt that abolition was a key issue in the 1807 campaign.[75] Another key factor in ending the trade was the bill to ban foreign slave-trading, a measure that was easy to achieve in wartime since, although aimed to penalise Britain's enemies, many believed that it would cripple the whole commerce.

The difficulties of advancing the abolition cause were even more acute in Scotland. As early as January 1793, the Crown's law officers embarked on a series of sedition trials in response to the growing movement for electoral reform and savage sentences were handed out by judges, notably by Lord Braxfield, who had so enthusiastically voted for Joseph Knight's freedom in 1778. The atmosphere of fear over any measure that might be seen to disturb the status quo, whilst already greatly increased after 1792, was hardly absent during that year, as is obvious from William Dickson's diary. Allied to that was the political power wielded by Henry Dundas, a man described as 'fierce and vigilant in protecting and expanding what he saw as his electoral interest' with the 'megalomania of the pure machine politi-cian'. His patronage all but assured control of the Scottish MPs for the Government interest and secured opposition to any changes, unless they strengthened his and its power.[76]

Given these circumstances, and the considerable commercial inter-ests enjoyed by Scottish merchants and planters, the contribution of Scotland to the petition campaign of 1792 was remarkable. Lord Auchinleck's simple appeal for right and freedom in the summing up of *Knight* v *Wedderburn* touched a basic chord in Scotland. Racism had been a powerful factor in England since Queen Elizabeth's exiling of 'blackamoors' and there was considerable prejudice against the presence of black 'vagrants' in London in the late eighteenth century. Scotland's treatment of those of African descent in her midst was as yet untainted by this – not perhaps out of any virtue, for Scots in the Empire were to exhibit some of the worst examples of racism, but simply because the comparatively few black people in Scotland at that time were not seen as a challenge to the livelihoods of communities amongst whom they lived and who often protected and supported their claims for freedom. In addition, pride in Scotland's forthright legal declaration in 1778 against slavery on its soil would have certainly counted for something amongst the educated Scots who were to formulate the petitions. The ground was therefore fertile in many a community for those who sought to evoke a natural sympathy for the victims of a horrific trade, once the facts about it were known.

In a study of a later campaign against American slavery it was claimed that two key factors in its success were basic humanity and what the writer called 'the religious cast of Scottish life' in the early nineteenth century, 'giving to the Church a social importance which it did not possess in England at this time'.[77] In 1788–92 ministers of the national churches of England and Scotland sponsored between 14 and 22 per cent of abolitionist petitions. But only 9 per cent of the English petitions came from Church of England sources.[78] That English figure included those from inhabitants of towns and communities jointly sponsored by clergy, and with that wider definition the Scottish figure would be considerably in excess of 50 per cent. Certainly there were a number of English bishops who supported abolition in the House of Lords and petitions came from a number of dioceses. But there was nothing comparable to the width of support from the national church in Scotland.

The organisation of the Church of Scotland was able to achieve a truly national campaign. A synod or presbytery petition is recorded statistically as one item in the Journals of the House of Commons, but it frequently followed an extensive debate within a large body of ministers and elders, and involved either prior meetings or consultation with Kirk Session or congregation, followed up by pulpit education. Historians have often given the impression that religious zeal for anti-slavery activity was limited to evangelicals, and the crucial role of the Clapham Sect in British anti-slavery, along with the more visible activity of Quakers and Dissenters in the late eighteenth century campaign, make this understandable for England. One of the most remarkable aspects of the Scottish campaign, however, was that it brought together leading members of the Moderate and Popular (Evangelical) parties in the Kirk. Enthusiasm for evangelism, concern for civilised and humane religion and devotion to a free constitution were aspects reflected in many of the petitions. The slave trade was seen as a fundamental challenge to all these, quite apart from its cruelty and inhumanity. In fact, at a local level, it is not immediately obvious whether the Church of Scotland ministers involved come from a Moderate or Popular stance, for the text of the petitions they sponsored does not indicate this.

There is a remarkable similarity in the arguments advanced against the trade in the Scottish petitions and those in England. In a study of anti-slavery in Britain it was claimed that 'religious considerations dovetailed neatly with what we might call a broad humanitarian approach'. That would be as true of the Scottish petitions as of those south of the border. Certainly divine judgement on sin and inhumanity featured widely in the Scottish petitions, as it did in the one from the Archdeaconry of Leicester.[79] The characterising of the trade as 'sinful', and as a barrier to Christian evangelism, finds a place in many petitions. In the religious climate of a Scotland that was at home with theological language, these very concepts could be powerful tools in anti-slavery campaigning rather than hostages to fortune that allowed the humanitarian cause of abolishing the slave trade to be diverted.

Such a campaign needed the dedication and commitment of certain individuals. To travel almost non-stop for three months in the difficult and at times dangerous terrain that was Scotland in 1792 took prodigious energy. Yet William Dickson kept totally focused on his task. He sought out the leading figures in each community, rather dramatically at times, as when he caught four town councillors curling on the ice in Dunfermline and signed them up to the campaign.[80] He carried large quantities of the *Abstract* with him and ensured that it reached some remote corners. His zeal to divert his supporters from any action that might rebound on the campaign matched Dundas's in its single-mindedness. No diary was left by Campbell Haliburton, the Secretary of the Edinburgh Abolition Committee, but other sources hint at a similar commitment to that of Dickson. Katherine Plymley noted that the Edinburgh Committee had sent a copy of the *Abstract* to every clergyman. This was a slight exaggeration, as Dickson was to discover on his travels, but Haliburton did all in his power to spread the word, not least by arranging to have the printing blocks of the slave-ship diagram sent up from London and from them made posters that were pasted up in strategic public places in Scottish towns and cities.[81] He was in regular contact with London, with Manchester – the second most powerful abolition committee in Britain – and with Glasgow, whose activity he did much to encourage. The documents from the Edinburgh Committee that survive in print show Haliburton's careful arguments about commerce and justice, the details of the trade and suggestions for lobbying those in power, all taking a great deal of his spare time and even risking his position as a Government employee in the Excise Office.[82]

The campaign to abolish the slave trade, and later on slavery itself, called not just for pressure on the legislature from a wide variety of sources, but also for the use of the rapidly expanding press to inform and stimulate public opinion on the issue. It required an almost super-human effort in the fields of communication and organisation, in philosophical and theological argument and through political and legal involvement to defeat the efforts of powerful interests and opponents. The contribution of Scots to this was not limited to those living north of the border. Scots in London, as throughout the world, were to make their mark in key events that shaped human history. Five of these, including William Dickson, were at the very centre of the abolition movement.

Notes

1 'Africanus' to James Beattie, 26 Jan 1788. AUL MS 30/2/55/561.
2 William Wilberforce to William Robertson, 25 Jan 1788. NLS MS 3943.230.
3 William Dickson, 'Diary of a visit to Scotland 5th January–19th March 1792 on behalf of the Committee for the Abolition of the Slave Trade', 16 Jan 1792. Friends Library London, Temp. Box 10/14.
4 Thomas Chambers, ed., *Biographical Dictionary of Eminent Scotsman* (Glasgow and Edinburgh, 1875), pp. 69–70.
5 Presbytery of Glasgow, Minutes, 7 Mar 1792. MLG, CH2/171/14.
6 Thomas Somerville, *A Discourse on our Obligation to Thanksgiving for the Prospect of the Abolition of the African Slave Trade with a Prayer delivered in the Church in Jedburgh on 15th April by Thomas Somerville D.D.* (Kelso, 1792), pp. 6, 18, 31.
7 Thomas Somerville, *My Own Life and Times 1741–1814* (Edinburgh, 1861), p. 263.
8 Somerville, *A Discourse*, p. 3.
9 *CM*, 22 Mar, 12 Mar 1792.
10 *CM*, 21 Feb, 19 Mar 1792.
11 Hugo Thomas, *The Slave Trade* (London, 1997), p. 524.
12 Katherine Plymley, Diaries 1791–2, Shropshire Records and Research, 1066/4, p. 6.
13 Thomas Clarkson, *The History of the Rise, Progress and Accomplishment of the Abolition of the Slave Trade by the British* (London, 1808), Vol. 2, pp. 196–7.
14 Dickson, 'Diary', inside cover.
15 Dickson, 'Diary', 24 Jan, 16 Feb, 13 Jan, 11 Mar, 12 Jan, 13 Jan, 23 Jan, 25 Jan, 2 Feb, 8 Feb, 14 Feb, 20 Jan 1792.
16 Society at Edinburgh for the Purpose of Effecting the Abolition of the African Slave Trade, bound pamphlets, 6 Feb 1789. NLS 3.873(2).

17 *EA*, 29 Feb 1792.
18 Dickson, 'Diary', 19 Jan, 23 Jan 1792.
19 Presbytery of Glasgow, Minutes, 7 Mar 1792.
20 *CM*, 28 Feb 1788.
21 *CM*, 29 Mar 1792.
22 Presbytery of Glasgow, Minutes, 20 Mar 1788; Synod of Angus and Mearns, Minutes, 22 Apr 1788. NAS CH2/12/9; Synod of Moray, Minutes, 9 May 1788. NAS CH2/271/8; Synod of Dumfries, Minutes, 15 Apr 1788. NAS CH2/98/5.
23 Presbytery of Hamilton, Minutes, 19 Mar 1792. NAS CH2/393/6.
24 *EA*, 25 Jan 1792.
25 Presbytery of Kirkcaldy, Minutes, 28 Mar 1792. NAS CH2/224/9.
26 *SM*, Jun 1788, p. 305.
27 *SM*, Jun 1791, p. 303.
28 *GC*, 26 May 1792.
29 *EA*, 14 Feb; *CM*, 6 Mar, 17 Feb 1792.
30 *CM*, 12 Mar; *EA*, 24 Feb; *CM*, 6 Mar 1792.
31 *EA*, 6 Apr, 12 Mar 1792.
32 *JHC*, Vol. 43, 1788.
33 Edinburgh Chamber of Commerce, Minutes, 1788. Edinburgh City Council Archives, ED005/1/3, p. 245.
34 *CM*, 27 Feb, 3 Mar, 15 Mar 1792.
35 *CM*, 7 Mar; *GC*, 21 Feb; *EEC*, 5 Mar 1792.
36 *EEC*, 17 Mar; *EA* 28 Feb; *GC*, 17 Jan 1792.
37 *CM*, 15 Mar 1792.
38 D.Adams, 'Trade in the Eighteenth and Nineteenth Centuries', in *The Port of Montrose*, G. Jackson and S. G. E. Lythe eds (Tayport, 1993), p. 127.
39 Presbytery of Kirkwall, Minutes, 14 April 1788. NAS CH2/1082/4.
40 Dickson, 'Diary', 14 Jan 1792.
41 Dickson, 'Diary', 14 Jan, 6, 7, 16, 20, 22 Feb 1792.
42 Presbytery of Glasgow, Minutes, 7 Mar 1792.
43 Presbytery of St Andrews, Minutes, 20 Mar, 2 May 1792. NAS CH2/1132/8.
44 Dickson, 'Diary', 21 Feb 1792.
45 Society at Edinburgh for the Purpose of Effecting the Abolition of the Slave Trade, *Reprint of Two Petitions from Scotland*, 1 Oct 1790. NLS 5.1965 (28).
46 Plymley, Diary, 3 Feb 1792.
47 *An Abstract of the Evidence Delivered before a Select Committee of the House of Commons in the years 1790 and 1791 on the part of the Petitioners for the Abolition of the Slave Trade* (Edinburgh, 1791).
48 *A Short Address to the People of Scotland on the Subject of the Slave Trade with a Summary View of the Evidence Delivered before a*

Committee of the House of Commons on the part of the Petitioners for its Abolition (Edinburgh, 1792).

49 J. R. Oldfield, *Popular Politics and British Anti-Slavery: The Mobilisation of Public Opinion against the Slave Trade 1787–1807* (Manchester, 1995), p. 114.

50 *CM*, 25 Jan; *GC*, 25 Feb 1792.

51 *CM*, 7 Feb, 23 Feb 1792.

52 Presbytery of Paisley, Minutes, 6 Mar 1792. NAS CH2/24/12.

53 Presbytery of Paisley, 'Letter from Mr. W. Wilberforce to the Moderator of the Presbytery of Paisley', 10 Mar 1792.

54 *Address to the Inhabitants of Glasgow, Paisley and the Neighbourhood concerning the African Slave Trade by a Society in Glasgow* (Glasgow, 1791). RHO MSS, 100.221 r.99 (2), pp. 11, 14, 15.

55 Dickson, 'Diary', 18 Jan, 19 Jan 1792.

56 *CM*, 1 Feb; *GC*, 9 Feb; *JHC*, Vol. 47, 28 Mar; *CM*, 9 Feb 1792.

57 Presbytery of Glasgow, Minutes, 20 Mar 1788.

58 *CM*, 15 Mar 1788.

59 Synod of Glasgow and Ayr, Minutes, 8 Apr 1788. NAS CH2/464/4, p. 229; Synod of Dumfries, Minutes, 15 Apr 1788; Synod of Ross, Minutes, 1788. NAS CH2/312/5; p. 238.

60 Presbytery of Aberdeen, Minutes, 19 Mar 1788. NAS CH2/1/2; Presbytery of Glasgow, Minutes, 9 Apr 1788; *CM*, 3 Apr; *EEA*, 2 Mar 1788.

61 Dickson, 'Diary', 4 Feb, 14 Feb, 6 Mar 1792.

62 *EEC*, 19 Mar; *CM*, 10 Mar, 23 Feb; *EEC*, 5 Mar 1792.

63 Presbytery of Glasgow, Minutes, 7 Mar 1792.

64 *EA*, 16 Mar; *CM*, 10 Mar; *EEC*, 20 Mar 1792.

65 Presbytery of Hamilton, Minutes, 19 Mar 1792; Presbytery of Stirling, Minutes, 8 Mar 1792. NAS CH2/722/16; *GC*, 21 Feb 1792.

66 *CM*, 11 Feb 1792; Presbytery of Edinburgh, Minutes, 29 Feb 1792. NAS CH2/121/19; *CM*, 1 Mar 1792.

67 Presbytery of Paisley, Minutes, 6 Mar 1792; Presbytery of Stirling, Minutes, 8 Mar 1792; Presbytery of St Andrews, Minutes, 20 Mar 1792; Presbytery of Hamilton, Minutes, 19 Mar 1792; *CM*, 21 Mar 1792.

68 *CM*, 23 Feb; *GC*, 28 Feb; *CM*, 7 Feb 1792.

69 *EA*, 16 Mar; *CM*, 15 Mar; *EA*, 20 Mar 1792.

70 *EA*, 6 Apr; *CM*, 10 Mar; *EA*, 24 Feb; 8 Mar; *EEC*, 6 Apr 1792.

71 *GC*, 18 Feb; *KC*, 17 Feb 1792.

72 *GC*, 23 Feb, 18 Feb, 25 Feb 1792.

73 *EEC*, 15 Mar; *CM*, 1 Mar; *EEC*, 10 Mar; *EA*, 13 Mar 1792.

74 *CM*, 10 Mar 1792.

75 Seymour Drescher, 'Whose abolition? Popular Pressure and the Ending of the British Slave Trade', *Past and Present*, Vol. 143 (1994), pp. 138, 140, 152.

76 Bruce Lenman, *Integration and Enlightenment, Scotland 1746–1832* (Edinburgh, 1981), pp. 100, 104.
77 George Shepperson, 'Frederick Douglass and Scotland', *Journal of Negro History*. Vol. 38 (1953), p. 308.
78 Seymour Drescher, *Capitalism and Anti-Slavery: A Critique* (London, 1986), p. 237, table.
79 Oldfield, *Popular Politics and British Anti-Slavery*, p. 115.
80 Dickson, 'Diary', 2 Feb 1792.
81 Plymley, Diaries, 3 Feb 1792.
82 Society at Edinburgh for the Purpose of Effecting the Abolition of the African Slave Trade, bound Pamphlets, 6 Feb 1789, 1 Oct 1790, 14 Oct 1791.

4

LONDON SCOTS IN THE MOVEMENT FOR ABOLITION

ɷ

Earl Bathurst will thus soon have an opportunity of perceiving with his own eyes and hearing with his own ears how sadly His Majesty's Government and this country have been deceived by a set of designing men, concerning the real situation of our colonies.

Glasgow Courier, 3 August 1826

In May 1804, the London Committee for the Abolition of the Slave Trade resolved to add the names of James Stephen, Zachary Macaulay and Henry Brougham to its membership.[1] That simple entry in the Minute Book scarcely reflects the significance of three men who were to become some of the key figures in the abolition movement. To these names might be added James Ramsay, 'the unknown abolitionist', and William Dickson, the Moffat-born campaigner. All received a Scottish education, and all but Henry Brougham had experience of the West Indies and had been close to the reality of its slave system.

Over a period spanning the second half of the eighteenth century and first half of the nineteenth century, these five drew on the ideas of the Scottish Enlightenment and displayed skills of analysis and collation of detail that had their roots in a traditional Scottish education. Key publications on the subject over this period emanated largely from these London-based Scots, and together they provided by far the bulk of the evidence used to attack the slave trade and slavery itself. One whose active years in the movement coincided with each of them was the man usually regarded as the doyen of abolitionists, William Wilberforce. Wilberforce did not always agree with their views and occasionally found them disturbingly radical, but he freely acknowledged the immense contributions of them all.

JAMES RAMSAY – THE ONE WHO LIFTED THE VEIL

On 21 July 1788, Sir Charles Middleton rose in the House of Commons to defend James Ramsay against another of the frequent attacks made upon him by members with West Indian interests. Sir Charles (later to be Lord Bareham, Comptroller of the Navy) said that he had known Ramsay for nearly twenty years, and he did not know a man of greater honour, integrity and talents. He went on to challenge Mr Molyneux, a former planter on St Kitts, to substantiate his accusation that the minister and surgeon had been dismissed for corruption and inactivity.

Folarin Shyllon described James Ramsay as 'The Unknown Abolitionist'. Born in Fraserburgh of an Episcopalian family, he studied at King's College, Aberdeen, where he became a lifelong friend of James Beattie, a contemporary. After medical training in London, Ramsay, who was also an ordained Episcopalian clergyman, served as a surgeon on the *Arundel* under the command of Sir Charles Middleton. In 1759 he boarded a slave ship, something that other surgeons were not prepared to do, to give medical assistance during an epidemic, but unfortunately, as he was leaving the ship he injured his leg, with the result that he was invalided out of the Navy. In 1762 Ramsay secured an Anglican living on the island of St Kitts, where he also practised medicine. He was called upon to treat both slaves and masters on the plantations and his care for and attitude to the former made him a marked man by the latter. After nearly twenty years in the West Indies, planter hostility necessitated his return to Britain and through Middleton's patronage he was given a Church of England living at Teston in Kent.[2]

In 1784 Ramsay published an essay of nearly 300 pages detailing the treatment of West Indian slaves and the missionary opportunities there. It began with an historical survey of classical and modern slavery, comparing ancient practice with that on the sugar islands. He detailed the harshness of modern slavery, especially with regard to women, and further argued that slave-owners who provided better conditions benefited from the improved results of their slaves' work. He described the practice on plantations of working slaves on the Sabbath day, refusing to allow them to receive any religious instruction or freedom to worship and arranging for mass baptism as a meaningless exercise except as a means of social control. Ramsay appealed to common humanity in a situation where many slaves had no rest from their toil, declaring that 'God is the God of bodies'.

He went on to attack David Hume's view of the inferiority of the negro race and offered the observation that if Hume and Lord Kames, whom he also criticised on this issue, had been enslaved and were on a West Indian plantation, they would not fare too well. The last part of the essay contained a detailed plan for better treatment, religious instruction and proper inspection to ensure that cruel masters were banned from public life and made to bear 'the mark of infamy'.[3] The essay was hardly a revolutionary document. Shyllon claimed that although 'he lifted the veil of plantation slavery', he did not tell the full story and included only what he thought might 'bear the light'.[4] However, to British readers, it was a revelation; and to his friend James Beattie, this was 'a spirited performance' that updated and filled out the evidence Beattie had used himself in his lectures to students in Aberdeen.[5]

Shyllon also claimed that it was Ramsay, more than anyone else, who had 'driven the matter [of slavery] close to Wilberforce's heart' after the two men met in 1783 at Middleton's house, and from then on Ramsay 'started to bombard Wilberforce with letters and memoranda dealing with every aspect of slavery and the slave trade, urging, explaining and advising'. A similar early influence was acknowledged by the young Thomas Clarkson, who in 1787 spent a month at Ramsay's vicarage and on departure pledged himself to devote his time to the abolition of the slave trade.[6] Ramsay can therefore be credited with being a major influence on the two best-known giants of the anti-slavery movement.

The first Abolition Society had been formed in London in 1787, with Granville Sharp as chairman. Ramsay was invited to attend in recognition of his publications, which included responses to James Tobin, a former planter from Nevis, now a leading figure in the West Indian community in England.[7] The following year, whilst the first petitions against the slave trade started arriving at the House of Commons, Ramsay and Clarkson gave evidence to a Privy Council inquiry on both the trade and slavery itself, and Ramsay published a point-by-point rejoinder to those who raised objections to abolition.[8] He was not the only one to provide Wilberforce and others in Parliament with detailed first-hand evidence on slavery, but at this stage he was the leading anti-slavery exponent. The threat he posed to the West Indian interests by continually providing fuel for the abolition case was attested by the verbal attacks made on him in 1788 by Lord Sandwich in the House of Lords and by James Molyneux in the Commons the following year. He was publicly defended in the press by the ex-slave and abolitionist Olaudah Equiano. Despite failing health, Ramsay published his last pamphlet, an appeal to the public, in which he painstakingly met every objection to abolition with a detailed response.[9] Shortly after the Molyneux attack on him in May 1789, he died in Sir Charles Middleton's home.

The year after Wilberforce made his first attempt in Parliament to abolish the slave trade, Ramsay published his *Objections to the Abolition of the Slave Trade with Answers*. In it, he anticipated not only the attempts to justify the trade with reference to Africa, but more importantly, to claim its necessity for British commercial interests and for Britain's defence. It was a theme that James Stephen was to take up much later in the different context of the Napoleonic wars.

Ramsay admitted that many of the inhabitants of African states were killed in war, sacrificed to placate rulers or enslaved for profit, but he argued that Britain's refusal to co-operate with the slave trade would halve these local evils. To the assertion that slaves were well cared for on the ships and placed in a happier situation in the West Indies, Ramsay asked whether the ships carrying five slaves for every space allocated to each soldier constituted proper care. In his observations to the Privy Council, he provided eyewitness evidence of the proportion of sick and emaciated slaves landed on the islands, devalued in price and described by the poor whites who bought them at cheap prices as 'refuse slaves'.[10]

All this would suggest that, apart from its inhumanity, the slave trade was wasteful and unprofitable. That point was central to Ramsay's argument. The annual cost of the importing of slaves he estimated at £750,000 and the value of West Indian exports amounted to not much more than double that amount. If the slave trade were stopped, he claimed, this would help to extend trade in staple commodities and provide a stable commercial enterprise. Ramsay was well aware of the argument that abolition would simply leave the way open for France and other nations to profit. His answer here was moral rather than economic, and he asked: 'suppose that others successfully rob and murder on the highway, must we join the lawless band?'[11] At one point Ramsay also argued controversially that if the sugar colonies were lost to France, Britain would be relieved of the present high costs of protective subsidies.

As we have already alluded to in Chapter 3, a popular justification for the slave trade was that it provided necessary training for Britain's seamen, a especially important factor given the ever-present threat of war. During his time in the navy, Ramsay had taken a particular interest in the physical and spiritual well-being of sailors, to which his written manuscripts testify. He described the slave trade as 'the very grave of seamen' rather than their training ground, estimated that twenty times the number of seamen died on slave ships than on the Newfoundland trade and referred to the extensive research on these statistics undertaken by Clarkson in Bristol and Liverpool. In a handwritten memorial from Teston entitled 'On Supplying the Navy with Seamen', in which he advocated trade with Africa and the development of Scottish fisheries, Ramsay wrote: 'instead of this our chief aim in our trade to that continent, the commerce of slaves which destroys our seamen annually by thousands, makes bankrupts of four out of five of those concerned in it and is chiefly applied to the improvement of the French sugar colonies'.[12]

To those who argued that regulation of the trade rather than abolition was the answer, he responded: 'regulate murder as you please, it still becomes murder'.[13] The impossibility of making regulations effective on the African coast thousands of miles away seemed to Ramsay to be an obvious invitation to evasion and he pointed out that the West Indians had opposed Sir William Dolben's 1788 bill to regulate conditions on the slave ships and hence deliver healthier slaves to the islands.[14]

Ramsay's moral passion was not limited to the trade itself. He argued that it was in the interests of the planters themselves to treat slaves with more humanity, building on his ideas in earlier works. However, to those who claimed that the master's interest was self-evident, Ramsay retorted: 'then his practice contradicts his opinion. Can it be in his interest to allow his slave neither food nor rest? Are six ounces of flour or five hours rest sufficient refreshment for twenty-four hours?' He also strongly reacted to the idea that slaves are better treated and happier than English peasants. Such an assertion, said Ramsay, insults common sense, and he continued: 'have peasants their eyes beat out, their flesh furrowed by the whip, their wives exposed to a bailiff's lust?'[15]

At the end of the day, though, Ramsay reluctantly accepted the limitations of the campaign against the trade. Although he rejected any racial inferiority, maintained that Christianity favoured liberty and denied 'that a man can ever be the object of property', he made it clear that in his view 'all our slaves are not generally in a state where full liberty would be a blessing', and he remained sensitive to the impossibility of achieving emancipation in the near future. In a carefully regulated statement, Ramsay wrote that 'the simple abolition of the trade, operating as a kind necessity on the interest and discretion of the planter, will do everything at present for the slave that humanity requires'.[16] With hindsight this was a naïve view, but it was one, as we have seen, held even by some who, such as Equiano, had been at the receiving end of slavery.

In 1788 James Beattie wrote to his friend, Bishop Bielby Porteus of London, who, despite owning slaves in Virginia,[17] had become a convinced abolitionist. Porteus had asked Beattie to provide a theological response to a recent pamphlet by a former Jesuit, Raymond Harris.[18] Harris had been commissioned by several Liverpool merchants to write a justification on biblical grounds for the slave trade and in 1788 he had published what became a widely circulated pamphlet.[19] Beattie offered some initial comments on it, but despite strong pressure from many in the movement, he did not produce a response. The only person who did so was James Ramsay.

'Few serious people', wrote Ramsay, 'will peruse his [Harris's] extraordinary positions without having their reverence for their creator shocked and their benevolence for their brother affected. . . . Mr. Harris considered himself "an enemy of injustice and oppression," but he keeps the humane and benevolent character for himself and sells tyranny and oppression to his friends of Liverpool.'[20] In his tract, Harris claimed to examine the scriptures with 'the utmost impartiality' and to show that the slave trade was consistent with the law of nature, the Mosaic Dispensation and Christian law. Jesus, he argued, affirmed Abraham, who practised slavery, and Hagar was an African transported from Egypt to Canaan. Equal weight for Harris should be given to both Testaments as the word of God and 'the practice of purchasing slaves was never accounted in the sight of God a violation of the laws of the religion of nature'.[21]

Many contemporary responses to scriptural justification of slavery depended on general appeals to the spirit of Christianity. However, Ramsay's response was more focused than that. He took seriously the problem of slavery in biblical times, but affirmed that this was a very different form from that found in the Caribbean. Even Egyptian slavery, he argued, permitted some rights to the slave. Hebrew domestic slavery was restricted by divine law and judged constantly by the prophets. Hagar, he said, 'was never cooped up in a guinea trader nor set to plant sugar cane'.

Ramsay argued that 'we can as little draw the doctrine of perpetual slavery from its permission to the Jews as we can the keeping of concubines from the thousand wives and concubines of Solomon'.

He also did not hesitate to discuss Pauline doctrine and concluded that care for Philemon stood in stark contrast to West Indian slavery, where only the master was considered and 'neither the feelings nor the happiness of the slave is taken into account'. He then centered on Jesus' ministry to set people free from sin: 'if any man be degraded or suffer under a disadvantage for the caprice or profit or will of another, that under whom he suffers is guilty of a sin', he wrote. In response to the questions 'Is slavery lawful?' and 'Is the present Liverpool slave trade lawful?', Ramsey responded: 'Mr. Harris's reasoning is all drawn from the first and is all applied to the second.'[22]

The reply to Harris was a skilful and measured one. By avoiding a blanket condemnation of slavery and drawing a distinction between ancient and West Indian conditions, Ramsay's pamphlet became a useful tool in the campaign against the trade. Although the details in the *Essay on the Treatment and Conversion of African Slaves* and the evidence that Ramsay provided for the Privy Council were not the only documents to hand, they were both timely and comprehensive. Ramsay's theological challenge to Harris was not the first on the subject, but he was the only person in Britain to make a specific response to what was a potentially influential, if intellectually flawed, document. Such was his effectiveness in neutralising it that he bore the largest share of the attacks on abolition from the powerful West Indian party. 'Mr. Molyneux', wrote James Stephen, 'announced the decease of the public enemy to his natural son in this island in these terms: "Ramsay is dead – I have killed him." '[23] This quiet and in many ways conservative man had threatened the system enough to gain the comment from the arch-critic Eric Williams that he was 'one of the earliest, ablest, and most diligent of the abolitionists'.[24]

WILLIAM DICKSON – LETTERS AND PLANS FOR MITIGATION

Duncan Rice described William Dickson as 'the Thomas Clarkson of Scotland'[25] for the prodigious work he undertook in the early months of 1792. The particular success he met with in the Aberdeenshire area that year was to some extent due to the support received from James Beattie. Dickson was given an introductory letter by Wilberforce warmly commending him and Beattie reported to Wilberforce that Dickson was 'indeed a most intelligent and worthy man', adding that 'for the important mission in which he was now employed he is particularly well qualified and he has been beyond expectation successful'.[26] This was underlined when the London committee heard

Figure 6 *William Dickson – a pencil sketch in the inside leaf of his 1792 diary.*
© *The Society of Friends, Friends Library, London*

Dickson's report and concluded that 'his assiduity and diligence in attaining the objects of his journey' was very acceptable to it.[27]

Marischal College, certainly at Beattie's instigation, awarded Dickson an Hon. LLD. in 1792. The university record designated him as 'the author of *Letters on Slavery*',[28] but when he offered these in

1788 to the London Committee with a view to publication, it was very cautious about accepting them. Two members, Messrs Barclay and Taylor, were appointed 'to inform Mr. Dickson that although the Committee consider his manuscript to contain much useful matter yet without it will be agreeable to him to submit to their alteration, they wish to decline printing it'.[29] These two were asked to keep the matter under review and James Ramsay was added to the group. In November 1788, the Committee ordered 1,500 copies of Ramsay's *Address on the Proposed Bill*, but delayed making similar use of Dickson's *Letters*. Meanwhile, James Phillips, an abolitionist printer and bookseller, himself a close associate of the London Committee, published the *Letters* in 1789. Much later the Board of the African Institution, successor to the London Committee, reported in 1815 that it had considered Dickson's *Mitigation of Slavery*, published that year. It enthusiastically concluded 'that it is calculated to further the objects of the Society', and directed that a number of copies be purchased 'which they propose to distribute in the West Indies and other places where such distribution may appear likely to be useful'.[30]

The *Letters* were addressed to Sir James Johnstone, the Member of Parliament for Dumfries, in whose constituency Dickson had been born. They contained a philosophical attack on slavery drawn from the example of Barbados, which was contrasted with what he judged to be the infinitely worse conditions for slaves in Jamaica. They were perhaps too strong for a Committee that was carefully targeting the slave trade in the 1790s and was anxious not to be seen to advocate emancipation. Although Dickson affirmed in his Introduction that he wrote with the caution of a man who expects to meet with the most 'pertinacious contradiction' and was keen to disabuse readers of any supposition 'that there are not persons with worth and humanity in the West Indies', there is no doubt where he stood on the general issue of slavery, denying 'that any man whatsoever is competent to hold, in the person of another man the same absolute property which he holds in a horse, a dog, or an inanimate piece of goods'.

The *Letters* also have many echoes of Ramsay's observations and Dickson himself paid an early tribute to 'that sensible, spirited and praiseworthy writer', directing his readers to the *Essay on the Treatment and Conversion*, where he claimed that the same data, with local variations, would apply to Barbados. Dickson struggled between his anger at the conditions that he knew so well and an attempt to avoid personal prejudice. He admitted enjoying kindness and hospitality from planters, but claimed that 'no private attachment can vacate or supercede a man's public duty'. The *Letters* were a blend of philosophical objections and factual condemnation. Despite a spirited response to the suggestions of negro inferiority from Kames, Voltaire and Hume, Dickson did not improve on the arguments of men such as James Beattie or William Robertson. Where he was particularly effective was in pleading the danger of abuse of the absolute power masters held over their slaves, a danger made inevitable by what he perceived to be sinful human nature. This was a key repost to those who argued that self-interest would lead to better treatment of slaves. In an appendix to his pamphlet, Dickson responded to a publication by James McNeil, a Scottish planter, who claimed that there had been great improvement in the conditions for slaves in Jamaica. Using local newspaper reports and first-hand accounts, Dickson gave detailed descriptions of the arbitrary floggings, mutilation, torture and sadistic killings of slaves. What he described as 'virtual murder by hunger, severity and oppression' led to his conclusion that only detailed and enforced legislation would have any effect on ameliorating the horrors of the system.[31] By the time that his second book appeared, such ideas were beginning to find some acceptance even within Government circles, though it would be another eight years before Lord Canning was to advance them in Parliament.

Dickson's later work, *Mitigation of Slavery*, a two-part document, took a more cautious approach. The first part promoted the ideas of a planter in Barbados, Sir Joshua Steele, whose practice Dickson saw as a model for what slavery could become. 'To advance above three hundred debased field Negroes who had never before moved without the whip', he wrote, 'to a state nearly resembling that of contented, honest and industrious servants and after paying them for their labour, to triple, in a few years, the annual neat clearance of his estates, these, I say, were great achievements for an aged man.' Dickson in this booklet acknowledged that the abolition of the slave trade had not remedied the evils, but he was careful to limit his immediate concern to achieving what the title implied. The second part consisted of a series of detailed letters to the leading abolitionist in London, Thomas Clarkson, providing evidence to support his view that the plantations, to be productive, required slaves who were well looked after. In his view the question was 'How can the acknowledged evils of West Indian slavery be mitigated without injury to the white colonists, the Negro slaves, or any other party concerned?' For him, 'every rational and temperate view of this great subject is bounded by two dangerous extremes – immediate emancipation and perpetual, unlimited, unmitigated slavery'.[32] Dickson's earlier account was certainly more dramatic and his appeal for remedies more urgent, but whilst *Mitigation of Slavery* showed the same restraint that he was later to display in his campaigning, in 1814 it was still ahead of its time.

These two works were William Dickson's main literary contribution to the campaign, but there were others. In 1797 he published what he termed 'addresses' to various groups in Barbados, essentially an updating of some of the materials in the *Letters*,[33] and in 1803, in a pamphlet written from Moffat and aimed at Scotland in particular, he gave a strong denunciation of American slavery in a land that espoused democracy. This was somewhat ironic, though, considering that the abolition of the slave trade was not yet secured in Britain.[34]

JAMES STEPHEN – LAW IN THE SERVICE OF LIBERATION

In a biography of William Wilberforce, the author observed of James Stephen that 'more than any other man he gave passion to the abolitionist movement'.[35] Stephen was born in Dorset of Scottish parents, but spent some of his early years with his grandparents in Aberdeenshire and went on to study at Marischal College, Aberdeen. David Brion Davis commented about this period in his life, 'like many other young Scots, Stephen believed in the abstract injustice of slavery and at Aberdeen had been impressed by the anti-slavery lectures of James Beattie'.[36] In his memoirs Stephen paid tribute to the influence of the Aberdeen philosopher when he wrote: 'I attended the Moral Philosophy class as it is called, under the celebrated Dr Beattie and here I certainly derived from his lectures much that has been useful to me in later life.'[37] Stephen's brother was a West Indian planter, who not only paid for his legal training in London after Marischal College, but also secured him a legal post in St Kitts in 1783.

James Stephen described the experience of witnessing a slave trial on his stopover in Barbados as the 'reversal of every principle that I had been taught to reverence'.[38] This 'Damascus Road' experience made him determined never to own a slave and he maintained this position over the decade that he spent in St Kitts. In the late 1780s he began to correspond with William Wilberforce, secretly providing valuable first-hand information on the colonies. The two men met when Stephen made a visit to Britain in 1788 and on his return from the West Indies he committed himself to using his legal expertise in the cause of abolition.

Stephen was elected to Parliament as Tory member for Tralee in

1808 and he represented East Grinsted from 1812 to 1815. In Parliament his close relationship with Spencer Perceval, the Prime Minister, enabled him to draft legislation aimed to check the excesses of slavery in the newly ceded colonies and to require registration of all slaves. He married Wilberforce's sister, was a neighbour of Macaulay and Wilberforce on Clapham Common, and is named alongside both in the plaque dedicated to the Clapham Sect in the local parish church. He is unique amongst that group, however, since he claimed that it was involvement in the anti-slavery movement that brought him to accept evangelical Christianity, rather than the other way round.

James Stephen's most significant contribution to the cause lay undoubtedly in his writings and his legal advice in the period that he was outside Parliament. By contrast his time at Westminster was characterised by frustration and failed plans. In the immediate build-up to the abolition of the trade in 1807, he was without doubt the principal architect of the complex stages that led to it finally becoming law. Ramsay's evidence had 'lifted the veil' and Dickson's campaigning secured the unprecedented number of petitions from Scotland in 1792, but it was Stephen who was able to combine detailed knowledge with political and legal skill.

Between 1802 and 1807, James Stephen wrote four pamphlets. In *The Crisis of the Sugar Colonies*, he not only argued that the slave trade made the colonies less secure, but that without a programme of amelioration of slavery, they could not be defended from France. This pamphlet was in the form of four letters to Henry Addington, Chancellor of the Exchequer. Stephen claimed that the object of the current French expedition to the West Indies was to restore slavery in St Domingue, despite Napoleon's promise to respect freedom. Massive resistance would render this aim unsuccessful. He then argued that 'the [sugar] consumption of France must in a considerable degree be supplied by the British planter' and that this intolerable situation would force her to seek to capture Jamaica. The result would be an increase in British taxes to provide a huge garrison of troops, many of whom would die of disease, and the risk of a ruinous naval campaign. 'Did the islands grow not only sugar but gold,' wrote Stephen, 'they might be bought too dear and the people of this country might grudge to give for the defence of their colonies another tenth of their income.' An alternative for him would be to equip and arm negro troops in the islands. The planters would oppose this and it is likely, he claimed, that black soldiers would regard the slavery of their colleagues 'with disgust'. For this to be viable, for him the slave trade must be abolished. Furthermore, since 'the extreme and unnatural bondage in which the great majority of the inhabitants of these populous islands is held, presents some obstacle to necessary measures of defence, is there no possibility', he asked, 'of going to the root of every evil at once and strengthening our colonies in the most effectual way, by interior reformation?'[39]

Davis claimed that, even at this stage, Stephen was 'the first abolitionist to move beyond images of individual domination and to think of slavery as a truly social system based on economic oppression'. Stephen also saw clearly that no planter 'could institute effective reforms without suffering ruinous losses'.[40] But while that may have been true, even in his much later work, *Slavery Delineated*, Stephen did not specifically advocate emancipation, contenting himself with a pragmatic plea for amelioration.

The Crisis of the Sugar Colonies was an appeal to national self-interest in a time of war and contained no polemic about humanity or threat of divine wrath, both of which featured prominently in the eighteenth-century campaign. In 1805, Stephen published what many consider was his most influential pamphlet in the campaign, the 250-page *War in Disguise: or the Frauds of the Neutral Flags*. As with *The Crisis*, it dealt with British commercial and defence interests. Stephen was now employed as a lawyer in the Prize Appeal Court of the Privy Council and had become an expert in maritime commercial law. He argued that the 'Rule of 1756' had not been enforced. (In that year, the Prize Court had ruled that a neutral nation could not be permitted to relieve a belligerent from the pressure of its enemies by engaging in a trade with it from which it was debarred in peacetime. Since 1793 France had opened her colonial trade to neutrals and Britain, having tried to enforce the Rule, yielded to American pressure. Thus France could ship her goods from her colonies without hindrance, using a neutral vessel.) The result, said Stephen, was that 'France and Holland have totally ceased to trade under their own flags . . . with the exception of a very small portion of the coasting trade of our enemies, not a mercantile sail of any description now enters or clears from their ports in any part of the globe, but under neutral colours'.

This, for Stephen, obviously enabled enemy commerce to thrive. He went on to argue that it weakened Britain's naval power, since an enemy's fleet would be supplied and supported by neutrals without having to stretch their resources in combat. Worse still, he maintained, 'our seamen, also, are being debauched into foreign employ, to carry on the trade of our enemies.'[41] For him, the answer was to return to a strict application of the Rule of 1756, despite the possible repercussions from America. In the entire document there is only a passing reference to slavery and that in connection with the expansion of agriculture in Cuba and the extensive importation of slaves. This seems extraordinary given Stephen's passionate commitment to abolition, but there is a plausible explanation given by the English historian, Roger Anstey. Anstey recognised how far down Britain's agenda the slave trade had slipped during the Napoleonic wars. Stephen's real purpose, he argued, was evidenced in a footnote in the *Life of Wilberforce*, in which Wilberforce commended this 'masterly pamphlet' aimed at the suppression of the neutral slave trade and claimed that Stephen confined himself entirely to the general question 'fearing if he mentioned the slave trade, that the effect of his argument might be diminished by a suspicion of his motives'.[42]

What followed certainly gives credence to this. The success of Wilberforce's renewed attempt to secure abolition of the slave trade was very much in doubt and he was convinced by Stephen to press for an end to the supply of slaves to foreigners and to conquered islands, on grounds of national interest rather than humanity. Those in Government who were unsympathetic to general abolition were won over and even some of the West Indian party were persuaded that such a measure might benefit them. Once the measure had passed the Commons, Lord Grenville, relying heavily on Stephen, piloted it through the Lords. The leading Whig, Charles James Fox, estimated that more than one half of the British slave trade had been destroyed; abolitionists claimed that the proportion was nearly two-thirds. Anstey himself, in his careful assessment of statistics, estimated that when the 1806 Bill confirmed and extended the 1805 Order-in-Council, the true figure was nearer three-quarters. At all events it was a substantial achievement for James Stephen whom, it was claimed, as a good evangelical, had ably followed the gospel injunction in Matthew 10:16 to be 'wise as serpents', thus succeeding in breaking the back of the trade through the more acceptable avenue of national interest.[43]

Stephen's other pamphlets contained very different approaches. In 1807, Stephen became the main drafter of the bill to abolish the slave trade, which was frankly promoted as a humanitarian act with the sanction of God's decrees. At the same time he published another pamphlet entitled *The Dangers of the Country*, in which he specifically argued that any delay would call down divine judgement and the 'anger of heaven'. 'The enormity of the aggravation of our sin since the first call to repentance,' he wrote, 'will perhaps be best estimated by a view of the actual increase in the slave trade since the year 1787', and he echoed later preachers on emancipation with his cry of 'When will this sad series end? Can we weary out God? Are we stronger than He?'[44] The same year yet another pamphlet appeared. It was simply entitled *New Reasons for Abolishing the Slave Trade* and it underlined the 'ruinous effects' of the trade. Although published anonymously, Dickson observed that it was 'generally ascribed to the masterly pen of Mr. Stephen'.[45]

Stephen was swimming with the tide in 1807, but there then followed a period of disappointment. From the House of Commons he attempted to promote the newly ceded colonies as models of free labour and to establish a register of slaves that would prevent illegal importation and enable all those unregistered to go free. Both schemes were advocated by pamphlets and both in the end were defeated. *The Crisis of the Sugar Colonies* carried a supplementary plan for the newly acquired island of Trinidad, whereby a portion of its land could be sold only to those who accepted the condition of cultivation by the labour of free negroes. When Stephen tried to introduce this in 1812, supported strongly by the African Institution, he wanted to link it with registration, but Lord Liverpool's government preferred to leave even ceded colonies to govern themselves without interference. In the same way, Wilberforce's attempt in 1815 to establish general registration, despite Stephen's strong support and the arguments in his *Reasons for Establishing a Registry of Slaves*,[46] were watered down to a meaningless voluntary code. Shortly afterwards Stephen resigned his seat.

But not his activity. In 1824 he finished the first volume of his massive *Slavery of the British West India Colonies Delineated*. In 1823 the first tentative steps towards amelioration were proposed by Britain to the colonies. To those who claimed that the recent insurrections had been caused by the public concern in Britain over slavery, Stephen responded 'that without public discussion in this country, slavery will never be abolished or effectively alleviated, no fair man who attends to the admitted facts of the case will dispute'.[47] He then examined in detail the legal systems of the colonies, demonstrating clearly the total lack of protection for the slaves. This time his work was enthusiastically welcomed by the *Edinburgh Review*, which claimed that 'of the numerous excellent works in which this important subject has lately been discussed, that of Mr. Stephen is the most comprehensive and in many respects, the most valuable'.[48]

It was 1830 before the second volume of *Slavery Delineated* appeared and it was to be Stephen's last major contribution to the cause. He was now seventy-two and was to die two years later. There was fire in it, though, as well as a minute examination of the lack of progress in the slave colonies, details that Macaulay and others were to find invaluable in the final stages of the campaign. Stephen noted in his conclusion that Britain seemed to have receded from 'the sacred principles of penitence and reformation' on which the 1807 Abolition Act was founded and had entered the blind alley by which 'we committed the fate of the oppressed to the discretion of the oppressors'. Uncharacteristically, he did not produce a plan for emancipation, but trusted in the parliamentary activity of Henry Brougham to obtain a hearing above the West Indian cries. Stephen proclaimed that the national voice, 'responsive to the call of religion, justice and humanity, will second our appeals to parliament in louder and still louder strains and without remission, till our legislators shall effectively listen to it and "let the people go" '.[49]

The measured, almost cold tones of the earlier pamphlets might call into question Furneaux's comment about Stephen's passion. Yet nowhere is this passion better demonstrated than in *England Enslaved by her own Slave Colonies*, a pamphlet addressed to the electors of Britain in 1826. It is an updating of his first volume of *Slavery Delineated* and it exposed the weakness of Canning's attempts in 1823 to persuade the colonies voluntarily to ameliorate the conditions of their slaves. 'Recommendation to the Assemblies!!!', thundered Stephen, 'you might as well recommend toleration to the Spanish Inquisitors, or Grecian liberty to the Turkish Divan.' He cited the trial and conviction of the missionary Smith in Demerara in 1823 and the continuing violation of the Sabbath by planters, despite their protestations otherwise. He further poured contempt on the attempt to make light of the cart-whip, 'the main spring of the machine', by styling it an 'emblem' or 'beadle's laced hat'. After a detailed argument of the cost to Britain of the colonies, he ended by encouraging electors not to believe that their interventions were unnecessary. 'Come forward with your petitions,' he pleaded, 'instruct your representatives; give or withhold your suffrages for the next Parliament; and use your personal influence throughout the country; all in such manner as may best promote the success of this great and sacred cause.'[50]

Eric Williams, for all his reservations about the work of the 'Saints', recognised Stephen's valiant efforts to check the excesses of the planters as 'a notable step in the protection of weaker peoples'.[51] For David Brion Davis, the passion identified by Furneaux was, in Stephen, accompanied by 'perhaps the most powerful intellect of the

British abolition movement, leading to a decisive influence over the abolition movement for more than thirty years'.[52]

ZACHARY MACAULAY AND THE AMMUNITION FOR THE CAMPAIGN

On 3 May 1825, Thomas Fowell Buxton, by now successor to Wilberforce in the leadership of the abolition movement, wrote to the Bristol poet and friend of the Clapham Sect, Hannah More: 'I concur with you entirely in thinking that few men have been persecuted and as unjustly calumniated, as Macaulay. But no matter. Man cannot rob Africa or the West Indies of his services, or him of the satisfaction of having rendered them.'[53] Zachary Macaulay was the son of the parish minister in Inveraray and after local schooling became a clerk in an office in Glasgow, enjoying a vigorous social life with students from the university. In his memoirs, Macaulay described his time there as filled with 'debauchery' and 'profanity'. At sixteen years of age, in 1784, he sailed for Jamaica on the advice of a relative, Sir Archibald Campbell, former Governor there. Macauley found a position as a bookkeeper or under-manager on an estate on the island and sailed for the Caribbean in 1784. He described this as 'a period of my life of which I scarce like to speak or think. It was a period of most degrading servitude to the worst of masters.'

Macaulay was immediately confronted by the extreme cruelty of plantation slavery, yet resigned himself to the role of overseer, developing what he described as a callous attitude to the slaves, 'with a levity which sufficiently marked my depravity'. One of his biographers judged that he was on a knife-edge between becoming totally demoralised by the humiliation of his lot and simply being absorbed in the system. Writing to a minister friend at home, Macaulay described graphically a scene in which he was 'cursing and bawling' in a cane field where slaves were being whipped at work, a scene which 'would make you imagine some unlucky accident had carried you to the doleful shades'. Yet he admitted that he resolved to 'get rid of my squeamishness' and to become 'the slave and the sport of the basest passions'. When an offer came from an uncle in London to return there, he did not jump at it, but had accommodated himself to Jamaica enough to hesitate before accepting.[54]

Macaulay returned from Jamaica in 1792. He was twenty-four. His father had died whilst he was abroad and he went to live with the Babingtons. Thomas Babington, who had married Macaulay's sister Jean, introduced him to Wilberforce and Thornton, and through the

Figure 7   *The memorial bust of Zachary Macaulay in Westminster Abbey.*
© *Dean and Chapter of Westminster*

abolitionist circle and for want of anything better to do, he embarked the next year on a voyage to the free settlement in Sierra Leone under the direction of a company formed by the Clapham Sect.

His presence in Sierra Leone impressed the directors of the company and in 1793 they appointed him second member of the council, or Deputy Governor. Sierra Leone in the late eighteenth century was regarded as a haven of freedom surrounded by some of the most concentrated slave-trading activity on the west coast. It was necessary to maintain a relationship with the slavers and especially with the slave station on Bance Island, since to some extent the colony was dependent on them for its supplies, especially during the war with France. Despite one incident in which he horrified the directors in London by returning five runaway slaves to Horrocks, a coastal trader, Macaulay acquitted himself reasonably well and was appointed Governor of the colony in 1794.[55]

The twenty-six-year-old Governor immediately faced a rebellion from settlers who found many of their hopes unrealised. This was followed by an invasion launched from French ships, whose crews looted and destroyed much of Freetown. Macaulay took leave the next year, returning to London via the West Indies. He then served for a further three years in Sierra Leone before his final return home in 1799. These were years of personal development in the anti-slavery field and of some success in the life of a colony that was plagued with problems from the start. They also included conflict with some of the ex-slave settlers and with the leaders of their religious groups, as well as difficulties in management that were used later by his enemies to discredit him.

Macaulay is often portrayed as a stern and unbending, even cruel dispenser of civil and religious authority in the colony, but he learned from his early experiences and became increasingly diplomatic. At the same time, he visited slavers and slave stations and worked hard at the delicate task of achieving a balance between maintaining a commercial relationship with them and ensuring that the colony was an example of commitment to freedom. Macaulay was prone to issue terse commands, even threats, but in contrast to the reaction to slave rebellions in the Caribbean, he granted a free pardon to most of those involved in the 1794 revolt, simply sending the ringleaders to England for trial. He introduced black juries into the courts and it was with one of those juries that a white schoolmaster was found guilty of cruelty and shipped home. With some negotiating skill, he saved many of the settlers' houses from destruction by French raiders and in his last years in the colony organised the kind of militia for defence against France that James Stephen had earlier recommended. In his defence, Hannah More, in a letter to Thomas Babington, spoke of Macaulay's character 'and the sacrifice made of his friends and country to the cause of Sierra Leone'.[56]

Macaulay's health had suffered in the punishing, fever-prone West African climate and he had to recuperate for a time in England before he began what was to be nearly thirty more years' service in the anti-slavery cause. From 1802 to 1816, he edited the Clapham Sect's journal *The Christian Observer*, in which anti-slavery played a major, though not overwhelming, role. For five of these years he acted as Secretary of the African Institution, which was both successor to the Committee for the Abolition of the Slave Trade and predecessor of the Anti-Slavery Society, of which he was a founding member in 1823. This marked the beginning of the periodic attempts of the British government to per-suade the Caribbean colonies to adopt reforms and the results fur-nished most of the material for the *Anti-Slavery Reporter*. The *Reporter* constantly monitored progress on 'amelioration', was a journal of anti-slavery activity throughout Britain and above all became a mine of factual information that was to supply those in Parliament with vital ammunition in their war against the entrenched interests of the West Indian planters. 'Every friend to slavery', wrote one of James Stephen's sons, 'well knew Macaulay to be his most dangerous foe.'[57]

The Anti-Slavery Reporter was the official organ of the 'London Society for the Mitigation and Gradual Abolition of Slavery through-out the British Dominions', the cumbersome and cautious title itself reflecting the stage of the campaign when it was launched in June 1825. From the start it was intended to be a regular means of com-munication with individuals, committees and organisations either sympathetic to the cause or with the potential to come on board. Within a few years the circulation of the *Reporter* rose to 20,000, and that did not include groups and individuals who borrowed copies, as they were encouraged to do. It became the standard reference for all throughout Britain who were engaged in anti-slavery activity, but especially for the campaign in Parliament, and led Wilberforce fre-quently to say, in response to queries, 'let us look it up in Macaulay'.[58]

Macaulay's lifelong obsession with facts was dramatically evi-denced after a year as Governor in Sierra Leone, when he decided to travel to England via the Caribbean to update himself on the state of plantation slavery. His biographers, relying on reports attributed to him and published after his death in the *Anti-Slavery Reporter*, describe his journey on a slave ship, the *Anna*, which left the Sierra Leone River in May 1795. Travelling on a slave ship would be entirely consistent with Macaulay's asceticism and his meticulons attention to facts, but his diary for 1795 indicates that he was already in the West Indies by May. The diaries are written in Greek script, possibly to keep his hand in with classical form, but more likely because, interspersed as they are with lists of supplies and comments on scriptural passages, they contain detailed comments and statistics on the reality of West Indian slavery. These very vital pieces of evidence required somewhat coded recording, in case they fell into the wrong hands.

From the start of his editorship of the *Anti-Slavery Reporter*, Macaulay collected statistics, reports, articles and reviews on issues relating to slavery, from voluminous Government tomes to small items in Caribbean newspapers or speeches at local anti-slavery meetings. The bulk of the *Reporter*'s material was collected and collated by Macaulay, but he engaged frequently in debate with apologists for slavery, generally using material which he regarded as much more impressive than his own words. Several aspects were crucial in supporting the anti-slavery campaign and building it up for the final push in the early 1830s. The first was a continual attempt to call the Government to account over the effectiveness of its reform of slavery. In 1826, Macaulay attempted what he described as 'a brief view of the real advance' since 1823, one which ran to over thirty pages. The current situation, island by island, was detailed and contrasted with the hoped-for reforms. Macaulay drew on reports from the legislatures and courts of each of the islands to provide his evidence.

The summary of the results that he gave to his readers were that none of the islands had done anything about religious instruction and none had abolished the flogging of females, two basic pieces of amelioration sought in 1823. Only Grenada, St Vincent and the Bahamas permitted slave marriages, only the Bahamas and Grenada prohibited the separation of families by sales, and only Tobago and Grenada had lowered the scale of arbitrary punishment by the master. The conclusion Macaulay gave to his readers was that, 'instead of having this flattering picture of improvement realised, it turns out that . . . only five of the colonies have done anything whatsoever towards carrying the resolutions of the 15th May, 1823, into effect'.[59] Such an indictment was key ammunition for the abolitionist group in Parliament. Just as importantly it fuelled the growing local committees and helped them look beyond hopes of an amelioration by persuasion towards emancipation by legislation.

Macaulay was well aware of the efforts made by the West Indian party to argue that improvements in the conditions of the slaves made by the planters rendered unnecessary what they termed 'interference' from London. The same cause was warmly endorsed by the monthly periodical *John Bull*, which regularly printed glowing reports from the West Indies, maintained a constant tirade against emancipation and claimed that the insurrections were a direct result of the work of the abolitionists.[60]

In response to this, Macaulay kept an up-to-date record of the West Indian slavery at the centre of the *Reporter* month by month. The sources that he used were incontrovertible. In 1826 and 1830, he reproduced a series of advertisements in the *Royal Jamaica Gazette* that detailed sales of slaves in payment of their master's debt, with the marks of whipping on their body that identified them and bore witness to their treatment. 'We will not cease', wrote Macaulay, 'to call the attention of our countrymen to these abominations, as long as they are suffered to exist.' When detailing particularly notorious cases such as that of Henry and Helen Moss in the Bahamas, who were found guilty of flogging and torturing to death several female slaves, Macaulay was careful to cite as his sources the dispatches of successive governors of the island to the Colonial Secretary.[61] In 1828, the *Reporter* carried an extensive review of a pamphlet entitled *The West India Question Plainly Stated*. The author was a Mr Fortunatus Dwarris, a planter who between 1822 and 1826 filled the office of a commissioner of legal inquiry and made lengthy reports on nine of the colonies. Dwarris totally rejected the idea that no improvements had been made. He boldly proclaimed that, in contrast to the representations made by 'persons as respectable as Master Stephen and Mr. Macaulay', the West Indies had changed out of all recognition in the last quarter century.[62] Instead of using his own words in response, Macaulay carefully researched Dwarris's reports, contrasted the information in them point by point with the glowing accounts in Dwarris's own pamphlet, and offered them to his readers. 'What motives', he asked, 'can have produced such extraordinary contradictions? Or who shall be dexterous enough to reconcile Mr. Dwarris the planter and pamphleteer with Mr. Dwarris the Lawyer and Commissioner?'[63]

All this was not without its cost. The opponents of abolition felt the threat posed by Macaulay's dogged effectiveness and throughout the 1820s he faced sustained attack in the columns of *John Bull*. Certainly he was often bracketed with Wilberforce, Buxton and

Stephen in what the journal claimed were false claims and hypocritical activities in 'Bible dinner snuggeries and Godly tea drinkings', claiming to care for black slaves whilst they cared nothing of Britain's labourers. However, Macaulay came in for special attention. 'Saint Zachariah' he was mockingly termed, and his suggestion of a sugar boycott let to a taunt of 'Zaccarine'. More seriously, *John Bull* was outraged at his presiding over the trial of whites in Sierra Leone with a black jury, seizing on every report of death rates in the colony as evidence of the utter folly of starting the colony and of Macaulay's incompetence. Above all, it accused him of 'feathering his own nest' in Sierra Leone by importing gunpowder, taking a bounty on captured slaves and monopolising trade. Much of their evidence came from Macaulay's successor in the colony, with whom he did not have a good relationship, and from Dr Robert Thorpe, a judge in Sierra Leone whom Macaulay had described in unflattering terms to Governor Thomas Thompson. 'We will never quit the subject', declared *John Bull*, 'until we have torn the veil [of hypocrisy] asunder and displayed the system of Macaulayism to the broad glare of day.'[64]

It was true that Macaulay and his less able nephew, Thomas Gisborne Babington, set up a company with Sierra Leone that provided a considerable income for him in earlier days, but when the anti-slavery cause took all his attention it fell into ruin and he lost much of his wealth.[65] However, that fact alone does not substantiate the allegations. Macaulay took time to write a pamphlet addressed to the Duke of Gloucester, patron of the London-based national anti-slavery Society, answering all charges against him. Encouraged by his friends, he sued *John Bull* for libel in 1824.[66] The journal responded by applying in Chancery for two commissions to take evidence in the West Indies and Africa. The action was then legally suspended until the result of the commissions, and with the advice of his friends, Macaulay chose to relinquish proceedings.[67] Macaulay continued with his work on the *Anti-Slavery Reporter* and *John Bull* kept up its attack on the abolitionists with bluster, but never with the same personal venom against Macaulay. In 1833, Thomas Fowell Buxton led delegates from throughout the United Kingdom to Downing Street with an address to the Prime Minister. That evening they met for dinner and Buxton ended his speech to them by 'gladly seizing a long wished-for opportunity of bearing testimony to the merits of the real leader of this cause – the anti-slavery tutor of us all – Mr. Macaulay'.[68]

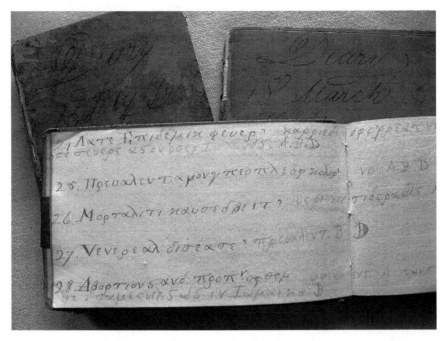

Figure 8   *Diary notes made in Greek script by Zachary Macaulay on slave conditions in Barbados in 1795. Terse comments on 'late epidemic' and 'venereal disease'. Photograph by kind permission of the Macaulay family*

HENRY BROUGHAM – REVIEWER AND PARLIAMENTARY DEBATER

It may seem strange to include Brougham in the company of the other four. Certainly he was active in the anti-slavery cause over many years. However, he alone of the five had no direct West Indian experience and his information was always second-hand. He was the only one who achieved high political office and that almost by definition meant that his efforts were dissipated among many other concerns and Government business, while Ramsay, Dickson, Stephen and Macaulay could concentrate on the one cause. When the bill to abolish slavery in 1833 was being discussed, Brougham, then Lord Chancellor, took very little part in the discussion and gave support to the provision which substituted apprenticeship for outright abolition. It may have been a safe tactical move, but it raised the question of whether he had trimmed his coat for reasons of personal political safety.[69]

There is a further reason to suggest that Brougham's name sits strangely amongst the others. It is to be found in an anonymous pamphlet which appeared in 1830 and claimed that in Brougham's most substantial work on colonial policy, he had been a defender of slavery.[70] The pamphleteer who was so keen to demonstrate these views appears to have some solid evidence. Negro slaves in the colonies, claimed Brougham, were 'utterly unfit for the relations of voluntary labourers in a regular and uncivilised state'. 'A perpetual terror of the lash is the only preventive of indolence', he wrote and 'nothing but the subdivision of the negroes and their subjection to the power of the masters armed with absolute authority, can prevent them acquiring that ascendancy to which decided superiority in numbers and strength naturally and invariably lead.' This reflected the classic argument of the planters for keeping every harsh measure in place. Brougham castigated the French abolitionist Abbé Reynal for his 'ridiculous fondness for savages' and his giving 'a favourable portrait of this degraded race'. 'The negroes', claimed Brougham, 'are the enemies to be most dreaded by all Europeans. They are the natural foes of white men.' It is hardly surprising, then, to find Brougham raising the spectre of St Domingue when he advised: 'let this branch of the imperial administration then be left to the care of those who are themselves the most immediately interested in the good order and government of those distant provinces and whose knowledge of local circumstances is more full and practical'.[71] In other words, leave the planters alone.

Such statements would appear to put Brougham firmly in company with Edward Long of Jamaica or James Tobin of Nevis, rather than with Stephen and Macaulay, his colleagues on the London Committee. In this light, the claim seems strange that *Colonial Policy* opened up the field for immediate action on the slave trade and that Wilberforce, on reading it, warmly welcomed Brougham to the cause, thus initiating a lifelong friendship.[72] However, that was not the full explanation. For there is another thread in the second volume that is in marked contrast to the first. In apparent contradiction of his earlier assertions, Brougham wrote that, however deficient in civilisation, negroes are endowed nonetheless with powers 'not only of body but of mind sufficient to render their improvement and high refinement a matter of absolute certainty under a proper system of management'. He continued by outlining a scheme of better management, maintaining that the lash led to 'a state of despair and not industry', that he was surprised that people did not recognise the 'gross impolicy' of cruelty and oppression, and that it was established beyond doubt that the most unprofitable plantations are not those with bad soil, but 'uniformly those which are cultivated by negroes subjected to a cruel and stingy system of management'. Basic to remedying this, for Brougham, was the abolition of the slave trade. 'We forget', he wrote, 'it is not a trade but a crime', and the only effective method of preventing the cruel treatment of slaves 'consists of cutting off that source which truly feeds the passions and caprices and shortsighted wishes of the planters'.[73]

Even a passionate concern for the abolition of the slave trade could, in 1803, be held comfortably alongside acceptance of the system of plantation slavery. Brougham may have accepted the system more easily than the other four Scots in this study, though, and in fact admitted this publicly in the 1823 debate on slavery, when he spoke of giving in to the 'delusion' that 'the abolition of the slave trade was all that was wanted for bettering the condition of the slaves'.[74] If that was so, it was no more cautious than the position taken by Wilberforce and many other abolitionists at that time.

In the autumn of 1802, Brougham founded, along with three legal and literary friends, the first Scottish journal of political and literary criticism since 1757. The *Edinburgh Review* from the start took a strong position against the slave trade, and with the exception of a piece which he commissioned from Wilberforce for the October 1804 edition, almost every one of the articles, book reviews and commentaries on the trade and on slavery itself for the next two decades were provided by Brougham. The highly controversial nature of the *Review* was reflected in its position on slavery above all and Macaulay frequently took material from it for the *Anti-Slavery Reporter*.

Early on in its life, the *Edinburgh Review* crossed swords with James Stephen, when Brougham reviewed *The Crisis of the Sugar Colonies*. He described Stephen's style as 'loaded with clumsy, or vulgar, or gaudy ornaments', but his main critique was directed to the content. Brougham challenged Stephen's central contention that British and French interests in the West Indies were hostile to each other and he claimed that Stephen had greatly underestimated the restoration of slavery in French colonies. For him, Stephen's scheme of cultivation by free negroes was not only impractical, but 'infinitely more dangerous and scarcely less cruel, than the old system with all its perils and horrors'.[75] The 'remedy' for the evils, in Brougham's view, was the abolition of the slave trade and it was this on that the *Review* mainly focused. In 1804, Brougham wrote a pamphlet on the trade.[76] This was on behalf of the London-based Abolition Committee and it was distributed to all members of the House of Commons prior to the first reading of Wilberforce's bill in May. It had such an effect that Pitt flourished a copy when speaking in the debate.[77] The summary of its contents in the *Edinburgh Review* and its commendation to the public were also from Brougham's own pen, as was a detail critique in October 1804 of an anonymous pamphlet in response to his, circulated to MPs, which the *Review* described as 'the last expiring effort' of the opponents of abolition.[78]

In 1807 the *Edinburgh Review* analysed Wilberforce's address to his constituents, congratulating its readers 'on the final and complete triumph of the great cause so often pleaded in this Journal'. The following year, in reviewing Thomas Clarkson's *History of the Abolition of the Slave Trade*, Brougham gave his readers brief biographical notes on Sharp, Wilberforce and Clarkson himself. This chapter in the anti-slavery movement appeared to be closed for the *Review*. But not for long. The prospect of a revival of the slave trade by the French was extensively dealt with in 1814, with a detailed description of documents that would have done credit to Macaulay. Early in 1823, Brougham led a rallying cry in the *Review*, this time for the mitigation and eventual abolition of slavery.

However prodigious Brougham's literary efforts may have been, his greatest contribution to the anti-slavery cause lay in his eloquence at Westminster. Elected as MP for Camelford in February 1810, he gave notice four months later that he would introduce a bill to make slave-trading punishable by transportation, instead of the small fines that were proving to be no deterrent to the slavers. He took the Commons by storm and justified the abolitionists' confidence that he was the parliamentary heir to Wilberforce.

Brougham reminded the House that it was three years since the trade had been abolished, but there had been an 'unaccountable silence of the law on this head' that permitted, by not prohibiting, the traffic. The time had come, he claimed, to 'let our indignation fall on those who dare to trade in human flesh' and to call them not traders and merchants, but murderers. Nor would he allow their crime to be compared to an ordinary murder through revenge or the like. Their courage threw 'a false glare over their crimes', but it was time, said Brougham, to give such traders and merchants in cities such as London and Liverpool 'the right name and call them cowardly suborners of piracy and mercenary murder'. He appealed, as he did in the conclusion of his *Colonial Policy*, to 'the Divine Legislator'. 'Whoever (says the scripture) stealeth a man and selleth him, or in whose hands he shall be found, shall surely be put to death', declared Brougham. By contrast, he claimed: 'Whosoever (says the English law) stealeth a man and tortureth him and killeth him and selleth him into slavery for all the days of his life, shall surely – pay twenty pounds. I trust that this grievous incongruity will at length be done away.' Next year it was, and largely because his first major speech to the house had established Brougham as a man to be reckoned with.[79]

In 1823, the Government took its first tentative steps towards the amelioration of slave conditions in the West Indies. The word 'amelioration' was set beside 'eventual emancipation' in many of the local anti-slavery societies, reflecting the extreme caution that was needed to gain public approval. Such approval seemed to receive a severe blow in October of that year, when reports came in of a slave rebellion in Demerara in which three whites had been killed. Two hundred and fifty blacks were either murdered by planters or executed under martial law in response. This reaction went almost unnoticed in the British press until word came of the death of Rev. John Smith, an English emissary of the London Missionary Society. The insurrection had started near Smith's chapel and a deacon, Quamina, was one of the leaders. There was no evidence of Smith's encouragement of the insurrection, let alone of his involvement in it. However, the planters seized Smith, who was court-martialled and condemned to death for complicity. After months in jail, Smith's health was broken and he died, thus giving the abolitionists a martyr.

Three weeks earlier, Brougham had raised the issue in the House of Commons through a motion of censure on the Demerara government and the court that had convicted Smith. In his speech, he seized on every legal irregularity in the case, pointing out that a sick and elderly man who had faithfully taught Christianity to slaves as his calling and appointment required was dragged from his house and held in an airless cell for weeks on end. He continued to argue that the trial itself was unconstitutional and that Smith had been permitted no legal representation. The death penalty was not even prescribed for the crimes with which Smith was accused. From a trenchant dissection of the case, Brougham then painted a picture of the planters under a triple fear – of a slave-free St Domingue on their doorstep, of their own slaves rising up, and now of 'Christians of the old world' as well as pagans of the new.[80] Furthermore, he ended by making a call for Parliament to recognise that such behaviour by Demerara struck at the foundation not just of law, but also of Christian evangelism. After a ten-day debate, Brougham's closing speech was even stronger. He argued that the word 'murder' was appropriate for on who was 'put to death by slow and wanton severity', and went on to appeal for direct intervention from Parliament into colonial legislation. 'That the rights of property are sacred' he did not question, but continued to state that 'the rules of justice [are] paramount and inviolable'. Brougham allowed that, 'for a season', it might be legitimate to accept property in human beings, but he was clear that 'we never for an instant forget that they are men and the fellow-subjects of their masters'.[81] The implication was that, at the end of the day, control rested in, and must be exercised by, the mother country.

Brougham failed narrowly to obtain a motion of censure, but the real work had been done. G. M. Trevelyan wrote that the trial and death of Smith 'was fatal to Slavery in the West Indies to the same degree as the execution of John Brown was its deathblow in the United States'.[82] The death of a missionary in this way touched a nerve with the British public, although James Walvin noted that the same public were hardly outraged over the death of hundreds of slaves at the same time.[83] Yet Brougham's publicising of the case focused considerable public feeling in preparation for the extraordinary popular petition campaign on slavery throughout the next decade. In 1830, although he once again failed to achieve a Commons majority, this time pressing for outright abolition, he was to highlight the popular groundswell that his own eloquence had helped both to create and foster. 'Let the planters beware,' he warned. 'Let the Parliament beware. The same country is once again awake – awake to the condition of negro slavery; the same indignation kindles in the bosom of the same people; the same cloud is gathering that annihilated the Slave Trade.'[84]

By the time of the Emancipation Act, Brougham was in the Upper House as Lord Chancellor. However, he seemed to take a step backwards on the issue, supporting the Apprenticeship Scheme to replace slavery. Yet when the truth of that scheme became evident he raised his voice again, proposing a bill to end it and addressing large public gatherings. His bill did not succeed, but Brougham used to the full well-attested reports of floggings, the treadmill and other atrocities. He helped to fix the final nails in the coffin of slavery, and the Apprenticeship Scheme was abolished at the end of July 1838. In the meantime, Brougham did succeed in what was a little noticed piece of legislation, but one that had dramatic effects. The 'bounty' system, by which rewards for captured slavers depended on the number of slaves carried, was replaced by one that, in his words, 'rewards men for preventing the slaver's voyage, not for interrupting it – for saving the Africans from the slave ship, not for seizing the ship after it has received them'.[85]

Thirty-four years after his first printed intervention on slavery, Brougham made his last spoken one. In that early writing, as we have seen, there is much that appears contradictory. He is alone amongst the five men discussed in this chapter in that anti-slavery was never his life's work and his public speeches on it might have been seen to be self-serving. But James Stephen, whose own work was savaged in the *Edinburgh Review* and who as a Tory had often clashed bitterly with Brougham, was in no doubt of his contribution to the cause. 'The colonists', wrote Stephen in 1826, 'would do anything to gain him or to suppress a voice which from his transcendent talents and commanding influence with a powerful party, cannot be easily put down.'[86]

The Scottish Stamp

It would be hard to exaggerate the effectiveness of the contribution of these five London Scots to the abolitionist cause. Certainly there were other giants of that movement: Granville Sharp was its pioneer, Thomas Clarkson was the engineer of many of its campaigns, William Wilberforce its leader in the House of Commons. Henry Thornton, Wilberforce's cousin, organised the Sierra Leone project. Thomas Fowell Buxton, Wilberforce's successor as leader of the movement, and Dr Stephen Lushington were parliamentarians who helped to steer emancipation finally through. However, none of them, with the possible exception of Sharp, were able to do their work without the skill and experience of at least one of the five Scots.

When Wilberforce made the first of his many attempts to secure the abolition of the slave trade in 1789, his answers to the response to his speech relied almost entirely on material provided by Ramsay. It has been claimed that the person who had more influence over Wilberforce in tactical terms was his son-in-law, James Stephen, and this was amplified in an account of the events of 1806 in a modern biography.[87] Macaulay's famed encyclopaedic knowledge was at the disposal of the whole campaign, and although Wilberforce often found him too radical on some issues, close family ties and unswerving devotion to the cause forged strong links between them. Macaulay once described Brougham as 'a kind of Solomon' and claimed that he appeared to know everything,[88] yet the latter's crucial place in the anti-slavery movement lay not in his detailed knowledge, but in his assuming the mantle of Wilberforce as the member of the House of Commons most able to command its attention on slavery.

All of these very diverse men owed more than is at first apparent to their Scottish background. Most historians accept the significance of religion in the abolitionist cause. These Scots who were active in that cause steered a middle ground between the antipathy to evangelical 'enthusiasm' in much of the Church in Scotland and the fervour of evangelicals. In their different ways, they were comfortable with religious concepts and were able effectively to use these in the cause. Ramsay and Stephen both experienced the University of Aberdeen's rigorous academic discipline and were influenced by James Beattie as a friend and teacher. Beattie's own strong, practical devotion to Christian ethics, not least in the matter of slavery, left its mark in different ways and at different times on both men. Macaulay's manse background enabled him to make a distinctive contribution within the community of the Clapham Sect. Although undoubtedly fervent for the spread of the Christian faith above all else, he brought a quality that is described in Scots as 'canny' to all his work, informing it with a measured coolness that some read as aloof and remote, but under which a fire burned. Dickson's familiarity with the Presbyterian tradition in Scotland enabled him to be trusted on his tour by churchmen and thus to enervate them to be effective agents of the cause. Brougham was by far the least religious of all five, and indeed one biographer reports a contemporary taking great pleasure in imagining him on his knees whilst attending family worship at James Stephen's home.[89] Nonetheless, his familiarity with theology is obvious in his speeches and in his articles in the *Edinburgh Review*, which make frequent open references to Christian doctrine and are peppered with scriptural quotations.

Scotland may not have been as egalitarian a society as has often been claimed, but it contrasted with its southern neighbour in the way in which men with ability could surmount the class barrier. This was particularly marked in education, which was in its ideal available to all males on merit. In turn, that education itself encouraged independent spirits. In a recent study of anti-slavery it was noted that some of the most prominent figures in the Manchester committee against the slave trade had been the recipients of a Scottish higher education.[90] This desire for freedom from an inflexible social hierarchy, and even contempt for it, as witnessed by the popularity of many of Robert Burns' poems, worked favourably for the abolitionists. Brougham's Edinburgh certainly had its snobbery, but it was much less pervasive than that of London. Being brought up in Fraserburgh, on a coast where there was a dependence on fishing and the work of the fishermen, gave James Ramsay a natural sympathy for ordinary seamen when he himself was a surgeon in the navy. The detailed attention to their welfare, evident in his early writings, was to be transferred to a similar passion for the well-being of slaves. Dickson's *Letters on Slavery* may have been too strong for the London Committee to publish, mainly because of its writer's passionate feeling against the reality of slavery for its victims, but Macaulay's letters to a friend at home expressing his horror that human beings could be treated so cruelly, and Stephen's report of the treatment of slaves on trial in Barbados, are further examples of how two young Scots enabled their grounding in humanity to remain intact. Much later both Stephen and Macaulay, with Brougham, sought to involve women in the movement, despite Wilberforce's strong opposition.[91]

All five were influenced not just by theology and egalitarianism, but by the belief in the progress of different societies within a single human nature that was central to the Scottish Enlightenment. Scots in England, as Boswell knew only too well, were often the butt of prejudice against their nation for its perceived lack of civilisation, especially in the north, and there was an implication that this was a natural state. One of the most telling aspects of Dickson's *Letters* was that it described the potential capabilities of those of African descent. When Dickson asked the rhetorical question 'What is the connection between the colour of the human skin and the faculties of the human mind?', his answer found no evidence to validate the theory of the innate inferiority of any race. It is true that he criticised Kames and Hume for implying the reverse, but he also clearly saw these ideas as aberrations within an agreed understanding of common human nature. Rather than accepting slavery as a legitimate response to a debased human nature, Dickson quoted with approval the Philadelphia Abolition Society's description of it as 'an atrocious debasement of human nature'.[92]

One of Macaulay's descendants spoke of 'the northern iron in his nature' that 'could not be consumed'. The nearest English equivalent to the Scots word 'thrawn' is stubborn. 'Thrawnness', allied to a singlemindedness that refuses to be deflected from its task, is a powerful combination and this was to a degree possessed by all five. Ramsay's friend James Beattie urged him not to reply to every piece of personal invective, but Ramsay replied that 'there was something in his temper that would not allow him to rest until he had done so'.[93] Stephen's massive *Slavery Delineated* in 1824 invited so much reaction that it took a very persistent man to publish a sequel six years later. He was that man, though, and his drafting of legislation exhibited the same dogged adherence to the task as he showed in pursuing the anti-slavery cause to which he committed his life. Brougham was well-known for his mercurial quality, and as the only career politician amongst the five, he was not above changing positions when this seemed advantageous. But to read his speeches on slavery, especially the one on the Smith case, is to be aware of a man who spoke without 'fear or favour', and once he had the bit between his teeth he was as thrawn as any of his abolitionist colleagues.

A Scottish education demanded a considerable amount of intellectual rigour. All five had experience of this. The encyclopaedic Macaulay set the pace with the most careful research and detailed attention to facts. The *Anti-Slavery Reporter* carried statistics and tables that would be a credit to a whole government department preparing a report, but the *Reporter* was the work of one man. Stephen came the closest to matching this with his *The Slavery of the British West India Colonies Delineated as it exists, both in Law and Practice and compared with the Slavery of Other Countries, Ancient and Modern*, whose very title indicates the extraordinary application of the author. The verbal and written attacks on Macaulay and Stephen were considerable. However, those attacks were habitually couched in personal terms, frequently relied on scorn and belittling, and very rarely attempted any detailed response to the evidence provided. It was no doubt too daunting a task for opponents to engage with them on ground that was so well-researched and collated. In earlier days, Ramsay's evidence to the parliamentary inquiry on the slave trade, Dickson's observations in his time as Secretary to Governor Hay in Barbados, and Brougham's continuous assault on the slave trade in the *Edinburgh Review*, together made a formidable yet varied contribution offered to audiences that would only be convinced by the highest standards of advocacy.

There were other Scots who made a significant contribution to the anti-slavery cause outside their own land. Ramsay's patron, Sir Charles Middleton, was an unswerving supporter of abolitionism in the House of Commons and his wife Margaret is credited in 1786 with persuading Wilberforce to first raise the issue of the slave trade in the Commons.[94] In the London Committee's Minutes of 1791, there are enthusiastic references to a Montrose landowner, Hercules Ross, who was elected an honorary member and encouraged to meet with them when in London. However, the contribution of 'the five' was outstanding. Furthermore, it was made in the teeth of powerful Scottish political interests that were far from sympathetic to abolitionism. Henry Dundas' control of all but a few of the MPs from

Scotland in the eighteenth century ensured that few Scots in Westminster broke ranks with the Government. The power of the West Indian interest in Scotland, always strong, became increasingly organised in the 1820s, and for the first time petitions were to reach Parliament from Scottish communities seeking to defend their commercial interests by maintaining plantation slavery. Signs of extensive West Indian influence were evident in the resistance encountered by Dickson in Scotland in 1792. To examine the popular movement and thinking that moved the nation from eliminating the trade to uprooting the system itself in the first half of the next century is to discover that it was a far from seamless thread, and that the abolition societies faced a similar opposition to that encountered by Stephen, Macaulay and Brougham.

Notes

1 Minute Books of the London Society for the Abolition of the Slave Trade, 23 May 1804, Vol. 2. BL, Add. MSS. 21256/208. f. 2.
2 Folarin Shyllon, *James Ramsay – The Unknown Abolitionist* (Edinburgh, 1977), pp. 7–12, 103.
3 James Ramsay, *An Essay on the Treatment and Conversion of African Slaves in the British Sugar Colonies* (London, 1784) pp. 2–90, 92–102, 113–30, 133–42, 145, 158–60, 178, 198–219, 245, 265–76, 282.
4 Shyllon, *James Ramsay*, p. 37.
5 James Beattie to Thomas Percival, 29 Jan 1788. Boston Public Library, MS Ch H.12. 21. I am indebted to the late Professor Roger Robinson of London for this reference.
6 Thomas Clarkson, *History of the Rise, Progress and Accomplishment of Abolition of the Slave Trade by the British* (London, 1808), Vol. 1, pp. 203–30.
7 James Ramsay, Papers, RHO. NA32 MSS, British Empire, S2, pp. 8–13.
8 James Ramsay, *Objections to the Abolition of the Slave Trade with Answers to which are Prefixed Strictures on a Late Publication entitled 'Considerations on the Emancipation of Negroes and the Abolition of the Slave Trade', by a West Indian Planter* (London, 1788).
9 James Ramsay, *An Address to the Publick on the Proposed Bill for the Abolition of the Slave Trade* (London, 1789).
10 Ramsay, Papers, pp. 6–7.
11 Ramsay, *Objections*, p. 51.
12 Ramsay, Papers, pp. 21–2.
13 Ramsay, *Objections*, p. 91.
14 Ramsay, *An Address*, p. 21.

15 Ramsay, *Objections*, pp. 38, 71.

16 Ramsay, *Objections*, pp. 8, 43, 86.

17 I came across a letter in the University of Virginia Library addressed to Rev. Bielby Porteus concerning the slaves on his plantation in Virginia in the mid-eighteenth century.

18 James Beattie to Bishop Bielby Porteus, 3 Jul 1788. NAS, Acc.4796, Fettercairn Box 92.WF 2.231.

19 Raymond Harris, *Scriptural Researches on the Licitness of the Slave Trade, Showing its Conformity with the Principles of Revealed Religion, Delineated in the Sacred Writings of the Word of God* (Liverpool and London, 1788).

20 James Ramsay, *An Examination of the Rev. Mr. Harris's Scriptural Researches on the Licitness of the Slave Trade* (London, 1788), p. 29.

21 Harris, *Scriptural Researches*, 5–7. Section 1, pp. 4, 6, 7.

22 Ramsay, Papers, pp. 30, 32, 81–2.

23 Stephen quoted in R and S. Wilberforce, *Life of William Wilberforce*, 5 vols (London, 1838), Vol. 1. pp. 234–5.

24 Eric Williams, *Capitalism and Slavery* (London, [1994] 1964), p. 180.

25 C. Duncan Rice, *The Scots Abolitionists: 1899–1861* (Baton Rouge, LA), p. 20.

26 Beattie to William Wilberforce, 2 Mar 1792. Yale, Osborn MS, 982.

27 London Society for the Abolition of the Slave Trade, Minutes, 3 Apr 1792. BL.

28 H. Scott, ed., *Fasti Academiae Mariscallanae Aberdonensis* (Aberdeen, 1897), Vol. 2, p. 100.

29 London Society, Minutes, 20 May 1788.

30 The African Institution, *Reports* (London, 1815) 9th Report, pp. 67–8.

31 William Dickson, *Letters on Slavery* (London, 1789), Introduction, pp. 3, 4, 6, 7, 36, 37, 55, 69–73.

32 William Dickson, *Mitigation of Slavery* (London, 1814), Introduction, pp. vii, ix, xii.

33 William Dickson, *Addresses to Whites, Free Negroes of Barbados and Accounts of some Negroes Eminent for their Virtues and Abilities* (London, 1797).

34 William Dickson, *Hints to the People of the United Kingdom in general and North Britain in particular on the Present Important Crisis and some Interesting Collateral Subjects* (Edinburgh, 1803).

35 R. Furneaux, *William Wilberforce* (London, 1974), p. 85.

36 David Brion Davis, *Slavery and Human Progress* (Oxford, 1984), p. 171.

37 James Stephen, 'Memoirs of James Stephen written by Himself for the Use of his Children, commenced 6 Jun 1819'. BL, Add. MSS 46443–46444, Vol. 1, p. 289.

38 James Stephen, *The Slavery of the British West India colonies Delineated as it exists, both in Law and Practice and compared with the Slavery of*

Other Countries, Ancient and Modern, 2 vols (London, 1824, 1830), Vol. 2, p. 28.

39 James Stephen, *The Crisis of the Sugar Colonies. An Enquiry into the Objects and Probable Effects of the French Expedition to the West Indies and their Connection with the Colonial Interests of the British Empire* (London, 1802), pp. 34, 61, 90, 110, 118, 121.

40 Davis, *Slavery and Human Progress*, pp. 173–4.

41 James Stephen, *War in Disguise: or the Frauds of the Neutral Flags* (London, 1805), pp. 58, 62, 63, 64.

42 R. and S. Wilberforce, *Life of William Wilberforce*, pp. 3, 234–5, cited in Roger Anstey, *The Atlantic Slave Trade and British Abolition 1760–1810* (London, 1975), p. 354.

43 Anstey, *The Atlantic Slave Trade*, pp. 354, 365–75, 376.

44 James Stephen, *The Dangers of the Country – We may be Conquered by France* (London, 1807), pp. 180, 208, 214.

45 Dickson, *Mitigation of Slavery*, p. 261.

46 James Stephen, *Reasons for Establishing a Registry of Slaves* (London, 1815).

47 Stephen, *Slavery Delineated* (London, 1824), Vol. 1, Preface, p. ix.

48 *ER*, Oct 1824, p. 464.

49 Stephen, *Slavery Delineated*, Vol. 2, pp. 397, 412–13.

50 James Stephen, *England Enslaved by her own Slave Colonies* (London, 1826), pp. 4, 5, 9, 45–51, 91.

51 Williams, *Capitalism and Slavery*, p. 180.

52 David Brion Davis, *The Problem of Slavery in the Age of Revolution 1773–1823* (Ithaca, NY, 1975), p. 366.

53 Arthur Roberts, ed., *Letters of Hannah More to Zachary Macaulay Esq containing Notices of Lord Macaulay's Youth* (London, 1860), p. 195.

54 Charles Booth, *Zachary Macaulay, his Part in the Movement for the Abolition of the Slave Trade and of Slavery* (London, 1934), pp. 4, 13.

55 Booth, *Zachary Macaulay*, pp. 36–58.

56 Hannah More to Thomas Babington, 28 Aug 1799. BL, Blakeney Collection, Vol. 6, Add. MSS 63084.

57 Sir George Stephen, *Anti-Slavery Recollections* (London, 1859), p. 52.

58 *Dictionary of National Biography*, Vol. 22, p. 419.

59 *ASR*, No. 11, Apr 1826, pp. 129–170.

60 *JB*, 20 Oct 1823.

61 *ASR*, No. 9, 1826, pp. 94–6; No. 47, 1829, pp. 462–8.

62 Fortunatus Dwarris, *The West India Question Plainly Stated* (London, 1828), p. 15.

63 *ASR*, No. 27, 1828, pp. 237–51.

64 *JB*, 27 Oct, 9 Nov 1823; 22 Feb, 12 Sep, 29 Nov 1824; 7 Feb, 30 May, 11 Jul, 29 Aug, 12 Sep, 28 Nov 1825.

65 M. Holland, Viscountess Knutsford, *Life and Letters of Zachary Macaulay* (London, 1900), pp. 396–402.

66 Zachary Macaulay, *Letter to his Royal Highness the Duke of Gloucester from Zachary Macaulay occasioned by a Pamphlet published by Dr Thorpe late Judge of the Colony of Sierra Leone entitled 'A Letter to William Wilberforce Esq.'* (London, 1815).

67 Knutsford, *Life and Letters*, p. 424.

68 Charles Buxton, *Memoirs of Sir Thomas Fowell Buxton* (London, 1850), p. 267.

69 Robert Stewart, *Henry Brougham 1778–1868: His Public Career* (London, 1986), p. 286.

70 *Opinions of Henry Brougham on Negro Slavery* (London, 1830).

71 Henry Brougham, *An Enquiry into the Colonial Policy of the European Powers* (Edinburgh, 1803), Vol. 2, pp. 120, 301, 310, 416, 451, 504.

72 Frances Hawes, *Henry Brougham* (London, 1957), pp. 41, 44.

73 Brougham, *Colonial Policy*, Vol. 2, pp. 445–6, 452, 454, 473, 475.

74 *Substance of the Debate in the House of Commons on the 15th May 1823 on a Motion for the Mitigation and Gradual Abolition of Slavery throughout the British Dominions* (London, 1823), p. 90.

75 *ER*, Oct 1802, pp. 217, 236–7.

76 Henry Brougham, *A Concise Statement of the Question regarding the Abolition of the Slave Trade* (London, 1804).

77 Stewart, *Henry Brougham*, p. 30.

78 The anonymous pamphlet was titled *A Defence of the Slave Trade on the grounds of Humanity, Policy and Justice* (London, 1804). Brougham's response was in the *Edinburgh Review*, Oct 1804.

79 Henry Brougham, *Selections from the Speeches and Writings of the Rt. Hon Henry, Lord Brougham and Vaux* (London, 1831), pp. 49–52.

80 Brougham, *Selections from the Speeches and Writings*, p. 102.

81 Henry Brougham, *Speeches of Henry, Lord Brougham*, 4 vols (London, 1838), Vol. 2, pp. 127–8.

82 Quoted in Stewart, *Henry Brougham*, p. 179.

83 James Walvin, *England, Slaves and Freedom: 1776–1838* (Jackson, MS, 1986), p. 140.

84 Brougham, *Speeches*, Vol. 2, p. 157.

85 Henry Brougham, *Lord Brougham's Speech in the House of Lords on 29th January 1838 upon the African Slave Trade* (London, 1838).

86 Stephen, *England Enslaved*, p. 69.

87 J. Pollock, *William Wilberforce* (Oxford, 1987), pp. 200–5.

88 M. Napier, ed. *Selection from the Correspondence of the late Macvey Napier* (London, 1879), pp. 98–9.

89 Stewart, *Henry Brougham*, p. 29.

90 David Turley, 'British Anti-slavery Reassessed', in *Rethinking the Age of Reform*, A. Burns and J. Innes, eds (Cambridge, 2003), p. 188.

91 Knutsford, *Life and Letters*, Henry Brougham to Zachary Macaulay, 1 Mar 1826.
92 Dickson, *Letters on Slavery*, pp. 61–2, 507.
93 Sir William Forbes, *Life and Writings of James Beattie* (Edinburgh, 1806), James Beattie to Mrs Montagu, 31 Jul 1789.
94 Pollock, *Wilberforce*, p. 53.

5

UNFINISHED BUSINESS IN EUROPE AND SCOTS COUNTERVOICES ON EMANCIPATION

୶

> The most odious allegations have been preferred against the colonists, accusations have been brought forward of cruelty, neglect, and injury to the people under their control . . . and the planters have been loaded with calumny for cultivating estates they were invited to hold and for following a system which was established and encouraged by the nation at large.
>
> Glasgow West India Association petition to the
> House of Commons, May 1826

In July 1814 two Edinburgh advocates, Henry Cockburn and Thomas Erskine, organised a petition against the slave trade after a meeting that Cockburn later described as 'made safe and respectable by the attendance of the humane and pious and even with this it excited great alarm'.[1] The last petitions from Scotland on this subject had been sent to Parliament in 1792, before the start of the war with France, and the suppression of any agitation for reform ensured that there were no anti-slavery meetings until the defeat of Napoleon in 1814. Even then, as Cockburn noted, reviving the subject of the slave trade, now abolished by Britain, had been done very tentatively.

The renewal of popular campaigning to prevent the renewal of the slave trade by France following the peace of 1814 indicated that slavery continued to be a subject that would rouse the passion of many Scots – but not all on the same side. The activity against the slave trade and later against slavery itself did not go unchallenged. Voices had already been raised cautioning against such political action not just on the grounds that it was inappropriate, but because tampering with the commercial status quo would set a dangerous and revolutionary precedent. One Scottish merchant, Archibald Dalzel, made a name for himself in the eighteenth century not by commercial success in his slaving enterprises or by effective administration in the West African trading communities, but by using his earlier learning to write on behalf of the Liverpool merchants a scholarly counterblast to the growing abolition movement.

Accounts from personal experience on the spot always carry a certain persuasiveness, and just as the Liverpool merchants used the pen of one who had been in the slave trade so the planters' representatives were keen to publicise sympathetic accounts of life in the West Indies. Another Scot with medical and judicial experience attempted to justify both a trade and an institution that were clearly under attack. Even in 1790 – and even more by the mid-1820s – strident polemical defences of a system whose extreme cruelties had been so well documented were unlikely to cut much ice. What was much more effective in advancing the more realistic aim of the planters to delay rather than prevent emancipation was any evidence that 'amelioration' of slavery was in progress and that intervention from Britain would be counter-productive. Alexander Barclay and John Stewart in their different ways provided this vital information.

Glasgow's West India Association was reckoned to be the most powerful group representing slaving interests outside London and its influence was seen in the lengthy counter-petitions of the kind feared by 'Africanus' in 1788, and in the cautious stance adopted by the Glasgow Abolition Society. Throughout the 1820s, as the anti-slavery campaign nationally moved up several gears, the West Indians in Glasgow city followed suit, even taking their case directly to the King on one occasion. The Association could rely on the support of the *Glasgow Courier*, an influential newspaper in the city that was at no time more sympathetic to the cause of slavery than under the editorship of a former manager of a plantation in Grenada, James McQueen. McQueen was not only retained by the Association, but also forged a close link with *John Bull*, the principal London organ of slave-owning interests.

UNFINISHED BUSINESS – THE SLAVE TRADE AND THE PEACE WITH FRANCE

In 1794 the government of republican France not only decreed the abolition of the slave trade, but also declared the emancipation of slaves in its colonies. Napoleon's accession to power had reversed this and there was strong pressure from the French government in the peace negotiations of 1814 to continue the slave trade for at least five years. James Stephen had successfully proposed a bill in the House of Commons in 1812 requiring all slaves held in the colonies to be registered. It was a recognition of the ease with which the act of 1807 banning the trade was being circumvented and an attempt to ensure accountability. The prospect of most European nations continuing to trade in slaves posed a severe threat to the enforcement of British abolition and if there was a chance of altering this situation in the case of France, it was one the abolitionists were determined to take.

A correspondent to the *Glasgow Chronicle* in July 1814 deplored the prospect of the British government sanctioning 'that most iniquitous of all traffic', expressed doubt that the French would abandon it after a five-year period and hoped that 'not a part of the population but the whole population, not one class of men but every class of men in this city will join in petitioning Parliament to consider what steps can be wisely and equitably taken for repairing the injury done to the cause of humanity'. A few days earlier, another Glasgow newspaper had been 'happy' to inform its readers 'that a public meeting is to be held on Friday of next week in order to petition Parliament to take the most effective mode of preventing the renewal of the slave trade in the colonies ceded to France by the Treaty'.[2]

The Glasgow meeting was chaired by the Chief Magistrate for the city, Charles Parker. Overwhelming distrust was expressed for the proposed five-year moratorium on French abolition and it was predicted that during those years the trade would be 'prosecuted with tenfold and increasing avidity and with tenfold accumulation of miseries' to the people of Africa. The meeting ambitiously called on Parliament to take every means 'to produce the immediate and entire abolition of the slave trade, not only in France, but in all the nations of Christendom'. Two days later, the Burgh of Gorbals held a similar gathering which expressed even stronger doubts about the likelihood of abolition after the five-year period, fearing that all that Britain had done to repair Africa's wrong would be undone and that 'we shall be still more criminal in the sight of God and man'. Their petition to Parliament urged 'all the nations of Europe' to unite in permanent suppression of the trade.[3]

The Edinburgh meeting to which Cockburn referred took place on 1 July. It was addressed by the Evangelical leader Sir Henry Moncrieff Wellwood, who moved a series of lengthy resolutions that set the tone for others throughout the country. Wellwood pointed out the inconsistency of stigmatising the slave trade in the Treaty of Paris, whilst at the same time permitting it, and argued that the years since abolition by Britain had demonstrated that even in terms of mercantile commerce its existence was neither necessary nor expedient. Earlier arguments had concentrated on the more philosophical grounds of morality and justice, but although it was unanimously agreed to petition both houses of Parliament to prevent the revival of the trade, the cautious tone of Cockburn was reflected in an agreement to print all the resolutions and appoint a supervising committee to draw up the petition for signature, 'that there might be no misrepresentation as to the real views of the committee'.[4]

The inhabitants of sixty-seven towns petitioned Parliament. These included all the main Scottish cities and small towns as far as Tain in the north-east Highlands and Langholm in the Borders. A public meeting in Paisley on 8 July requested Parliament to take steps 'for averting the many evils that must result' from the proposed treaty, and the inhabitants of Leith looked 'with horror at the revival of that inhuman traffic'.[5] Half a dozen petitions came from local government officials. The Magistrates and Councillors of Musselburgh minuted the receipt of a letter from Thomas Clarkson urging, on behalf of the revived London Committee, all the burghs and towns in Scotland to petition Parliament for 'the immediate and universal abolition of the slave trade'.[6] They were one of the first to take action by unanimously agreeing to this and collecting 600 signatures in May 1815, although strangely their petition did not arrive in Parliament until February of the following year. Inverkeithing had the most consistent record amongst Scottish towns in sending petitions against both the slave trade and slavery in every active year of the campaign. A report of a meeting there on 14 July observed with approval that the women of Hawick had given them a lead in gathering signatures for the cause. Inverkeithing's women, it claimed, 'obtained 200 signatures in 24 hours'.[7]

The hope of the writer to the *Glasgow Chronicle* that all classes would petition was partly realised. The Royal College of Physicians and Surgeons did so on 21 July and they were followed the next week by the Incorporated Trades of Rutherglen and of Aberdeen and the Hammermen of Edinburgh. On 5 July, a notice appeared announcing a special meeting of the Grocers of Glasgow to consider petitioning Parliament to prevent the continuation of 'the horribly cruel traffic in human creatures'.[8] This may have encountered opposition, as there is no record of any subsequent petition being received from the Grocers at Westminster.

Only 6 of the 141 Scottish petitions came from the churches. For the first time Methodist congregations sent petitions, from Edinburgh and Dalkeith on 22 July and from Glasgow and Paisley four days later.[9] The Presbytery of Cupar meeting on 12 July agreed unanimously to a deliverance moved by the evangelical minister of

Kilmany, Thomas Chalmers, later to be a prominent Scottish church leader.[10] The Presbytery of Kirkcaldy claimed to respond to the 'alarm that has been so powerfully awakened amongst the friends of humanity by the prospect of the slave trade being renewed by France'. They declared that such a sentiment was representative 'among the inhabitants placed under their ecclesiastical superintendence' and that 'the desires of all the friends of humanity, justice and religion' were to see 'the total abolition of the said trade without delay'.[11]

Both Napoleon, on landing in France the following year, and the fugitive Louis XVIII before the battle of Waterloo, which would bring him to the throne, committed themselves to abolish the French slave trade immediately. The new Treaty of Paris of November 1815 included an article confirming this, leaving only Spain and Portugal amongst the European powers holding out. In the spring of 1824, four Scottish petitions were sent to the House of Lords from Inverkeithing, Bo'ness, Denny and Alloa. All prayed for their lordships to 'take such measures as may lead to the final and general abolition of the slave trade'.[12] By this time, despite the official ban by every European nation except Portugal, few countries were taking effective measures to stop the trade. The Duke of Wellington was the leading British delegate at the European Congress of Verona in 1822 and there he claimed that the slave trade was then at a higher volume than ever. At a time when some were considering taking petitions to the next stage and seeking the abolition of slavery, there was still work to be done. It was therefore not surprising to find petitions to the Lords against the trade alongside those to the Commons against slavery in the same year.

SPEAKING UP FOR THE MERCHANTS – ARCHIBALD DALZEL, SLAVE TRADER AND HISTORIAN

On 13 April 1771, Archibald Dalzel wrote to his brother, the Professor of Classics at the university of Edinburgh: 'I am conscious, Andrew, I shall never make a good M.D. Perhaps I never discovered to you that I never was fond of my business.'[13] That 'business' was soon to be changed for another, one that carried considerably more risk than the practice of medicine and a good deal of potential for adventure. If it did not necessarily bring Dalzel more pleasure, it certainly was to bring him considerably more profit.

Born in 1740, Dalzel saw his early years in Kirkliston, West Lothian. He was the oldest of four brothers and a sister. His father was a local carpenter but his mother persuaded the local minister,

Figure 9   Sierra Leone token commemorating the abolition of the slave trade, issued by Thomas Babington and Kenneth Macaulay in 1816. Both were nephews of Zachary.

Rev. John Drysdale, to support his education and he went on to study medicine at the university, entering the service of the navy as an assistant surgeon just a few years after his compatriot James Ramsay (whose subsequent involvement with slavery was to be so different). Dalzel saw action during the Seven Years War and was paid off in January 1763 when HMS *Minerva*, on which he served, was decommissioned at the end of the conflict. That month he wrote to his brother, then a fledgling lecturer at the university, that to save the family and himself from penury he was prepared to go 'to the uttermost part of the globe' to work. He had considered becoming a West Indian planter but had no capital, and decided that the Guinea coast might be his best bet. Despite the fears of his mother and brothers that West Africa was indeed 'the white man's grave', Dalzel applied for a job as surgeon with the Royal African Company, which he obtained in March 1763. For the next fifteen years, the African coast was to be his livelihood and his enrichment.

To his surprise, as Dalzel wrote to his school friend the career diplomat Robert Liston, he found life on the Gold Coast much better than expected. His medical work was light, since the whites at Annomabu seemed to keep reasonably healthy. With time and energy, and above all with the need to make money, Dalzel embarked on the business of slave-trading for the next few years. The moral paradox of this could hardly be lost to him, but alongside so many of his compatriots in the colonies he allowed the necessity and perhaps the self-evident right-ness of commerce to outweigh any reservations he might have had. In a letter to Liston in May 1764, he confessed: 'I have at last come into the spirit of the slave trade and must own (perhaps it ought to be to my shame) that I can now traffick in that way without remorse. I have already gained a trifle by it and shall make all the haste I can to revisit my native clime.'[14]

In 1767, Dalzel was appointed Director of the Royal African Company's fort at Whydah in today's Benin. Again he wrote in glowing terms to his brother Andrew about 'the most pleasant country on the coast of Guinea'.[15] This was ironic for a man who was later to use what he described as the horrors of life in this African kingdom as a justification for the slave trade. But no doubt for him the pleasantry lay in the luxuries of life that he enjoyed and the asso-ciations with French and Portuguese neighbours with whom he built up a profitable trade in slaves, earning him a handsome annual profit.

In 1770, he left Whydah to venture further into slave-trading. He had hoped to be able before long to retire in style back home, but his correspondence with his brother demonstrates that this was over-optimistic. A short spell in London in 1771 persuaded him to under-take a joint enterprise with Mr Shoolbred, a London merchant, and Mr Devaynes, formerly of Whydah and later to become an MP. The partnership was short-lived, though, and in the next few years Dalzel purchased and ran three ships, making enough money to buy sub-stantial land in Jamaica. However, on his return to Britain in 1778, pirates seized the ship and with it all that he had. Facing ruin, and attempting to take financial responsibility for his family and espe-cially for debts incurred by his brother William, Archibald Dalzel turned his hand to various ventures including the wine and tea trade in Spain and for a brief spell even piracy, the very 'profession' that had deprived him of his gains.

By 1783, Dalzel was being financed by his brother Andrew and there is no surviving correspondence that indicates how he was employed in the next eight years until he was appointed Governor of Cape Coast Castle, the chief British settlement on the Guinea coast in what today is Ghana. His task was to set in motion administrative reforms and to sort out the accounts. He stayed there for more than ten years, a remarkable spell of endurance, only punctuated by a break at home in 1799. By all accounts, he was neither popular nor effective, attempting to obtain better trade concessions for Britain and labouring hard over the accounts but receiving little cooperation from either the British Government or his colleagues at the fort. He resigned from the post in 1802, returned to Britain and died in bankruptcy around 1810.

Although Dalzel's voluminous correspondence with his brother Andrew gives us an insight into this roller-coaster life of a slave trader and administrator, his story is paralleled in less colourful ways by many other Scots. What marks him out in the history of slavery is a book he wrote just before embarking for Cape Coast, but which drew on his earlier experience in Whydah and became a seminal document in the efforts of the Liverpool merchants to defend the slave trade.

William Dickson's 1792 tour showed the powerful effect of the evidence given to the House of Commons on the slave trade when communicated to the public. The merchants in Liverpool realised that they needed to have articulate and well-versed allies testifying before the committee as well, and they were glad to include Dalzel amongst those deputed by them to do just that, giving him in June of that year the Freedom of the Borough in recognition of such services. Few merchants and slave traders who could speak with the authority of experience would be men of letters, but Dalzel was an exception. In early 1763, preparing for his first voyage, he told his brother that books were a priority in his budget. Having considered writing a history of the Gold Coast when on his first appointment, he then did just that for Dahomey, fifteen years after leaving Whydah.

Incredibly, one of the standard arguments for the slave trade was that of bringing men from the horrors of primitive Africa to the civilisation of Western society. Despite the protests of Dalzel's contemporary James Ramsay, who asked whether Guinea captains murder, burn and pillage in order that one in fifty Africans may find a good master, the tales of cannibalism, human sacrifice on a grand scale, superstition and heathen practices only needed to be given concrete account to sow doubt in the minds of those who were critical of the middle passage and life on the plantations. In the crucial last quarter of the eighteenth century, Archibald Dalzel served the slave-owning interests well by providing this in his detailed *History of Dahomey – an inland Kingdom of Africa*, which he subtitled *Compiled from Authentic Memories'*.

Archibald Dalzel claimed from the outset that such a volume enabled the reader to learn through the history of 'ruder nations' to demonstrate the values of enlightened Western civilisation. He was not the first to argue in this way, nor would he be the last. Many apologists for some of the worst excesses of nineteenth- and twentieth-century colonialism justified it in these terms. Not surprisingly, just as Zachary Macaulay let the eyewitness accounts of Caribbean slavery stand as evidence for the untenability of slavery, so Dalzel spent much of the book cataloguing the customs of the Dahomeyan kingdom. Many of his accounts are shocking and intended to shock. He detailed the ritual murders before the King on each festival, with the victims hanging from gibbets throughout the palace and others staked out on the ground to be beheaded. The graves of the ancestors, said Dalzel, are 'watered with the blood of many human victims'. Young boys of seven or eight years old, he claimed, were employed as executioners of prisoners of war and examples made by mass murder when any had dared to challenge the King in any way.

None of these public examples were exactly unknown in recent European and indeed British history, of course, but Dalzel further argued that superstition and ignorance made Dahomey prefer war and slaughter to commerce. He introduced the spectre of cannibalism (even though a modern editor claims that he reads the word for 'using' as that of 'eating'), and instanced such practices to argue that there is a natural tendency in West Africa to abandon any civilised behaviour for unrestricted barbarity. 'The haughty ferocity of a people bred to war and rapine' were claimed by Dalzel to be 'incompatible with the mild and steady spirit of commerce'.[16]

A key argument used by abolitionists was that slave traders encouraged war amongst the peoples of Africa in order to obtain slaves from the losing side. Dalzel spent much of the *History of Dahomey* in meeting this argument. Far from conflict being initiated by the European adventurers, he claimed to find that Dahomey had, 'with very little intermission, been engaged in wars with its surrounding neighbours for near seventy years'. In case his readers did not take his word for it, Dalzel relates a report of a conversation between the Governor of Whydah, Lionel Abson, and King Adahoonzou, who reigned between 1774 and 1789. 'In the name of my ancestors and myself, said the King, 'I aver that no Dahomean man ever embarked in war merely for the sake of procuring wherewithal to purchase your commodities.' He continued to assure Governor Abson that even if the slave trade was abolished Africans would still go to war and that the charge that women and children were sold 'for a few kegs of brandy' was malicious and insulting.

It was therefore a short step from the graphic picture of relentless cruelty and the refutation of European responsibility for African conflict to justifying another barbarity. 'In this light,' he wrote, 'Asiatic pomp and European necessity for labourers inured to a tropical sun, appear to have been the only effectual instruments of mercy, the only means whereby the lives of many of these unfortunate people have been saved.' The alternative for the Dahomeyans was obliteration. 'If there be no ships to receive their captives [in war] what will become of them? I answer for you, they will be put to death.'[17] For Dalzel, the slave trade then became an act of benevolent rescue, although an objective observer might have asked what evidence there was of Africans embracing the escape from the horrors of their lot in the bowels of a slave ship and why strong measures had to be taken to prevent the numerous slaves on the ships choosing death through drowning than the horrors of the middle passage.

The accounts of cruel practices in West Africa detailed in *The History of Dahomey* provided not just a justification for the slave trade as a better alternative, it also gave ammunition to those who claimed that freedom for Africans was not just impossible but irresponsible. In the early pages of the book the argument was advanced that the actions of human beings under little other control than that of their own will could only be civilised if controlled by the influence and restraint of the laws of refinement. Once again there was considerable irony in associating the slave trade and plantation slavery with influence, restraint, or laws of refinement. As abolitionists were later not slow to argue, it was these very restraints that were necessary to place on the unlimited power of planters over slaves. In the end, far from the contention that West Africans were incapable of emerging from savagery unless tamed by the plantations being the telling argument, it was when the nation rejected any reformation of a system that gave unlimited powers over other humans that the end of the institution was assured.

One modern African historian, L. A. Akinjogbin, has described *The History of Dahomey* as impressive in its 'eloquence and power', to be compared 'favourably with the best literary traditions of the eighteenth century'.[18] J. D. Fage, however, in the introduction to a modern reprint of the book, observed that it is 'as much a pro-slave trade tract as it is a history'.[19] Both are probably true. Dalzel's life and work demonstrates another aspect of this curious dilemma of enlightened and educated Scots becoming involved in such a barbarous trade in human beings. In the end there is little evidence that it had a significant impact in delaying the abolition of the trade – the war with France was already doing that – but it is a unique example of a Scottish merchant steeped in books drawing on his educational roots to persuade thoughtful people that the slave trade was not as destructive or cruel as might be thought. Dalzel was employing Scottish skills to justify the institution as Dickson, Stephen and Macaulay were to do in order to destroy it.

Scottish Voices from the Colonies – James Adair from Antigua; Alexander Barclay and John Stewart from Jamaica

Three years before Dalzel published his *History of Dahomey*, a book appeared with the lengthy title *Unanswerable Arguments against the Abolition of the Slave Trade with a Defence of the Proprietors of the British Sugar Colonies*. The author was a Fellow of the Royal College of Surgeons in Edinburgh who had served for many years as a doctor in Antigua and combined with that the role of a Judge of the Kings Bench court on the island. *Unanswerable Arguments* was part pamphlet, part manual of medical and administrative care for slaves. In fact, it was very little about the slave trade and much more about giving detailed advice over diseases and how to avoid them.

James Adair claimed on the title page that it was published 'for the benefit of the starving tin-miners of Cornwall'. In doing that, he reflected a common assumption that the suffering of slaves was less than that of British labourers. Later, when discussing the necessity of corporal punishment for slaves, Adair claimed that this was more regulated and milder than the treatment of those who served in the British army or navy, a point he had already made when looking at the conditions faced by sailors on the West African coast and soldiers in the West Indies.[20] Despite its title, however, *Unanswerable Arguments* is devoid of any such thing, and when Adair attempted to struggle with what clearly for him was an ambiguous subject, he wrote rather quaintly in the third person:

> Adair does nor presume to defend or even palliate the species of traffick which has been carried on between Africa and America; but begs leave to observe that the present generation of our West Indian planters is not responsible for the consequences, provided they do all in their power to render the situation of those poor people as comfortable as possible.

Welfare, if not comfort, of the slaves is a theme throughout Adair's work. From advice to feed slaves on vegetables rather than Indian corn to positioning slave houses on healthier ground, Adair seems to be a man ahead of his time. He argued that the decline in numbers of slaves – a key factor in the defence of planters' rights to replenish 'supplies' – was often due to a lack of proper medical care and want of attention from absentee proprietors. He recognised that overwork was a large factor in reducing numbers even though he denied, rather strangely, that there was any difference between slaves and whites in life expectancy in the West Indies. Conveniently for the merchants, however, this claim that estates could not be worked by an insufficient number of Africans being pushed beyond their abilities was of course an argument against abolition of the trade.[21]

Adair was well aware of the philosophical and moral arguments against the trade and slavery itself, and even cited the very arguments used in the petitions that were at that time being sent to Parliament. 'The enthusiasts', he wrote, 'exclaim *fiat justitia ruat coelum* and argue that it must be abolished because it is "incompatible with our duties as Christians" and "with the genius of the British constitution"'.[22] These points he countered by the familiar appeal to the Bible. For him, the fact that the Old Testament allowed slavery and Jesus never opposed it made the unchristian charge invalid, although he added: 'Adair wishes that such a traffic had never been established', claiming that it was inhuman and led to war between states.

This paradoxical reasoning led Adair to take comfortable refuge in the contention that cruelty was rare and that it was in the interests of masters to treat slaves with 'assiduous attention and indulgence.' He mirrored Dalzel in claiming that although he had never been in Africa, he learnt that the coast there was full of 'small despotic monarchies' that 'frequently engage in war'. From his observations in Antigua, he knew that slaves 'often amuse themselves with singing and dancing' and concluded from this that 'there is no reason to suppose that they regard bondage as a great evil'.[23]

Unanswerable Arguments is in many ways a shallow and naïve publication, uncertain in what it is promoting and lacking the robustness of Dalzel's *History of Dahomey*. It would be unlikely to win many converts to the slave trade, although its detailed treatment of medical conditions, which occupy more than half of the book, could stand as a useful tract on medical treatment of slaves. Yet it is a testimony of a Scot who made a good living and gained a position in West Indian society, bringing some of the basic humanity of his upbringing as a leaven into that society. He was not uncritical of its practices, but by humane reasoning rather than the rampant racism of so many West Indian spokesmen or the pictures of savagery given by Dalzel, Adair made the trade and the institution of slavery seem more palatable. And it was then easy for him to strongly oppose any idea of emancipation, which he did.

In 1826, Alexander Barclay, a resident of Jamaica for twenty-one years, sought to provide a detailed response to James Stephen's *Slavery Delineated* of 1824. Barclay read Stephen's account just before leaving for home and drafted a response to it on the voyage from Jamaica. In this, he claimed that he had no intention of publishing his comments until he learnt that there was a new ferment in Britain over slavery and that the issue was being raised in Parliament once again. His authority was that of one who knew slaves 'in daily intercourse', and it was the thought of the 'fatal consequences' of measures proposed in ignorance of their 'condition, habits, and dispositions' that led to his seeking to publish what he saw as the true facts on slavery. Barclay termed his book *A Practical View of the Present State of Slavery in the West Indies*, and in the preface he complained that no subject had been more misrepresented than West Indian slavery through a class of authors in Britain who had been 'aiming more at effect than truth'.[24] James Stephen, in particular, was cited.

For Barclay, Stephen's facts were not so much erroneous than outdated and based on the situation before the abolition of the slave trade. Yet having made the old accusations of cruelty, even if they were out of date, they would still stick in the minds of the readers. Stephen, for him, may have been ready to plead the cause of humanity and religion, but Barclay claimed that he had simply stirred up 'engines of oppression against a few offending individuals'. He continued by saying it was impossible that the old cruelties could now exist 'because these things cannot be done in secret – the damning facts would soon become public'. The whip in the hands of a driver, he said, 'has become little more than a badge of his office'. Barclay admitted that there was some room for improvement, such as allowing evidence from slaves in court, but his book took Stephen's arguments clause by clause on slave codes, treatment on plantations and opportunities for religion, marriage and manumission. Chains that were in common use in Jamaica at the turn of the century, he said, were now almost unknown, punishment was limited to thirty-nine lashes and the generous clothing allowance provided by so many masters was reflected in the finery of dress observed on Sundays at worship.

Many apologists for slavery used the argument that the cruelties detailed by abolitionists could not possibly be carried out by decent and civilised men. In the light of imperial history from ancient times, this is a curious defence, but it is one hinted at throughout Barclay's work. He painted slavery in feudal terms, where the rights and obligations of the masters and slaves were bound up together, not least in the precarious enterprise of a sugar plantation. A slave-owner, for him, was bound to be beneficial to his slaves, since both were tied to the land. These ties were evidenced, he claimed, by the taking of the names of white people by slaves at their baptism, taking whites as godparents and by playing and dancing in the master's house at Christmas or harvest time. At another point Barclay argued that Stephen's complaint of 'breeding by a white keeper' involved no degradation to female slaves, since he considered that they had little concept of marriage.[25]

In an age where the life of agricultural labourers in Britain was often little distinguishable from serfdom, and where miners in Scotland had only recently been released from their bondage to owners, it was not difficult for apologists for slavery to draw parallels with the lot of workers at home. This argument was strengthened by the insecurity of those working in new industries in which freedom of labour often meant the liberty to starve. William Cobbett, the English reformer, continually claimed in his *Political Journal* that West Indian slaves were better off than labourers at home. However tortuous an argument this was, and one that ignored the violence and humiliation, the absolute power and degradation of slavery, it was one easily adopted in the colonies and Barclay argued that, compared with the starvation of a British labourer who could not work, the conditions of a slave, fed and clothed, cared for when ill, enabled them to think themselves free of worry.[26]

An issue often raised by abolitionists in an era in which Sunday observance was an obligation of Christian societies was the refusal of masters on the sugar estates to allow slaves time off work for worship and for cultivating their own ground for food. Barclay pointed out that the working of the sugar mills on Sunday was now illegal and that the law provided for slaves to have twenty-six working days a year, in addition to Sundays, free for their own use. Twenty years previously, baptism of slaves was almost unknown and few slaves were permitted to be married. There had been very little recognition of the ties of kinship when slave sales were made in the past. Now, he claimed, the situation was very different. Despite later comments, he stated at the beginning of his book that almost every slave was now baptised, marriage was common and the tearing apart of families was a thing of the past, which had in any case been outlawed since the middle of the previous century.

In case his readers doubted the effectiveness of the laws protecting slaves, Barclay stressed that there was now a council of protection appointed by the magistrates. This had replaced the individuals – themselves often planters or friends of the slave's owners – who were previously the only sources of redress. In response to Stephen's claim that any complaints made by slaves brought a vicious revenge from overseers and that there were no laws to prevent women being abused in the masters' houses, Barclay quoted a case from the *Jamaica Gazette* of 19 January 1819, in which a master was indicted and imprisoned for torturing, branding and flogging his female slave Amey, who was subsequently freed. For him, this proved not only that the slave laws were effective, but that the climate of opinion had changed.[27]

Barclay's book reflected the bitterness of colonists who felt that they shouldered the blame for slavery whilst Britain continued to reap its benefits, and its author was keen to point out that the slave trade started in Elizabethan England before any colonies existed. When the legislature in South Carolina attempted to ban further imports of slaves into the colony in 1760, and Jamaica to restrict the trade in 1774, Britain vetoed both these measures. This, for Barclay, showed not just hypocrisy but inconsistency in the nation's public posturing. Yet, given the dominance of slave-owning interests in the British Parliament throughout most of the seventeenth century, it possibly indicated a dispute more about management than morality.

A Practical View was mainly written in order to demonstrate the changing nature of Caribbean slavery, although Barclay admitted at the beginning that there was still considerable room for improvement. At one point he stated boldly that 'Slavery is an evil and therefore it should be abolished.'[28] It is tempting, in the light of this, to see him ahead of his time in making such an unequivocal statement until we recall that many of his fellow Scots were easily able to hold in tension the philosophical objection to slavery and acceptance of its practical and commercial necessity. By 1826, as was evident from the petitions to Parliament in support of slavery, outright opposition to abolition had become recognised as impractical. Despite stubborn resistance to change from many in the colonies, most sensible planters and their friends at home recognised that the institution could not last for ever.

It was therefore important to delay emancipation for as long as possible. Barclay's book, in its insistence that slaves were totally unfit for freedom and that the economic and social consequences of abolition would be disastrous for all, simply expressed the sentiments of the merchants who sought throughout the 1820s and 1830s to delay the inevitable. Therefore, far from being a supporter of abolition, Barclay clearly sided with those who wished to milk everything possible from the last days of slavery.

John Stewart, a former resident of Jamaica now back in Scotland, published a substantial survey of Jamaica in 1823 in which he included a survey of the condition of slaves. An anonymous account published in Glasgow in 1828 in the form of reminiscences was very possibly also written by Stewart. But they are two very different documents.

A View of the Past and Present State of the Island of Jamaica claimed to 'fairly and impartially' state the truth between the reports that said slaves were suffering 'under every species of the most revolting tyranny' and those that argued they were 'a happy and contented people, uniformly treated with mildness and humanity and enjoying comforts beyond those of a British peasant'.[29] In the same way that Barclay was keen to highlight supposed improvements in the treatment of slaves, so Stewart claimed that the Slave Code in Jamaica over the last thirty years had protected free time, limited whipping and provided obligations on masters to feed and clothe slaves adequately. Although highly critical of Wilberforce for what he regarded as blanket condemnation of supposed cruelty in the West Indies, Stewart commended him for securing the abolition of the slave trade. In company even with abolitionists in earlier days, he regarded the suppression of the trade as a prelude to better treatment of existing slaves in the colonies, and claimed that it had been more effective than any laws enacted to protect slaves.

Stewart was similarly critical of James Stephen for his introduction of the Slave Registration Act, whose imposition on the colonies Stewart regarded as high-handed, leading to a strong reaction there; but he also admitted that the Act had brought benefits and had helped to reduce fraud. Throughout the book there are what seem to be a number of contradictions caused no doubt by the tension between a man caught between two cultures, recognising the intrinsic evil of slavery, but accepting the need for it and frightened by the possible consequences of abolition.

Unlike Barclay, John Stewart was unwilling simply to highlight improvements in treatment of slaves. He claimed that the use of the cart-whip was fading, but admitted that it was often replaced by the cat-o'nine-tails or the birch. Whilst slaves were simply classified as property they could be, and were, uprooted at the will and whim of the master, thereby destroying family life. He recommended that slaves be enabled both to hold property and to be legally attached to the same place. In addition, he recommended that slave testimony in court should be accepted, citing in support of this a West Indian proprietor, now resident in Britain, who saw this as a 'wise, safe, and salutary step' that should be taken by the Jamaican Assembly rather than have it imposed by Westminster.[30]

Stewart had detailed plans for religious instruction and was far more critical than Barclay over the failure, particularly by the established Church of England, to provide both teaching and the ordinances of baptism and marriage. This may partly reflect his own Presbyterian background, since he argued for 'full and free toleration' for all churches in the colonies, but he further pleaded for 'a positive law obliging proprietors and others to have their slaves baptised and instructed', citing Bielby Porteus, the abolitionist Bishop of London who had written to governors and proprietors in the West Indies, reminding them of their responsibility for the physical and spiritual welfare of the slaves in their care.[31]

Stewart's survey at times gave weight to the same issues that defenders of slavery used – the spectre of chaos in St Domingue after the slave rebellion, the need for approximately £100 million compensation for the planters, the loss of West Indian trade and of the 'nursery for our seamen', the latter an old argument made for the trade rather than slavery itself. This appears to indicate a certain degree of confusion for Stewart, not least because, unlike Barclay, he recognised the potential in ex-slaves and even cited Toussaint L'Ouverture, the leader of the rebellion in St Domingue and bête noire of the planters, as an example of leadership through the benefits of education.[32]

Marly: or the Life of a Planter in Jamaica provided a fictional, but perhaps autobiographical, account. It too was full of contradictions and its hero fairly soon left to become a plantation clerk. Marly was both shocked at the arbitrary nature of punishments and the flogging of elderly people for lateness in the field, yet comforted by his conviction that it had no lasting effects on the slaves. He made observations on the happiness of the slaves who knew nothing else and had food, shelter and medical help provided for them. At the same time, he recognised that half the slaves on the Water Melon Valley sugar estate would exchange that satisfaction for freedom.[33]

The accounts of discussions with numerous characters in the text of *Marly* are interspersed with polemical pieces of comment that are similar to those in Stewart's account. These too appear to be contradictory. As Stewart described slavery as a 'state of degrading bondage' and 'revolting', so Marly termed it 'detestable' and carrying a curse. He continued by arguing that when the victims of slavery suffer degradation, the whole of society is degraded.

Yet the very recognition of the slaves' humanity provided an Achilles heel. 'Man', argued Marly, 'is not a machine to be managed like a piece of clockwork or a steam engine. He has too many passions and prejudices to submit to be treated like a piece of inert matter.' Yet it was those very passions and emotions that Marly saw would be released by the prospect of emancipation. In what would be music to the planters' ears, he declared that to abolish slavery would be to let loose upon society 'a host of idle, immoral and profligate wretches, who would instantly become pests of society and who would be a perpetual burden on the community until they ceased to exist'.[34]

If this forthright declaration of the likely consequences of abolition would commend itself to the planters, so too would Marly's opposition to action from the British Government. In contrast to the abolitionists, who, by the late 1820s, were getting increasingly impatient over Westminster's refusal to intervene with legislation, the assemblies in the colonies clung to their independence. Jamaica, Marly claimed, had the right to refuse to listen to and comply with instructions sent to them by a body in which they were not represented. As a footnote to the book, the author claimed that the Jamaican legislature recently had taken significant steps to revise the slave laws and to improve the condition of slaves. He was critical of the Colonial Secretary's attitude in sending the legislation back to Jamaica, 'thereby annulling what has been done in favour of the slave'.[35]

John Stewart was a Scot who genuinely struggled with the contradictions of the two societies in which he found himself. In the midst of his book there is a curious theological passage. Immediately after a lighter passage on humour, with a slave poking fun at the inability of a Guinea captain, so expert in navigating the seas, to find his way to a house in the land of Jamaica, he observed of slaves that they could not reconcile with justice that God should have 'shown so marked a predilection for the whites as to give dominion to them, while He placed blacks, who have no wish to offend Him, in a state of perpetual bondage under them'.[36] Far from seeing this as a reasonable response, though, Stewart's dogmatic Presbyterianism leads him to condemn the slaves for not learning to submit to the will of providence, despite their boast of being Christians. Others, equally grappling with the theological puzzle as we will see, came to the conclusion that slavery was a standing rebuke to the divine will and that every second of its existence involved the nation in corporate guilt.

In no sense could Stewart's writings be reasonably seen as proslavery documents. They stand in contrast to Alexander Barclay's apologia, which was summarised by the *Glasgow Courier* as part of its campaign in support of the West Indian cause. In 1823, to argue for amelioration of slavery and gradual steps towards eventual emancipation was exactly what the majority of anti-slavery petitions demanded and echoed the efforts of the abolitionists in Parliament. Nonetheless, Stewart and the fictional or autobiographical character Marly used some of the very arguments that were to be found at the core of those petitions that sought to postpone abolition indefinitely and to eke out the life of slavery. The opposition to 'interference' from Westminster in colonial legislation, the lack of readiness amongst slaves for a life of freedom, the improvements made by the colonies in slave conditions, the need to pay massive compensation to planters, the spectre of revolution, havoc and bloodshed – all these are outlined by Stewart. And all are to be found in the arguments made by those who profited from slavery by delaying emancipation.

THE GLASGOW WEST INDIA ASSOCIATION GOES ONTO THE OFFENSIVE

In 1823, the planters and merchants of Edinburgh and Glasgow sent petitions to the Commons. Edinburgh expressed concern about rumours that the sugar subsidies were to be removed, putting the West Indies on the same footing as the East and argued that such drastic measures would reverse the more 'liberal policy' towards the slaves that was gradually taking hold amongst the West Indian estates. The proprietors, it claimed, in properly providing for themselves and their children, would, albeit reluctantly, be forced to abandon comforts for the slaves, including 'the advantages of moral and religious instruction'. Glasgow's petition was concerned about an inquiry by the Government into slavery with the 'avowed intention' of effecting emancipation, a course they judged would deprive the slaves of 'the means of comfortable subsistence which they now possess' and expose them to the 'consequences of that indolence and inactivity which from their natural constitution they are too apt to indulge'. If there should be any inquiry, argued the merchants, it should be entrusted to 'the local legislatures of the colonies whose experience would lead them to lessen the public danger'.[37]

The planters often complained about the danger of what they termed 'agitation' or propaganda at home. Simply raising the issue of slavery, however cautiously, would, they argued, lead to unsettling the slaves and ultimately to rebellion. There was some basis for this view, but in a rather different way than they expected. James Walvin attributed 'plantocratic outrage' in the local press and over the dinner tables in response to Stephen's Registration Bill as a factor in encouraging the 1816 slave revolt in Barbados, convincing the slaves that their promised freedom was being obstructed.[38] Certainly the timing of the Demerara slave rebellion in 1823, blamed by the planters on the missionary Smith, followed the first news of Canning's proposals. The Jamaican uprisings in 1831–2 followed hard on the spectacular growth of anti-slavery activity at home and its suppression in the West Indies.

Such 'agitation' concerned the prominent citizens of Cromarty and Tain, who petitioned the Commons in 1824. Both burghs argued for a system of amelioration by 'the gradual influence of time', but warned about exciting the slaves 'by delusive hopes'. Cromarty detailed the consequences to trade, the injury to Britain's naval strength by 16,000 seamen being unemployed and the burden to the army and navy if called upon to subdue rebellion.[39] In 1826, a petition was sent to the Commons from planters and merchants in Glasgow and Greenock. Its language betrayed an urgency and fear of change. The petitioners reiterated the current economic distress in the West Indies and claimed that this also impacted on the 'well-being and existence of the very slaves, whom it was the object of these proceedings to ameliorate and protect'. The rights of any British subject to hold property freely was emphasised, with the perceived injustice of selective interference with property held by West Indian citizens. The petitioners expressed their anxiety that 'the plan of compulsory emancipation is now seriously entertained', speaking of Britain seeking to 'fetter' the colonies 'with restraints which can paralyse their industry and even crush their existence', despite the commercial and maritime value of 'one of the brightest gems in the crown'.[40]

Sensing the inevitability of abolition, planters resident in Edinburgh who petitioned in 1827 trusted that they would receive 'full and fair indemnification' of such losses that they might sustain by future legislation, whilst proprietors of estates in the West Indies resident in Aberdeen prayed that any alterations in existing laws 'as shall affect the petitioners' property' would be accompanied by 'full and ample compensation'.[41] Planters' petitions at this time all called for the Government to set up a commission to inquire into the treatment of slaves and their moral and religious state. Clearly this was a tactic to delay what was described as 'any further measures of interference with lawful property'. The Glasgow West India Association recommended that the members of the commission be those 'practically acquainted with tropical agriculture and the control of agricultural labour in the colonies' – in other words, former planters and estate managers. As if to guarantee a favourable outcome for them, the Association also inserted in their petition a requirement that the commissioners submit their reports on each colony to the Governor and Council, 'for their perusal and attestation'.[42]

The Glasgow West India Association was formed by merchants and planters in the city with an expressed purpose of protecting the interests of the tobacco and sugar trades. Its inaugural meeting was held on 22 October 1807 in the Tontine Tavern. It was hardly a coincidence that this was a mere seven months after the bill for the abolition of the slave trade had received the royal assent. The London West Indians, who also met in a tavern, had been divided in their tactics over the bill the previous year and the need for a body to address the particular concerns of those who were involved in the sugar business was evident to the Glasgow businessmen who attended the meeting. The economic problems caused by the war with France, the blockade of ports and the aggravation of this by the increased volume of sugar being imported from islands captured by the French, all added to the claims of such an Association.

For the first part of its life, the Association concentrated on lobbying for the lowering of tariffs and discussing local arrangements for transportation into Glasgow. There was little discussion of slavery in the early years of the nineteenth century and Glasgow's merchants were, if anything, supportive of the attempts in 1814 to ensure a ban on the French slave trade. In 1823, the Association noted that 'the misfortunes of the West Indian planters have been greatly aggravated by the prosecution of the foreign slave trade' from which they were barred.[43] If there had to be prohibition, it was only just, they felt, that all be penalised in this way.

That same year the Association pre-empted the new movement that agitated on slavery by presenting itself as a benevolent organisation, not least for the slaves. A petition in April to the Earl of Liverpool at the Treasury seeking a more sympathetic view of the need to relieve their economic plight and stressing the benefits of the sugar trade to Britain contained the assurance that 'these benefits depend on the orderly and contented state of the negro which your memorialists have been ever anxious to promote by attending to their comfort and happiness'. Later in the year the committee received documents from the Church of England Society via the London West Indians regarding religious instruction for slaves in the Caribbean and voted to contribute £100 to this object.[44]

From then on, however, this benevolent approach gradually receded. In the annual report for 1824, the complaint was found that East Indian sugar interests 'united with the party of Mr. Wilberforce' to threaten the existence of the colonies. The East India Party was accused of representing the planters in 'a most hideous light' and encouraging petitions for amelioration and ultimate emancipation. In 1825, the directors of the Association reported to members that because of the numerous societies now formed to campaign for abolition, they planned to establish an organisation to defend 'the colonial interest in Scotland', with the purpose of 'opening the eyes of the public and diffusing correct information relative to the condition of the negro population'. The petition sent to the Commons in 1826 complained that some West Indian properties had lost up to 50 per cent in value. It went on to make the extraordinary claim that the planters had welcomed any suggestions for improvement of the slaves' conditions and had implemented religious instruction. They further proclaimed their confidence that if the attacks on the colonial legislatures ceased, they would 'cheerfully concur with His Majesty's Government in the adoption of every salutary scheme'.[45]

In 1825, the Association approached the King directly, requesting that he use his prerogative to veto an Act of Parliament that, if implemented, would compromise their 'vested interests'.[46] They sent a further petition the next year to the King in Council specifically warning about Colonial Secretary Bathurst's plan to impose manumission on the crown colonies of Demerara and Bernice. 'Such a measure', they argued, 'if carried into effect, would be a danger to the whole West India colonies.'[47] At the same time an urgent appeal was made for money to fight 'agitation'.

For the rest of the decade, the West Indian supporters in Glasgow swung from complacency to panic and then from frenzied activity to acceptance of the inevitable. By 1827, the Association reported a victory for the colonists when the British Government refused to impose direct rule, a move advocated by some abolitionists. They claimed with satisfaction that things had improved in terms of the status of West Indian property and proclaimed that although the danger was not yet over, 'the nation is beginning to see that it has been imposed upon by a set of designing men'. That perhaps indicated the relative inactivity of Government and the absence of abolitionist petitions from Scotland that year. In 1829, the same mood was reflected in a report that whilst neither Government nor people had 'abandoned altogether the dangerous theories and innovations on the West Indian concerns', things were seen by the Association to be 'in a more satisfactory state'.[48]

That perception was to change dramatically before the next year was out. By 1830, the Association was mobilising, petitioning the new King William IV about the danger to the 'peace and prosperity 'of his colonies, proposing to set up local associations for the defence of West Indian interests and gathering signatures for a gradualist approach. An air of panic is obvious in the call to take prompt action to prevent 'the spread of evil, so much to be dreaded'. As anti-slavery petitions mushroomed all over Scotland, the Glasgow West India Association discussed legal action against the now likely British Government's interference in the West Indies, appointed a Mr Milne as their agent in London, sent £100 towards the election expenses of a sympathiser in his attempt to win Forfar in the 1832 General Election and paid for space in six Scottish newspapers to carry a paper explaining the case for keeping slavery. They further recommended 'Rev. Mr. Brown' of 26 Scotland Street, Edinburgh, whose experience in Demerara would make him a good witness 'for the present enquiry'.[49] Yet in the end there is a terse notice in the 1833 minutes which carried the factual announcement that slavery was to be abolished in British possessions and that £20 million had been set aside to compensate the colonists for the loss of their property. The report to the AGM in January of 1834 had a tone of capitulation.[50]

Given Glasgow's economic stake in the West Indies, and the perception that the city's West Indian influence was regarded as second only to London, it is surprising that the Association were not more effective in their cause. In 1826, the economic downturn caused the city's abolition society to be more cautious in its approach and in that decade Edinburgh's Society was clearly in the lead as far as anti-slavery activity was concerned. Yet the petitions from the West of Scotland continued to flow and to be signed in large numbers. The West Indians had the support of the *Glasgow Courier* and also of the editor of the *Free Press*, who offered to organise a petition in 1830 against any immediate moves towards emancipation.[51] But they did not have the competence to mobilise public opinion. In 1825, the Association had reacted to the formation of abolition societies by seeking to unite those who had a financial stake in the Caribbean, inviting them to a public meeting in Edinburgh. It was a damp squib. Many of the invitees sent their apologies, others complained of inconvenience, and there were such differences of opinion over how to proceed that the directors decided to abandon the project for the time being. The 1830 proposal to set up local associations in defence of the West Indian interest met with an equal lack of success. By that time the abolition campaign was in top gear and the Glasgow West Indians were unable to counter it.

THE PRESS DEFENDING SLAVERY – JAMES MCQUEEN'S *GLASGOW COURIER*

By and large, the Scottish newspapers were sympathetic to abolition, with varying attitudes to its urgency. The major exception was the *Glasgow Courier*, whose editor during the 1820s was James McQueen. In February 1825, it was proposed by the Glasgow West India Association that 'a handsome remuneration' should be made to Mr McQueen 'for the great service he has rendered the West Indian interest in general'. The 'service' referred to was both in Britain and the West Indies, and in recognition of the expenses that he had incurred in journeying to London it was resolved to pay him £250 guineas, by the standards of the time a handsome remuneration indeed. The following year the sum of £262–10/- was recorded in the annual accounts as paid, presumably an increase of his expense, and to this was added £92–12/- for 600 copies of his book, *Colonial Controversy*, which the Association undertook to distribute.[52]

James McQueen, a native of Crawford, had been the manager of a sugar plantation in Grenada at the turn of the eighteenth century. He had clearly managed to save some money as, around the beginning of the 1820s, he became part-proprietor and editor of the *Glasgow Courier* throughout most of that decade. Although there was a report that towards the end of 1825 he had been appointed 'to a London paper in defence of the West Indian colonies', he either did not stay long there or possibly combined the two positions, since the style of the *Courier* remained consistent until the 1830s, by which time his successor had taken over.

McQueen took an interest not only in Caribbean matters, but also in Africa. He had been captivated by the published travels of Mungo

Park and had become a keen student of the geography and current situation of the West African coast. It was this, above all, that led him to become a staunch ally of *John Bull*, the London journal that was fiercely opposed to the abolitionists. From time to time thoughout the 1820s, the *Courier* carried a number of articles from *John Bull*, reproducing its attacks on Sierra Leone and Macaulay's time of governorship of the colony.

The attack on the abolitionists began from the report on the parliamentary debate on slavery in May 1823. Thomas Fowell Buxton was accused of a 'virulent declamation' of the white population in the colonies, although a close look at the reporting of the debate would revealed no such targeting.[53] Yet even a mild critique of slavery was, for McQueen, enough to constitute an attack on the character of every colonist in the West Indies. The *Courier*, for the next few years, busied itself with lengthy testimonies to the uprightness of the West Indian planters and to the exemplary treatment of the slaves under their control. If McQueen could use testimony from those who would be known and respected at home, so much the better. The *Courier* referred continually to Rev. George Bridges, the Anglican priest in Jamaica who had mounted a vigorous defence of slavery, although the editor would no doubt have realised that this would cut little ice in Presbyterian Scotland, even before Bridges was accused of terrible cruelty to his cook and other practices which eventually led him to leave the island. A far safer bet was Rev. Archibald Browne from Paisley, minister of St Andrews Scots Kirk in Georgetown, Demerara.

Mr Browne published three sermons in pamphlet form in 1824, entitled *On the Duty of Subjects to their Sovereign and on the Duties of Slaves to their Masters*. These were serialised in the *Courier* at a particularly apposite time. The 1823 rebellion on the island and the trial and death of John Smith had excited public opinion and these counter-blasts were exactly what the West Indians wanted. In December, the *Courier* announced 'we have pleasure in being able to state that the excellent discourses recently delivered by Revd Mr. Browne . . . will by the entreaty of those who heard him, be published as soon as possible'.[54] In fact, it was July of the next year before these sermons found their way into the newspaper, but in the early part of the year Archibald Browne wrote several letters justifying the action of the Governor of Demerara in putting Rev. John Smith on trial and claiming that the London Missionary Society, his employers, had been responsible for encouraging the stirring up the slaves and fomenting rebellion in the island.

The *Courier* was also keen to cite attacks on abolition from other journals that might be seen to be more moderate. In July 1824, McQueen reproduced a article from *Blackwood's Magazine* condemning John Smith and the London Missionary Society for not maintaining a strict and silent neutrality on the issue of slavery in order to preach the gospel.[55] This followed an article the previous month taken from *John Bull* attacking Smith and the other missionaries in the West Indies for their 'interference' in matters the paper regarded as of no consequence to them. Later in the year, the *Courier* published a long extract from the *Quarterly Review* citing St Domingue as a clear example of the dangers of abolition.

McQueen was to use reports from St Domingue as he did those from Sierra Leone to demonstrate to his readers the dangers of slaves taking charge of their lives, claiming the African country was a drain on national resources providing no profit to Britain. Sierra Leone was going through a period of economic and social instability and it was a soft target for the anti-abolitionists. Zachary Macaulay's *Anti-Slavery Reporter* had quickly became an effective organ of the campaign and James McQueen used *John Bull* as a source for accusations of Macaulay's profiteering in his time as governor of Sierra Leone.

In contrast to the 1792 debate in the *Courier*, where letters for or against the abolition of the slave trade had given a balance to its columns, the paper under McQueen carried letters almost exclusively from planters in the colonies or those who had just returned from them. An exception was 'M', who in 1823–4 criticised the position of the *Courier* as 'one sided' and produced a detailed analysis of slavery in the West Indies. But with every column printed from 'M' at least two were offered by the editor in refutation. In January 1824, James McQueen, suspecting, perhaps correctly, that Zachary Macaulay was the author of the letters, addressed his reply to 'Our correspondent "M"' and 'the scribe of the African Institution', whose Secretary at that time was none other than Macaulay.[56]

In the latter part of 1824, James McQueen serialised his own polemic, *Colonial Controversy*, which, as was usual with such writings of that time, took the form of a series of letters.[57] These were addressed to the Earl of Liverpool, the Colonial Secretary, and were not a direct defence of slavery in the same way that other pamphlets had been. Starting with a strong criticism of what he regarded as the folly of setting up the Sierra Leone Company, McQueen continued with a critical analysis of Joshua Steele in Barbados, the planter whom William Dickson used as a model for good practice in *Letters on Slavery*. He then ventured into an analysis of apprenticed Africans, China and the East Indies, taking nearly half a page of the newspaper to proclaim his ideas. The following year saw extracts from Alexander Barclay's *A Practical View of Slavery* published in the *Courier*. At the same time McQueen produced an attempted refutation of some of Zachary Macaulay's views on Slavery, addressing this characteristically to 'Zachariah Macaulay, Esq.'.

In 1826, James McQueen was incensed at the suggestion from the abolitionist Member of Parliament Dr Stephen Lushington that he and *John Bull* were agents paid by the West Indian colonists to defend slavery, and that they attacked 'with the most scullirous abuse, all who differed in opinion from them on this point.' In a pained yet vigorous piece in which the 'great Whig lawyers of Edinburgh' were similarly accused of slander and abuse against the newspaper, the *Courier* complained that neither Mr McQueen nor the editor of *John Bull* (who may by this time have become one and the same) were able to defend themselves and proclaimed that the charge that McQueen was an agent of the slave interests 'as Dr Lushington knows is pure Tom Adamson, scurrility and information' (sic).[58]

Tom Adamson was claimed by the newspaper to be a fictitious signature on the 1826 petition organised by the Glasgow Abolition Society. At the end of May, the *Courier* invited 'a discerning public' to judge for itself the authenticity of anti-slavery petitions sent to Parliament in their name. It claimed that extensive investigation of the Glasgow Directory showed no such person, and that 'multitudes' of the petitions were 'written in London, sent down to the country for signature and only heard of when they were presented in the House of Commons'. Like an overheated engine, the article gathered steam to end in a journalistic style that mirrored *John Bull*.

> Why! Were not the signers lashed into the work with a coach-whip at 160 Trongate – physicked into it at our *friends* in the Candleriggs – carried captives at the old Spanish ship, among the sweetcakes, at the Bazaar, *led* into it at the Old Bridge, and *coerced* at the timber Bridge, as we ourselves were attempted to be; and lastly, *denounced* into it in a certain chapel in John-street – sign or go to the devil, was an alternative which every nerve was not sufficiently firm to oppose.[59]

The *Courier* was the only newspaper to report a meeting in April 1826 of the Glasgow Auxiliary Moravian Society. It complained that hardly any public discussion took place in the country without attacks on 'our fellow subjects in the West Indies' taking place, and that Moravian missionaries had been 'eagerly received in the West Indies' and had made 33,000 converts among the slave population. The newspaper was at a loss as to why the meeting attacked slavery as 'degrading and disgraceful'. The main speaker at the meeting was Rev. John Smyth of St George's Parish Church, later to be active in the 1830 campaign, and the *Courier* challenged his biblical analysis at length, citing Abraham, Jesus and Paul for their acceptance of slavery.[60]

In August 1826, a correspondent from the Bahamas congratulated the *Courier* for 'your steady and honourable efforts in support of the persecuted and betrayed colonists'[61]. But McQueen was shortly to concentrate more on the controversy over the Apocrypha, which at that time was an important issue in the churches. By November, he felt that the fervour for anti-slavery had sufficiently calmed down for an editorial to declare 'that the hour of the anti-colonial folly and interested philanthropy is passing away and that reason is fast resuming her seat in the minds of our countrymen[62]'. In the next few years, the *Courier* concentrated on other issues, notably Catholic Emancipation. By 1830, William Motherwell, a sheriff-clerk from Paisley with a reputation as a Tory Orangeman and fanatical anti-radical, was appointed editor. Motherwell had neither experience of the West Indies nor close contacts with the slave interests, but the *Courier* continued in the same tradition. By October of that year, battle was joined in earnest with the abolitionists as a new stage in the campaign began.

Even though he had ceased to be editor, McQueen continued to make his mark in the *Courier*. In late November 1830, he returned from London and did battle in the newspaper with Dr Patrick Macfarlane, minister of St Enoch's in Glasgow. In the *Courier* of 28 October a letter appeared that referred to the petition sent that month to Parliament from the Synod of Glasgow and Ayr. The writer signed himself 'D.C.' and his address 'Banks of the Clyde'. He warned the ministers of the Synod that they were dependent for their livelihood on the colonial interests supplying the public purse. They should be aware, said 'D.C.', that in their determination to 'take away the property of fellow-subjects, that there was an equal or more just case for "the dissenter and the liberal" to demand of the legislature to strike away these stipends'.

This none-too-subtle attempt to divide anti-slavery campaigners on the contentious issue of religious establishments was taken up by

Dr Patrick Macfarlane at the Glasgow anti-slavery meeting on 11 November, whose speech was taken from the *Chronicle* and reproduced in the 30th November issue of the *Courier*. Macfarlane claimed that he was not a member of the Society, although a fervent supporter of abolition, but that Committee had invited him to speak. He would not have attempted to answer 'D.C.' had the letter simply attacked the views of the Synod, but felt obliged to reject what he called 'the foul insinuation' against the integrity of the ministers of Glasgow, who were of the same mind as he. Macfarlane went on to suggest that 'D.C.' was to be interpreted as 'Defender of the Colonies' living at South Wellington Place (McQueen's address) and was none other than 'this redoubtable journalist – this pampered and well paid supporter of the West Indian interest – this declaimer against the rights of 800,000 black men and as has been shown, of white men too'.

James McQueen's letter published that day was specifically addressed to Macfarlane. He identified himself with every word written by 'D.C.' and asked when Defender of the Colonies was anything other than an honourable position. He accused Macfarlane of total ignorance of 'the colonial subject', simply by his own admission of coming to the meeting to attack 'a public Journal of this city', and of ignoring the ties between the colonialists and the national church. McQueen also associated Macfarlane with 'bloodthirsty and firebrand interpreters [of scripture]'. Furthermore, said McQueen, Dr Macfarlane attacks the Glasgow West Indian interests but 'without the trade to these colonies and to countries also cultivated by slaves' there would have been no money to take him from Polmont 'to dazzle [Glasgow] with his eloquence'.

The 1830 correspondence from 'D.C.', which was not limited to Macfarlane, was a robust swansong from James McQueen, whilst the *Courier* continued in a tradition that would meet with his approval. But the next spring he was cited by another journal in arguing that 'ages of progressive improvement must precede the establishment, among such a race, of that rational freedom which is established in civilised states'.[63] As the pro-slavery interest began to realise that the prevention of emancipation was a lost cause, the tactics switched to that of delay. It was necessary for their interests to spin out the continuation of slavery using the argument of gradual improvement. And it was to take a sustained attack on this seemingly sensible and secure doctrine of 'gradualism' to move the anti-slavery campaign on to a new stage.

AN UNCERTAIN SOUND

In the white-ruled states of Southern Africa in the 1960s, Scottish immigrants played a significant role, not least in the semi-autonomous colony of Rhodesia. Those who sought at home to challenge the structures of racist regimes and to persuade the public to put pressure on the British Government were met with strong resistance from those who had relatives or friends in that part of the world or who had themselves lived and worked there before returning to Scotland. The picture, the folks at home were assured, was not as it was portrayed by some radicals, and the consequences of 'majority rule' would be the destruction of an idyllic way of life, if not a blood-bath for those whose skills and capital had turned the country from primitive barbarism to civilisation.

Such a script could easily be translated to the British Caribbean in the early nineteenth century. Just as apologists for even the harshest of colonial regimes in Africa had compared these with the alternatives, so Dalzel had written of the benefits of ordered slavery over the wanton murder of Dahomeyan society. Correspondents from Southern Africa who distanced themselves from hard-line racists hastened to assure readers and listeners that although there was much that was wrong and many evils from the past, considerable progress had been made, but which could be arrested by too speedy changes, especially if imposed by Westminster. James Adair, Alexander Barclay and to a lesser extent John Stewart would have identified with such perceptions. Just as opponents of colonial freedom in modern times were quick to point out what they saw as the disastrous results of independence – citing the religious bitterness in India after the Raj or the massacres in the former Belgian Congo – so the *Glasgow Courier* under James McQueen increasingly highlighted the volatile state of Haiti and the failure of Sierra Leone to measure up to the ideals of its founders.

The opponents of emancipation of slavery in the nineteenth century had plenty of material to work on. There were few investigative journalists at the time and no newsreels or television film that could demonstrate a different picture. Given the economic power of West Indian interests in a small country such as Scotland, and the educational background that provided literacy skills for so many of its citizens, why were they so unsuccessful? Part of the answer is that they were not. With hindsight it is easy to see the abolition of the slave trade in 1807 and the proclamation of emancipation in 1834 as defeat for those who profited by human traffic and property. But the converse of the argument, that without careful and sustained organisation and massive public pressure slavery would have continued for many more years, is that without the pro-slavery propaganda and the counter-pressure the abolitionists would have achieved their aims much earlier.

Of course it was not a simple battle between opposite extremes. Many of the petitions both of the early campaigns and those that led up to emancipation reflect great variety in their aims, from extremely radical positions to those so hedged with provisos that they demand hardly anything. The fact that Britain was at war over much of the earlier period and under the threat of internal revolution during the later years was a huge contributing factor to the timescale for the abolition of slavery.

On the other hand, there is little doubt that the anti-abolitionists sowed some of the seeds of their own destruction and that they faced a formidable array of skilled opponents. So keen were some of their apologists not to be seen to be identified with drink-sodden colonists who daily wielded the cart-whip without limit and nightly violated slave women that their very ambivalence over defending the system lost them the cutting edge.

Hesitancy and complacency marked their campaign and none more so than in the Glasgow West India Association's belief in the late 1820s that the threat of abolition had become so diluted as to be no longer effective. Indeed, campaign would perhaps be a misnomer, since there was no sense of co-ordination. The work of associations of planters and merchants who occasionally petitioned Parliament could not be compared to that of the anti-slavery societies in so many Scottish cities and towns. Nor did they enjoy the support of ministers and churches, with the exception of a very few. Dalzel's *History of Dahomey* may have commended itself to some readers, but it hardly compared in effectiveness with the *Extract of Evidence* Thomas Clarkson distributed throughout England and William Dickson took throughout the length and breadth of Scotland. The *Glasgow Courier* may have had a circle of readers in the country's commercial capital, but Macaulay's *Anti-Slavery Reporter* provided the ammunition not just for the parliamentary campaign but for hundreds of communities who were to flood Parliament with petitions in the 1830s. It was a trickle at the start, and it took its time to get going, but in the end it was a flood that could not be stopped.

Notes

1 Henry Cockburn, *Memorials of his Time* (Edinburgh, 1856), p. 282.

2 *GCH*, 5 Jul; *GC*, 30 Jun 1814.

3 *GH*, 11 Jul, 15 Jul 1814.

4 *CM*, 2 Jul 1814.

5 *GC*, 15 Jul; *EEC*, 7 Jul 1814.

6 Musselburgh Council, Minutes, Jul 1814. NAS B52/3/5.

7 *JHC*, 9 Feb 1815; *EEC*, 21 Jul 1814.

8 *JHC*, 21, 22 Jul; *GCH*, 5 Jul 1814.

9 *JHC*, 22, 26 Jul 1814.

10 Presbytery of Cupar, Minutes, 12 Jul 1814. NAS CH2/82/20.

11 Presbytery of Kirkcaldy, Minutes, 6 Jul 1814. NAS CH2/224/10.

12 *JHL*, 17, 29 Mar, 5 Apr, 11 May 1814.

13 Archibald Dalzel to Andrew Dalzel, London, 13 Apr 1771. EUL, Dk.7.52.

14 Archibald Dalzel to Robert Liston, 26 May 1764. EUL, Dk.7.52.

15 Archibald Dalzel to Andrew Dalzel, 20 Apr 1768.

16 Archibald Dalzel, *The History of Dahomey – an Inland Kingdom of Africa. Compiled from Authentic Memories* ed. J. Fage (London, [1789] 1967), pp. 22, 25, 121, 130, 158.

17 Dalzel, *History of Dahomey*, pp. 217–21.

18 L. A. Akinjogbin, 'Archibald Dalzel: Slaver Trader and Historian of Dahomey', *Journal of African History*, Vol. 7 (1966), p. 78. Other articles that are helpful in understanding the life of Dalzel are: C. Duncan Rice, 'Archibald Dalzel, The Scottish Intelligentsia and the Problem of Slavery', *Scottish Historical Review*, Vol. 62 (Oct 1983); L. K. Waldman, 'An Unnoticed Aspect of Archibald Dalzel's *The History of Dahomey, Journal of African History*, Vol. 6 (1965).

19 Dalzel, *History of Dahomey*, Introduction, p. 9.

20 James Adair, *Unanswerable Arguments against the Abolition of the Slave Trade with Defence of the Proprietors of the British Sugar Colonies* (London, 1790), pp. 141, 225–8.

21 Adair, *Unanswerable Arguments*, pp. 195–9, 220.

22 Adair, *Unanswerable Arguments*, p. 139. 'Let justice be done, whatever the consequences.' This was a maxim often quoted in petitions and dramatically used during the large anti-slavery meeting in Edinburgh in October 1830.

23 Adair, *Unanswerable Arguments*, pp. 143, 146, 148.

24 Alexander Barclay, *A Practical View of the Present State of Slavery in the West Indies or an Examination of Mr. Stephen's 'Slavery in the West Indian Colonies' containing more particularly an Account of the Actual Condition of the Negroes in Jamaica* (London, 1826).

25 Barclay, *A Practical View*, pp. 2, 43, 91, 104.

26 Barclay, *A Practical View*, Introduction, p. xvi.

27 Barclay, *A Practical View*, p. 74.

28 Barclay, *A Practical View*, Introduction, p. xiii.

29 Stewart, *A View of the Past and Present State of the Island of Jamaica; with Remarks on the Moral and Physical Condition of the Slaves and on the Abolition of Slavery in the Colonies* (Edinburgh, 1823), p. 220.

30 Stewart, A View of the Past, pp. 337, 226–7.

31 Stewart, A View of the Past, pp. 268–99.

32 Stewart, A View of the Past, p. 265.

33 Anon., *Marly: or the Life of a Planter in Jamaica; Comprehending Characteristic Sketches of the Present State of Society and Manners in the British West Indies*, ed. Karina Williamson (Oxford, [1826] 2005), p. 81.

34 Anon., Marly, p. 222.

35 Anon., Marly, p. 325.

36 Stewart, *A View of the Past*, p. 260.

37 *GH*, 11 Apr; *JHC*, 12 May 1823.

38 James Walvin, *England, Slaves and Freedom*, (Jackson, MS, 1986), p. 129.

39 *JHC*, 26 May, 10 Jun 1824.

40 *JHC*, 19 May 1826.

41 *JHC*, 9, 20 Jun 1827.

42 *JHC*, 1 Jul 1827.

43 Glasgow West India Association, Minutes, Mar 1823. MLG, Mic.P, 3290–3294.

44 Glasgow West India Association, Minutes, May, Sept 1823.

45 Glasgow West India Association, Minutes, Jan 1824, May 1826.

46 Glasgow West India Association, Minutes, Jan 1825.

47 Glasgow West India Association, Minutes, Aug 1826.

48 Glasgow West India Association, Minutes, Jun 1827, Jan 1829.

49 Glasgow West India Association, Minutes, May 1832.

50 Glasgow West India Association, Minutes, Oct 1830, Jun 1832, Mar 1833, Jan 1834.

51 Glasgow West India Association, Minutes, Nov 1830.

52 Glasgow West India Association, Minutes, Feb 1825, Jan 1826.

53 *GC*, 22 May 1823.

54 *GC*, 2 Dec 1823.

55 *GC*, 10 Jul 1824.

56 *GC*, 6 Jan 1824.

57 James McQueen, *The Colonial Controversy containing a Refutation of the Anti-Colonialists addressed to the East of Liverpool with a supplementary letter to Mr. Macaulay* (Glasgow, 1825).

58 *GC*, 25 May 1826.

59 GC, 25 May 1826.
60 GC, 22 Apr 1826.
61 GC, 8 Aug 1826.
62 GC, 7 Nov 1826.
63 *Blackwood's Magazine*, Mar 1831.

6

COMING OUT OF SIN – THE ROAD FROM MITIGATION TO THE CALL FOR IMMEDIATE ABOLITION

༄

It is dictated by unchangeable truth and rectitude, and is therefore put beyond the reach of controversy, that slavery is a crime; that to engage or to persist in it is to contract guilt in the sight of heaven; and consequently being aware of this, we are bound to make no delay in hastening out of the transgression, and putting an end to it, whenever it has obtained a footing in our dominions.

Dr Andrew Thomson, 19 October 1830

In the autumn of 1830, two meetings took place in Edinburgh that marked a new watershed in the anti-slavery campaign. The central figure in both was Dr Andrew Thomson, minister of St George's, Edinburgh, who had been a member of the Committee against the Slave Trade in 1814 and was the recognised leader of the Church of Scotland's Evangelical wing. Thomson was founder and editor of the *Christian Instructor* and under his guidance it had since 1824 continually promoted the abolition of slavery. These meetings followed seven years of activity by an abolitionist movement that had seen little progress since its inception. Early in 1823, Zachary Macaulay had written a note to the editor of the *Imperial Magazine* seeking contact with the author of an article on West Indian slavery that month and declaring his deep interest in the subject.[1] Twelve days later, the 'Society for the Mitigation and Gradual Abolition of Slavery' was launched in London, with Macaulay as a leading member.

Scotland produced fewer petitions against slavery during the 1820s than the country had mobilised against the trade in the late eighteenth century. The strong reaction of the Glasgow West India Association meant that although Aberdeen, Edinburgh and Glasgow had active abolitionist societies, the most effective meetings took place in the east of Scotland. For the first time organised groups with commercial interests in maintaining slavery became active in petitioning, some from the very same towns that had seen anti-slavery petitions, underlining the tensions throughout Scottish society on the issue.

The 1830 meetings in Edinburgh were therefore pivotal points in the campaign, surrounded as they were with a number of smaller gatherings and resolutions sent to Parliament. Andrew Thomson's *Christian Instructor*, Zachary Macaulay's *Anti-Slavery Reporter* and the *Edinburgh Review* had kept not just the Scottish intelligentsia informed of the facts of Caribbean slavery, and these facts were disseminated from pulpits or specially convened meetings to a much wider audience. As with the campaign against the slave trade, church ministers played a crucial role. This time, however, it was the Secessionist congregations and those of other denominations that tended to eclipse the national Church of Scotland in activity. One of the most prominent and most vocal ministers from outside of the Kirk was Dr John Ritchie of the United Associate Secession congregation at Potterrow in Edinburgh. At the same time there was a reaction from more cautious churchmen who feared revolution and provided a philosophical challenge to what they saw as a headlong and irresponsible rush towards emancipation. Such sentiments were seized upon by those who represented the interests of West Indian planters, including, not surprisingly, the *Glasgow Courier*, albeit now under a different editor.

Nonetheless, the failure of the West Indian legislatures to implement the reforms recommended by the British Government throughout the 1820s, and their obdurate defence of every detail of the system, led to increasing frustration amongst those concerned to see an end to slavery. This was reflected in petitions that became less conciliatory as the decade wore on. If the planters had given some ground, it is probable that they would have been able to delay abolition by some years. If the moment had not been seized in 1830, the abolition movement might similarly have had to endure a longer timescale. There was much to be done and a considerable struggle that lay ahead in the years between 1830 and 1833, but the die was firmly cast.

MITIGATION AND FRUSTRATION – THE PETITIONING OF PARLIAMENT IN THE 1820s

On 15 May 1823, Thomas Fowell Buxton moved a resolution in the Commons, 'that the state of slavery is repugnant to the principles of the British Constitution and of the Christian religion and that it ought to be abolished gradually throughout the British colonies, with as much expedition as may be found consistent with a due regard to the well-being of the parties concerned'.[2] It had now become obvious to the leading campaigners against the slave trade that its ban and James Stephen's registration system, with its attempt to prevent importation, had not produced any better conditions for slaves on the plantations. This sense of frustration was expressed in what was described as 'a numerous and respectable meeting of the Inhabitants and Householders' in Edinburgh that year. The meeting 'deeply deplored' that so many years had passed without effective means being found to ameliorate the lot of slaves in the colonies, and instanced the prevention of marriages and the destruction of slave families, the denial to them of the 'hallowed sanctity' and 'peaceful repose' of Sabbath day and the exposure of any slave to the 'ignominy and cruelty of the lash, often at the wanton caprice of the basest of our race'.[3] Buxton's motion was partly designed to address similar concerns. The first proposal was that all children born after a certain date should be declared free. Thus, as he put it, 'slavery would burn itself down into its socket and go out'. The second part dealt with amelioration and preparation for freedom. This included the security of attachment to the same place, provision for marriage and religious instruction, no Sunday work, time allowed for the cultivation of provision grounds, limitation on punishment and the use of the whip, and the purchase of freedom by instalments. Perhaps the most crucial proposals, however, were those that said no one who held a judicial function should own slaves and that the testimony of slaves should be valid in law.[4]

George Canning, the Foreign Secretary, in his response to Buxton's resolution, claimed that many cruelties had now ceased. Evading any mention of emancipation, he assured the West Indians that their interests could be safeguarded. However, he also committed the Government to most of Buxton's proposals for amelioration, adding a ban on the flogging of female slaves, and through the Colonial Secretary, Lord Bathurst, he sent two dispatches to that effect to the West Indian colonies on 28 May and 9 July. Because most of the colonies had their own assemblies and had long since passed their own legislation, Canning was reluctant to impose legislation from Britain and even the subsequent Orders in Council, with which the Government in the next few years attempted to effect amelioration, were drafted in consultation with the West Indians. Only in the Crown Colonies of Trinidad, Demerara and St Lucia, where legislation was under more direct control from London, did the Government feel confident of imposing its policy of amelioration. Although Grenada, St Vincent and St Kitts received the dispatches with some kind of favour, the most populous slave islands of Jamaica and Barbados did not. The Jamaican Assembly hinted at a complete break from Britain if the Government continued to interfere, one Assemblyman asked for the removal of Bathurst and one of the committees appointed by the Assembly declared that Britain sought to dispose of the property of the colonists and urged members firmly to defend their rights.[5]

From then on, events throughout the early 1820s followed a predictable pattern. More and more Orders in Council were proposed, often seeking to amend in minute detail the slave codes that had been crucial to administration in the islands. These were almost invariably followed by strong and often violent resistance by the West Indians – which in turned fuelled the anti-slavery campaign at home. The death of the missionary John Smith in Demerara was well-publicised in sympathetic newspapers. In 1825, a Methodist minister in Barbados, Rev. William Shrewbury, incurred the wrath of the planters, who incited poor whites to break up his meetings, demolish his chapel and force him to flee to St Vincent. The Smith and Shrewbury cases were instrumental in bringing public pressure to bear on the Government.[6] The carefully researched work of Zachary Macaulay for the *Anti-Slavery Reporter* tried to ensure that atrocities against slaves were documented.

In 1823, Scotland provided 23 petitions on slavery out of a total of 226 sent to the House of Commons. A correspondent to the *Glasgow Chronicle* pointed out that many English towns had petitioned supported by the editorials of their newspapers, and he regretted not only that Glasgow – which 'justly prides herself as the most attached to religion and humanity in the world' – should not have done so, but that in Presbyteries and Synods 'not a word is whispered on behalf of the injured of the human race'.[7] The next week a reply was printed indicating that at the same moment that the original letter was being written, the Synod of the United Associate Secession Church had resolved to petition and encouraged its 280 congregations to do the same. No less than twenty responded at that time and in years to come the Secessionists were to produce by far the majority of church petitions calling for emancipation.

The British campaign against slavery had been launched at a public meeting in London at the end of January 1823. This led to the founding of a 'Society for the Mitigation and Gradual Abolition of Slavery throughout the British Dominions', although the emphasis on abolition was played down. In fact, it was virtually absent from a pamphlet that Wilberforce produced for the Society,[8] and Buxton's motion held out hopes for it only in the long term. The Synod of the United Associate Secession Church had sought simply 'the immediate mitigation and ultimate abolition of slavery',[9] but many of its congregations were less cautious. Lanark and Brechin called for an end to slavery 'as soon as it shall be practical', Lilliesleaf, Crail, Rathillet and Muckart spoke of 'that particularly malignant species of slavery which prevails in the West Indies', and Braehead and Carnwarth demanded its 'speedy abolition'.[10]

Alongside petitions to the Lords in 1824 on the slave trade, Scotland sent 49 out of a total of 460 to the Commons praying for 'the gradual abolition of slavery in the colonies'. More than half of these were from United Associate Secession congregations, three of which – Dundee, Linlithgow and Peebles – had also petitioned in 1823. They were joined by the cities of Glasgow and Edinburgh and towns mainly located in central Scotland, Fife and Ayrshire, with Kelso alone in the Borders, which petitioned from its Associate Trades. In 1824, only a small handful of petitions were sent to the Commons, with none coming from Scotland, but in 1826 the pattern changed. All the major cities were involved in the 66 petitions from Scotland, and out of the 46 from public and civic bodies, 10 came from the north-east, reflecting renewed anti-slavery activity in that area. St Andrews University Senatus petitioned and so did Glasgow University's students. Alongside ten Associate Secession churches, Church of Scotland Presbyteries of Dundee, Kirkcaldy, Lauder and North West England and the Synod of Merse and Teviotdale all sent petitions. There are no statistics of signatures on any but the Edinburgh petition, but the *Caledonian Mercury* reported that the one from Dundee 'measured 63 feet in length and the signatures are five column inches deep'.[11]

Dundee's petition was to the House of Lords alone, as were those from Paisley, Auchterarder and the Presbyteries of Forfar and Paisley. This may have reflected what was clearly a growing frustration at the ineffectiveness of legislation originating from the Commons. Certainly there are signs of impatience in texts that have survived. The Synod of Merse and Teviotdale observed 'with deep concern the keen opposition by the planters to the wise and humane regulations' made by Parliament. The Presbytery of North West England declared that they 'strongly deprecate the determined opposition of the colonial authorities to the united wishes of the government, parliament and the people of this country'.[12] Whilst still relying on the 1823 measures to lead to gradual abolition, the petitions now began to seek to replace the voluntary and cooperative approach towards the West Indies with legal enforcement.

In 1827 there were only 9 petitions to the House of Commons and all came from England; 1829 saw only 6, again none from Scotland. In 1828, England and Ireland sent 196, including those from two major centres of slave-related commerce, Liverpool and Bristol. Scotland contributed 8. Apart from the cities of Edinburgh, Aberdeen and Glasgow, all but one were from the north-east. Aberdeen urged both houses 'to fulfil at length the just expectations of the public by carrying into complete effect in every slave colony belonging to His Majesty, those reforms that have been promised' and recommended in the meantime doing away with any subsidies in favour of 'slave grown produce'. Montrose, the former slave-trading town, stopped short of demanding immediate abolition, but urged the Commons and Lords to use the 'direct exercise of their legislative powers' to correct an evil they claimed was, 'opposed to the national interests, damaging to the "temporal and spiritual interests" of the colonists and offensive to God'. The parish of Old Deer called for the sugar duties to be withdrawn in order not to uphold 'a system so injurious to moral feeling and so directly opposed to one of the first principles of Christianity', and sought the ending of slavery certainly in a manner 'compatible with the safety of all concerned', but not at a far distant time or 'gradually' but 'at the earliest period'.[13]

SOCIETIES, ASSEMBLIES AND CHURCHMEN ACTIVE IN THE CAUSE

The power-houses for the campaign during this period were without a doubt the abolition societies in the major cities. Not only did they organise mass petitions, they also printed pamphlets and appeals and key public figures were among their office-bearers. As in the campaign against the slave trade, Edinburgh had the strongest Committee, followed by Glasgow and Aberdeen. Alongside the public meetings organised by the societies, which could draw thousands of citizens, there were debates in the General Assembly of the Church of Scotland and the Synod of the United Associate Secession Church.

Shortly after the London Society was formed, Edinburgh followed suit with the claim to bring together all who, 'whatever differences of opinion they may entertain on other points', wish to put an end to 'this most grievous outrage on humanity', and characterised as its sole object 'the present and eternal interests of the negro population'. At its first annual meeting in February 1824, the Edinburgh Society resolved to petition and did that in March.[14]

Edinburgh's *Annual Report* requested that the House of Commons 'resume the consideration of the important question of the mitigation of slavery', and 'take such further steps as may seem to them expedient for carrying their unanimous resolution of last Session into effect'. In a series of resolutions, members of the Society congratulated the administration for 'promptly redeeming their pledge' and noted that Tobago, Nevis and St Kitts had responded positively to plans for improvement in the treatment of slaves. The Society strongly deprecated 'the rash and premature emancipation of the negroes', but also deplored 'the ill judged and intemperate opposition by some other of the Colonial legislatures' and warned that this would not only impede progress towards the moral and religious education of the slaves, but would also prove hazardous to the interests of the colonists by forcing the slaves to take matters into their own hands.[15] The Committee's recommendation to members was to accept the Canning proposals to the West Indies on the amelioration of slavery as embracing everything desirable in the present circumstances and to concentrate on campaigning to see them effectively implemented. However, frustration at the continual failure of this approach was soon to drive the Edinburgh Society towards a more urgent call for emancipation.

In January 1826, the Society held a public meeting chaired by the Earl of Rosebery. Key speeches were given by Committee members James Moncrieff and Henry Cockburn, both leading advocates. Moncrieff claimed that numerically there had never been such a large meeting and that those there formed an unprecedented representation of the nation. He then outlined slave conditions on the various islands. 'Hopes were entertained', he reminded them, 'that after the expression of the sentiments of the Government had been known, measures would have been taken for the gradual abolition of slavery, but how fallacious had these hopes been.[16] Henry Cockburn, in presenting the petition for agreement urged them to read a recent pamphlet produced by the anti-slavery movement drawn from the colonists' own sources, which he claimed presented a damning picture of slavery.[17] But perhaps the most telling point was made by Moncrieff early in the meeting. Although he granted that there were good masters and plantations where the slaves were well treated, 'was it not plain', he asked, 'that the power was in their hands? That one set of men were subjected to the power of another, their caprice, their passion, their selfishness; or that of their subordinate agents. It was the power that was the evil and it was to that, as to their most precious jewel, that the West Indian planters showed such an eagerness to cling.'[18] This recognition that slavery could not be reformed and the only way forward was to break the evil was to be developed in anti-slavery debates six years later. The implications of that, however, were a little premature in 1823.

In 1824, the Edinburgh Society published a pamphlet entitled *Considerations on Negro Slavery*, in which it sought to inform its members and other readers about the progress made towards amelioration. Detailing the colonial obstruction to the 1823 measures, it sounded a cautious note that the object of the associations in London and Edinburgh was to 'raise the character of the negroes, by religious instruction and by political regulations, as to gradually fit them for the enjoyment of personal freedom'. The pamphlet expressed the hope that the West Indies would gradually become a place that, 'like Scotland, has been taught to consider religion as the first and freedom as the next, blessing it has derived from the bounty of God'. Then its white population 'would see that it was not consistent with honour and duty to debar six hundred thousand of our fellow subjects from the slightest participation in these blessings'.[19]

A different note was found in the Society's pamphlet of 1826, entitled *The Necessity of Abolishing Negro Slavery Demonstrated*. It declared that recent communications from the West Indies indicated clearly 'that slavery will never be mitigated, much less abolished, but by the direct interference of Great Britain; and that all the means for securing this interference ought to be immediately employed'.[20]

The approach of the Glasgow Society was more cautious. It organised a petition in 1824 from 'The City and its vicinity', which sought 'the gradual abolition of slavery in the British Colonies.' But in February 1826, there was a strong feeling within the Committee that it would not be appropriate to call a public meeting at that time because of what they described as 'the unprecedented gloom that has spread itself over its [the city's] commercial interests'. Instead, they decided to advertise a petition in the newspapers, with copies made available for signing at various locations in the city. The Committee reassured the public that there was not the 'slightest abatement of their zeal in regard to the great cause on which they are embarked, but [the decision was made] solely from the consideration of the peculiar delicacy of the present situation'.

The lengthy petition itself reflected something of this caution. It rehearsed the commitments made by the government in 1823 and affirmed support for 'the attainment of these desirable ends in such ways as may not only consist with the real welfare of the slave population and the safety and benefit of the colonies, but they may also leave unanswered, no fair and equitable claim on the part of the proprietors'. However, it included a clause that recognised, as indeed the planters did, that the inevitable consequence of the extension of civil rights to slaves was 'the ultimate, though gradual, extinction of slavery'. Declaring the Government's own commitment to both as 'judicious and temperate', and recognising a 'determined and vigorous' enforcement of these measures, it nonetheless declared that 'having thus far been faithfully redeemed by a display of the most conciliatory deference to the Colonial Governments', it was time to meet the latter's complete disregard of the advice by being 'effective and vigorous'. The petition ended with the declaration that 'nothing can give [the measures] real and permanent efficiency short of some direct and authoritative interference of the Imperial Legislature'.

However much the Glasgow Society's action in 1826 appeared to be attempting to keep a wide spectrum of opinion on board, the size of the petition sent to Parliament in April represented a remarkable achievement for the Committee. The Earl of Rosebery, in presenting it, remarked that the 39,000 signatures appended to it represented a quarter of the city's population in a part of Britain that had a substantial West Indian connection, and that the total was only two thousand short of that of Manchester, for so long a pioneer in anti-slavery activity.[21] He might have added that it was in the same city where one of the principal newspapers, *Glasgow Courier*, vigorously represented the interests of the West Indian planters.

'The philanthropist and the Christian must be gratified by observing the zeal which is still displayed in this country for completing the work of abolishing slavery in the West Indies' – so wrote *The Scotsman* in January 1826, and it continued by claiming that 'on the 16th inst an example was set to the rest of Scotland by the Abolition Society of Aberdeen'. The meeting was described as 'numerously attended and ably conducted' and the resolution was perhaps the most strongly worded from any city in Scotland. It may well have been responsible for Aberdeenshire producing the bulk of the Scottish petitions in what was a thin year in 1828. The petition read:

That the system of slavery maintained in the West Indian and other colonies of Great Britain, which degrades many hundred thousands of our fellow men to the conditions of chattels, to be bought and sold at pleasure and frequently subjected to grievous oppression, appears to this meeting to be altogether incompatible with the indisputable rights of men, with the precepts of the Bible and with the principles of the British Constitution and is therefore altogether indefensible and ought to be speedily terminated.[22]

Congregations of the United Associate Secession Church produced a substantial proportion of the early petitions from Scotland. The Synod addressed the issue of slavery in 1823 and returned to it in 1829, when a committee was set up to report on progress. The 1823 motion called on Synod to not only express its 'deep abhorrence of slavery', but to recommend to the members 'and to those under their charge, to take all scriptural and habile means for turning the attention of the moral and religious public to this great evil and to the fittest means for its speedy abolition'. This proved a little too radical for the members of Synod at that time and an earlier motion proposing that a Committee be set up was carried in its place,[23] but the correspondent to the *Glasgow Chronicle* noted a fervent description of 'the horrors of the system in all its bearings' by two of its prominent ministers, Dr John Brown of Rose Street, Edinburgh and Rev. John Ritchie of Kilmarnock.[24] This was a prelude to a very substantial contribution to the campaign in the early 1830s, in which two Synodical petitions led the way for no less than 118 from individual congregations of the United Associate Secession Church.

The General Assembly of the Church of Scotland never petitioned against either the slave trade or slavery. In 1823, Principal Nicol, whilst claiming that he 'should feel exceedingly anxious that it [the abolition of slavery] could be done consistently with the peace of the country', resisted the idea that the Assembly should include the issue of slavery within the traditional loyal address to the King. Professor Jardine on the first day of the Assembly was unsuccessful in proposing that, but he returned with another motion for a separate address on this issue alone. It expressed satisfaction with 'the pledge given [by HM Government] that effective and decisive measures will be adopted for ameliorating the condition of the slave population so as ultimately to prepare them for the enjoyment and rights of British citizens', and continued to express the 'utmost confidence' of the Assembly that 'such preparatory steps will be commenced as early as possible'. Although during the debate there was considerable overlap in references and continued hesitation from some on the propriety of addressing the King on these issues of the slave trade and slavery, a committee was appointed to investigate the matter and the text was agreed five days later.[25]

The Assembly was not to debate the issue again that decade and this silence is perhaps the main reason why only four presbyteries and one synod petitioned during the period. Yet the Address to the Throne in 1823, albeit guarded and cautious, provided a marker for the Establishment to which it alone amongst churches in Scotland had access and the deliverance was copied to the Secretary of State for the Colonies.[26] The representative range of petitions from presbyteries and synods made them almost mini-Assemblies and that kind of activity was unparalleled in Britain, except for the very occasional Diocesan petition from England. Above all, the role of churchmen from different denominations in the anti-slavery cause was to be seen in their participation in the large public meetings in the cities and on the Committees of the Societies. In these ways, the Church of Scotland was as prominent as might be expected.

The Edinburgh Committee to supervise the presentation of the city's petition in 1814 included the current Moderator of the General Assembly, Dr David Ritchie of St Andrews Church, Rev. Andrew Thomson, Sir Henry Moncrieff Wellwood and four other ministers. Leith's committee numbered three Doctors of Divinity and was chaired by Dr David Johnston of the North Kirk, a Chaplain to the King. Dr Stevenson McGill, Thomas Chalmers' predecessor at the Tron Kirk, took a leading role in Glasgow that year, as did Dr Robert Balfour of St Paul's, continuing to support an issue that he had raised before his congregation in 1788. Paisley had three ministers on its committee, Dr John Findlay of the High Kirk, Rev. William Smart of the Abbey Close Burgher congregation and Rev. Jonathan Rankine, successor to Dr Snodgrass, who had been won over to abolition in 1792 by William Dickson.

When the new Societies were formed in the 1820s, Edinburgh had seven clergy on its Committee of twenty-seven. Most were Church of Scotland, but included on it were Rev. John Brown of the United Associate Secession Church and Rev. C. H. Terrot of the Scottish Episcopal Church, who presented the first *Annual Report* of the Society. The President was Dr Thomas Davidson of Muirhouse, Minister of the Tolbooth Kirk.[27] There is no record of Glasgow's Committee, but in gathering the substantial number of signatories in 1826, twenty ministers and congregations agreed that their vestries or session houses should be added to the eighteen shops at which copies of the petition would be held for public signatures.[28] Two academics who were also clergymen were prominent in the Aberdeen Committee at this time – Robert Hamilton, Professor of Natural Philosophy at

Marischal College since 1779 and President of the Society until 1829, and Rev. William Jack, Principal of King's, who was one of the Society's Vice-Presidents. At the founding of the Aberdeen Society in 1825, six of the Committee of seventeen were parish ministers and they included the Principal of Marischal College and minister of Greyfriars, Dr W. L. Brown, and Dr George Morison of Banchory, who at his death in 1845 was the longest-serving minister in the Kirk.[29] Although there were latterly a few Secessionist petitions from Aberdeenshire, throughout the campaigning years in Aberdeen all ministers active on the city's Committee belonged to the Church of Scotland.

ANDREW THOMSON AND THE IMMEDIATISM DEBATE IN 1830

On 8 October 1830, according to a report in *The Scotsman*, 'as numerous a meeting as could be', full of the 'respectable, enlightened and fashionable' citizens, took place in Edinburgh's Assembly Rooms.[30] The meeting was organised by what was then called the Edinburgh Society for the Promotion of the Abolition of Negro Slavery. The Lord Provost of the city was in the chair and a number of distinguished speakers had already paid tribute to the efforts of those such as William Wilberforce, Granville Sharp and Thomas Clarkson in the anti-slavery campaign, and to William Robertson and Adam Smith in the Scottish Enlightenment's attitude to slavery. Francis Jeffrey, Dean of the Faculty of Advocates, proposed a motion to petition Parliament for the abolition of colonial slavery 'at the earliest possible opportunity', and for legislation that would free all children born of slave parents after January 1831. These resolutions reflected the increasing public impatience with the slow speed of parliamentary action to end slavery, and the need to set a date to begin that process. The motion was seconded by Dr John Ritchie, of Potterrow. The stage was thus set for what would appear to be a unanimous call for the abolition of slavery.[31]

Then, to his feet rose Dr Andrew Thomson. The Chairman indicated that he should come up to the platform. William Cousin, a young eyewitness who was later to be minister in Duns, described the scene. 'It had been observed with amazement', he wrote, 'that Dr Thomson, of all men in the world, was not on the platform. But at last the well known face was seen rising from the body of the hall and was received with acclamation mingled here and there with some slight tokens of disapproval.' In response to the Lord Provost's invitation, he said, 'No, my Lord. I cannot come to the platform this time; I am going to speak against your resolutions.'[32]

Figure 10   *Dr Andrew Thomson (1778–1831). Portrait by George Watson in the* Biographical Dictionary of Eminent Scotsmen. © *The Trustees of the National Library of Scotland*

The reaction to this was described as 'the bursting of a bomb'. Thomson then began what was to be the first of two landmark speeches in the anti-slavery movement, by explaining his position. He described the resolutions as excellent and gave credit to the Committee. However, his reasons for opposition, he declared, were that they did not go far enough. To argue that abolition should take place 'at the earliest possible opportunity', for him, gave leave to the West Indian planters to extend its life indefinitely, and to set a date for the emancipation of children recognised the legitimacy of their parents' enslavement. He would move to insert the word 'immediately' in the resolution. 'I am astonished', he said, 'that anyone could acquiesce in the premises laid down, or in the soundness of the arguments we have heard, without seeing the necessity of immediate abolition.' And, according to one report, he turned to John Ritchie and 'twitted him' by suggesting that if he knew him aright, immediate emancipation would better serve his purpose than the gradual abolition suggested by the resolutions that he had supported.[33]

Another eyewitness, Henry Cockburn, the judge and literary figure, saw such a dispute as trivial. In his memoirs, Cockburn described the chaotic scene that followed, in which Thomson declared that if abolition meant the shedding of blood, it was a necessary price for ending the slavery of 800,000 human beings. The Lord Provost departed from the chair, with a declaration that, as chief magistrate of the city, he could not preside over a meeting where such sentiments were expressed and the meeting decided to reconvene on 19 October to petition for immediate abolition. 'After all', wrote Cockburn, 'the difference was verbal, for *immediate*, as explained, meant only *with all practical speed*, which was exactly what the cautious meant by gradual.'[34]

Was this a matter of semantics or was there a fundamental principle involved? Andrew Thomson was in no doubt that it was the latter, and although not nearly as hot-headed as many in the hall, he seized the moment that was to draw a line in the rather static sand of amelioration and move beyond it to a position that would have radical consequences for the abolition movement.

Exactly a week later, two notices appeared in *The Scotsman*. One announced a meeting in three days' time with a view to 'petitioning Parliament for immediate emancipation' and requesting all friendly to that object to attend. At the same time another was placed in the name of several of the old Committee, calling on support for 'the petition for the abolition of slavery at the earliest period at which it may be found practicable'. The subscribers argued that very many of the inhabitants of Edinburgh are 'of the same mind' in believing that it would be 'unsafe to grant immediate emancipation to 800,000 individuals', and stated that to press Parliament for this would be 'impolitic and injurious to the general cause of emancipation'.[35] Copies of that petition were made available in the Council Chamber, the Merchants House and in eleven shops.

On 19 October, the Assembly Rooms provided the venue for

what was again described as 'one of the largest and most respectable meetings we have ever seen in Edinburgh'. Rev. James Buchanan of Leith moved a series of resolutions on behalf of the Committee. These affirmed that slavery was contrary to natural rights, the British Constitution and revealed religion, and recognised that 'the voice of the British Nation both in and out of Parliament has been raised in vain'. No amelioration of a slave's condition', stated the resolutions, 'could ever make his bondage just' and 'no mitigation of his suffering should ever make it tolerable'. Therefore, they continued, 'the instant and unqualified abandonment of evil is absolutely demanded by the supreme and unbending principles of revealed truth' and the meeting agreed 'to petition the British Legislature for the immediate and total abolition of slavery throughout all the colonial dependencies of the Empire'.[36] One voice was raised in dissent, from a person with experience in the West Indies. He was ruled out of order by the Chairman on the grounds that the meeting was advertised for the sole purpose of promoting anti-slavery. The Chairman then called on Dr Thomson to propose the text of the petition to be sent to both Houses of Parliament.[37]

In the previous week before the meeting a letter that was highly critical of this new direction had appeared in several newspapers. It was from the celebrated Edinburgh phrenologist, George Combe. Combe claimed that 'among humane and enlightened men there cannot be two opinions about the necessity of abolishing slavery', but declined the invitation to attend the meeting since he regarded 'gradual emancipation as the only practical course'. His caution was, he claimed, based on a realistic view of human beings. 'Undoubtedly if man were a perfect being', he wrote, 'it would be safe as well as glorious and delightful, to discover the principles of justice and to carry them into complete execution.' From this, he argued, there was a need to prepare slaves for emancipation and, in the same way, to prepare the planters for such an act. Combe then accused advocates of immediate abolition of subverting West Indian society and of seeking 'a total revolution in the state of property in the colonies'. Although he admitted that property in human beings sat uneasily with justice and with the divine order, he concluded that this justice was, in the light of human imperfection, 'an abstract principle'.[38]

Andrew Thomson replied directly to these arguments not in the press, but in a speech that formed the centrepiece of that meeting in the Assembly Rooms on 19 October. In the early part of his remarks, Thomson responded on the question of property. He claimed that the proposition that 'man cannot hold property in man' was self-evident, and the absurdity of the reverse would lead logically to blacks holding whites in slavery, 'a doctrine which as soon as it is carried into operation, breaks up the whole frame of society and reduces all things into absolute anarchy and confusion'. He proposed, however, to concentrate on the examination of the 'abstract principle for which we contend'.[39]

In a sermon published in 1829, Thomson had spoken of the danger of separating spiritual and temporal freedom, of portraying blessings and evils as words of 'mere vague and general import' rather than 'definite and impressive', and above all of concluding that ideas of slavery in the Bible are abstract and not concrete. 'When our Lord spake of false teachers', he affirmed, 'he did not say that they would be *like* wolves in sheep's clothing, but he spake of them as though they had been these animals themselves.'[40] Continuing this theme in his speech, Thomson cited the views of a Mr Hinds in Barbados, who claimed that 'all the evils of slavery are abstract and all its blessings positive'. He suggested that this might be the source of Combe's contention and continued,

> What he calls an abstract principle, is nothing more nor less than this, that to make any man a slave, or to keep him a slave, is to violate his essential rights – to transgress eternal justice – to break the first laws of religion and morality. There is nothing abstract in this . . . To adopt the views which Mr. Combe seems to avow, would in my opinion, lay every moral obligation at the feet of worldly expediency . . . That we should obey the will of the Almighty and that we should not continue to do what he has forbidden, is not an abstract principle – it is a concrete principle, for ever dwelling in the Christian's mind, pressing upon his conscience and influencing his conduct. Slavery – being in direct hostility to that will and an impious defiance of it – is a crime which must be immediately and unreservedly abandoned, as much at least as any other species of criminality whatever.[41]

When Thomson turned to the subject of mitigation, such a central part of abolitionist and government strategy in the 1820s, he argued that it had not only been minimal and ineffective, but a dangerous diversion. It both furnished the slave-owners with a delaying tactic and at the same time deluded the public into believing that effective steps to abolition were being taken. Although he did not deny 'that the evils of practical slavery can be lessened' and welcomed any relief to the slaves, he characterised slavery as a malignant disease. Thomson began then to reach his most radical conclusions about slavery, literally going to its foundations. With a flourish he described the institution as a 'sepulchre, full of dead mens' bones and all uncleanness', remaining so, however much the sepulchre was white-washed and adorned with flowers. He then gave a verbal picture that was to be translated into graphic illustration and borrowed by later generations of abolitionists on both sides of the Atlantic:

> Why, Sir, slavery is the very Upas tree of the moral world, beneath whose pestiferous shade all intellect languishes and all virtue dies. And if you would get rid of the evil, you must go more thoroughly and effectively to work than you can ever do by these palliatives, which are included under the term 'mitigation.' The foul sepulchre must be taken away. The cup of oppression must be dashed to the ground. The pestiferous tree must be cut down and eradicated; it must be, root and branch of it, cast into the con-suming fire and its ashes scattered to the four winds of heaven. It is thus that you must deal with slavery. You must annihilate it, – annihilate it now, – and annihilate it for ever.[42]

At the beginning of the meeting, James Buchanan alluded to a pam-phlet written in 1826 by Dr Thomas Chalmers, now Professor of Moral Philosophy St Andrews. Chalmers had commended a scheme suggested by a West Indian planter whereby slaves could earn their freedom in seven or eight years by voluntary labour, for which the planters would be compensated by the Government. Buchanan, in rejecting this, maintained that freedom was an absolute birthright of every British subject. In his speech, Thomson warmly supported Buchanan and opposed not only the idea that 'freedom must be wrought out by your paying a price for it', but also that compensa-tion should be paid. 'We have been subjected to a kind of poll-tax to uphold their iniquitous system', he claimed and continued: 'if com-pensation is still proposed as a *sine qua non*, I appear in the name of the slave, who is surely the most aggrieved party in this case and is entitled to compensation before all others'.[43]

The absolute clarity with which Thomson saw divine sanction for human freedom was matched by his perception of slavery as sin. 'For if it be unlawful, iniquitous and unchristian, to steal a man and force him into bondage', he declared, 'it must be equally unlawful, iniquitous and unchristian to retain him in that state, whether he has been purchased, or received as a gift, or got by inheritance, or obtained in any other way whatever.'[44] But in his concern to convince his opponents of the urgency of abolition, Thomson had to take into account the fact of slavery in the Bible. During his sermon *Slavery not Sanctioned*, he granted that permission was given in the Old Testament to practise it in some circumstances, but claimed both that it was limited in time and to a particular people, and that God's deliverance of the Israelites from Egypt demonstrated the real core of divine will.[45] Writing in *The Christian Instructor*, he challenged the anti-abolitionists who claimed authority from the Old Testament not to be conveniently selective and to remember that a Hebrew slave-owner must pay for any violence done to the slave by emancipation, an interesting concept for the West Indians.[46] In his October 1830 speech, whilst conceding that slavery was not forbidden in the New Testament, he pointed out that Paul did not attack the patently evil tyrant Nero nor condemn the Roman practice of putting deformed children to death. Instead, he fastened on the Great Commandment and asked 'do we follow this golden rule, or do we despise it, when we make others slaves? . . . is it a token of brotherly affection – is it not a contempt of the very phrase, when we retain anyone, who is bone of our bone and flesh of our flesh, in the condition of a slave?'[47]

For Christians, according to Thomson, two further factors needed to be recognised. First, that the slave had a soul 'for which, as for ours, the Saviour died and which, like ours, is destined for immortality'. If that was acknowledged, then the consequences were radical, since slavery struck at the roots of the faith.[48] The second was the increasingly accepted concern with the absolute power of the slave-owners and its damaging effects, not only on the slaves, but also on their masters. No doubt there were merciful and kindly slave-owners, but Thomson's realistic understanding of human nature led him to warn 'that absolute power must be abused where it is held and exercised for purposes of aggrandizement'.[49]

All these arguments were the basis on which Andrew Thomson gave his forthright call for immediate abolition. The logic was two-fold. If slavery was a sin and a violation of divine law, just as mitigation or amelioration was no substitute for destruction, any delay in bringing it to an end was unacceptable. Consequently, for him:

We are bound to make no delay in hastening out of the transgression and putting an end to it, wherever it has obtained a foothold in our dominions. To say that we will come out of sin by degrees – that we will only forsake it slowly and step by step – that we will pause and hesitate and look well around us before we consent to abandon its gains and pleasures . . . that we will postpone the duty of 'doing justly and loving mercy,' till we have removed every petty difficulty out of the way, and got all the conflicting interests that are involved in the measure reconciled or satisfied; – to say this is to trample on the demands of moral obligation, and to disregard the voice that speaks to us from heaven. The path of duty is plain before us; and we have nothing to do but to enter it at once, and to walk in it without turning to the right hand or to the left. Our concern is not with the result that may follow our obedience to the divine will. Our great and primary concern is to obey that will. God reigns over His universe in the exercise of infinite perfection: He commands us to let the oppressed go free and to break every yoke.[50]

Andrew Thomson regarded no price too high to achieve abolition. At the close of his three-hour speech he stood by the statement that had led to the Lord Provost's withdrawal from the chair twelve days previously. If he was still to be pushed on the issue of insurrection and bloodshed, albeit 'more indebted to fancy than to fact', he agreed that he would accept that. *Fiat justitia ruat coelum* once again found a place in abolitionist rhetoric. 'Righteousness, Sir,' he proclaimed, 'is the pillar of the universe. Break down that that pillar and the universe falls into ruin and desolation', continuing: 'if there must be violence, let it come. Give me the hurricane rather than the pestilence.' He ended:

> Give me that hurricane, infinitely rather than the noisome pestilence, whose path is never crossed, whose silence is never disturbed, whose progress is never arrested by one sweeping blast from the heavens; which walks peacefully and sullenly through the length and breadth of the land, breathing poison into every heart . . . and which from day to day and year to year, with intolerant and interminable malignancy, sends its thousands and thousands and its tens of thousands into the ever-yawning and never-satisfied grave.[51]

When Thomson sat down, *The Scotsman* reported 'cheering and waving of hats for several minutes'. A Mr Maclean from the Methodist Church seconded the petition, which was unanimously adopted. The Society was renamed The Edinburgh Society for the Abolition of Negro Slavery to reflect the shift in policy before 'the immense assembly then dispersed from the hall, all apparently highly gratified'.[52] He had indeed carried all before him. Not the least of his achievements that night had been to move the formation of a Ladies Association and to ensure that a committee was nominated. The wind of change was blowing strongly.

It has been said that Andrew Thomson 'moved to an immediatist view on slavery because of his position on personal accountability',[53] but that is not by any means the full story. In common with other Evangelicals, he held individual accountability to God very highly and his sense of individual sin was strong. But he was equally attuned to the corporate sin of a system and had a very strong grasp of the practical and political realities that kept it in place. His espousal of the cause of abolition was far more driven by human concern for justice than by the hidden agenda of the salvation of souls, a charge that was often laid at Wilberforce's door. Of course he prayed devoutly for the salvation of planters and slaves, and there is no doubt that his evangelical faith was the mainspring that inspired his abolitionism. But it is inadequate to cite one theological doctrine as the explanation of a radical political position.

Only four months after the October meetings, Dr Thomson died of a heart attack. We can only speculate on what his contribution might eventually have been to the abolitionist cause in the 1830s; but one historian claims that the publication of his speech 'probably did more to push the British movement into its immediatist phase than any other publication'.[54] Another wrote that it was his 'fire and brimstone speech' that provided an ideology for later abolitionists in the 1830s.[55] But for his intervention and subsequent oratory on 8 October 1830, there is little doubt that the Edinburgh Society would have settled for a considerably trimmed policy.

A THEOLOGICAL ATTEMPT TO PUT THE BRAKES ON

'That slavery should have ever been permitted to exist under the sanction of Britain is itself a fact deeply humiliating to our national pride.' The words could apply to many a sermon, speech, or petition at this time. They were in fact in the introduction to a series of letters to the Colonial Secretary, George Murray, that appeared in the pages of the *Dumfries and Galloway Courier* in 1829 and were published in pamphlet form the following year. The author, Dr Henry Duncan, was the founder and editor of the newspaper and the minister of Ruthwell Parish Church, and he would later be Moderator of the Kirk's General Assembly. Duncan claimed to have 'entertained only one desire on the subject of slavery from an early age' and that was for 'the final emancipation of the Africans'. Such an avowal was perhaps a necessary preface to a published collection that marked him not only as a gradual abolitionist, but gave much support to those who continued to resist emancipation and to use biblical and theological arguments to do so.

For all his earlier statement, Duncan claimed that the call by abolitionists to 'once and for all wash this foul stain' was an emotional one that assumed that the very institution was an offence to God. He argued that the law of Moses 'not only permitted but sanctioned by express statute, the holding of heathen slaves' and even allowed perpetual slavery 'amongst the chosen people themselves'. Nothing in the New Testament, he claimed, condemned slavery. He pointed out that the Greek word *doulos*, used by Jesus and translated as 'servant', in fact meant 'slave' and claimed that if St Paul had asked Philemon to manumit Onesimus it would be as a favour, not a Christian obligation. From this Duncan went on to argue that slaves were unfit for freedom. The example of Haiti was held up, wherein 'the demolishing influence of free revolutionary principles' gave rise to 'wild and brutal passions'. After the revolution there, he claimed, former slaves had to be driven to work at the point of a bayonet. For him, reports from Sierra Leone showed the necessity of 'coerced labour' and a recent dispatch from Demerara indicated that liberated slaves spent their time in idleness and petty theft.

Duncan's fourth and fifth letters argued that considerable progress had taken place in 'the improvement of the negro race' within the last few years in the West Indies. His source was Alexander Barclay and he claimed that religious education, church attendance and baptism had increased whilst the use of flogging and working in chains decreased. Duncan ascribed this to a change in the character of many of the planters and their agents, who, 'far from being tyrants, are rapidly becoming the benevolent protectors of slaves'. For him, the policy of amelioration had made great strides and emancipation would not be long delayed. But his concern for what he saw as the disastrous economic state of the West Indian colonies led him to advocate caution by the British Government in its dealings with the planters. For Duncan, the planters' prejudices against the missionaries had all but disappeared and the 'sweeping censures' ignored the many examples of good slave-owners. He recommended a committee of inquiry into the state of the West Indian colonies, but maintained that it was 'the duty of government to abstain as much as possible from direct interference with the internal regulation of West Indian affairs' and to 'confine itself to friendly advice and gentle guidance'.[56]

There were two long reviews in response to Henry Duncan's letters in the anti-slavery *Christian Instructor*. The first appeared in the January 1831 edition and was the last written contribution to the cause of immediate emancipation made by Andrew Thomson before his death the following month. Duncan delayed his response until the end of March out of respect for the memory of his 'much valued and deeply lamented friend, by whose ardent, sensitive and uncompromising mind the critic was indicted'.[57]

Thomson claimed that Duncan, whilst proclaiming his opposition to slavery, allowed himself to be used by its defenders. Although he did not question Duncan's desire for emancipation, he found it 'an unfortunate proof of this that he has published a work which has been hailed and eulogised by those whose interests and prepositions are favourable to slavery'. Thomson noted how the letters had been eulogised in the *West India Reporter* and questioned whether the funds of the West India Association, often expended to promote the anti-abolitionist campaign, were used in printing and distributing them.

Thomson then turned to the plea made in *Presbyter's Letters* for citizens to look at the subject from all sides and not be swayed by emotional statements heard at 'fervid speeches delivered at public meetings' and in 'the *ex parte* statements of tracts and periodical publications'. 'Does the Doctor', he asked, 'recollect a meeting that was called at Dumfries some time ago for the purpose of petitioning Parliament against slavery?' He challenged Duncan to recall who it was that 'made a fervent speech to extinguish its fervour and to break it up and to frustrate its holy purpose'.

But the core of the *Instructor*'s review rested on a theological critique. The question of slavery was, for Thomson, 'a religious and moral question', and he claimed that political issues were subordinate to that. Duncan was criticised for devoting too much space in the *Letters* to 'worldly interests and pecuniary consequences – to determine what ought to be done by the maxims of secular expediency'. Only a few pages were to be found, in the second letter, taking up the question of a biblical and theological approach to the subject. Such marginalisation, for Thomson, had led to 'so much bad theology, so many misinterpretations of scripture' given by the 'Anti-Abolitionists and by the Gradualists – between whom there is a very suspicious agreement on this point'.

For Thomson, it was obvious that God had given liberty as one of the 'natural rights'. The Bible, he claimed, proceeded on this recognition, giving no general allowance to slavery – 'far less does it give allowance to the white men in our colonies to enslave their black brethren'. Thomson examined the Old Testament in detail, concluding that when slavery was found, it was permitted only within particular contexts and hedged round by safeguarding laws relating to manumission, by the year of jubilee when freedom was granted and by the strict prohibition in Exodus 21 against any violence done towards slaves. He took issue with Duncan over the latter's refusal to condemn planters and slave-owners as sinners. For him, this was fallacious. Even if they had taken no part in the capture and transporting of African slaves, for Thomson 'they have been buyers or receivers of stolen goods'. The 'essence of the sin', he wrote, was 'every successive hour that they [the slaves] are held and deprived of their natural liberty'.[58]

Duncan made a rather weak, if lengthy, response to the review. He repeated his plea for recognising planters and merchants as 'men of liberal education and enlightened understandings'. The present West Indian proprietor, he claimed, 'is surrounded on all sides with influences and connections which tend to enlighten his mind and lead him to view the system of slavery in its true light.' He therefore asked their opponents to treat them with 'tenderness and feeling' and with 'proper allowances to be made for their natural prejudices.' Duncan stood by his assertion that slavery 'only becomes sinful when it is inconsistent with the temporal or spiritual welfare of the bondman', but agreed with the reviewer that the logic of this is that 'the system may be innocently perpetuated'. If slavery cannot be permitted under any circumstances, he wrote, and if 'it be admitted that the relation between master and slave is, like blasphemy, perjury and murder, sinful in itself, the whole argument must be conceded and nothing remains for the Christian but immediate, absolute, unconditional manumission without consideration of the consequences'.[59]

A second review of *Presbyter's Letters* appeared in the September 1831 issue of the *Christian Instructor* some months after Thomson's death. This one also dealt with the New Testament and slavery, but with rather a different emphasis. The reviewer argued that the lack of explicit condemnation of slavery in the gospels was more than compensated for by the general teaching of Jesus. In contrast to the specific and literal meaning that Thomson gave to freedom in the gospel, this new reviewer claimed that Jesus avoided judgements on questions of society and gave his disciples 'no power to regulate the usages of society by positive *precept*'. This seemed to dilute the case against slavery. The reviewer's assertion that St Paul in the New Testament only sent back the slave Onesimus because Philemon was a Christian, and thus the Deuteronomic prohibition against returning runaway slaves did not apply, simply muddied the waters.

The reviewer was on stronger ground, however, when he challenged Duncan's optimistic view of amelioration and preparation for freedom. Any improvement in the condition of the slaves, he argued, had come as the result of pressure and coercion. He claimed that few of the planters were active Christians and detailed some of the worse recent cases of cruelty towards slaves, including the infamous case of Rev. George Bridges of Jamaica, who had been accused of viciously beating his slave.[60] Duncan's plea for non-interference and gradual improvement, said the reviewer, simply echoed the views of the planters, few of whom seriously resisted the idea of eventual emancipation.

FERVOUR AND REACTION AS THE TEMPERATURE RISES

The Edinburgh meetings were both catalyst for and reflection of considerable public fervour in the cause of abolition. Between September 1830 and April 1831, Scotland sent 388 petitions to Parliament, 56 of which went to both Houses. They represented more than 7 per cent of the British and Irish total. Although the majority called for immediate abolition, there were many that had a gradualist flavour. Dissenting voices were heard in church circles, in the press and from the Glasgow West India Association. But nationally, there was a new mood of optimism when the Whig Government under Lord Grey, which replaced the Tories in November 1830, promised some break with the inertia on slavery of the previous seven years.

The Edinburgh petition for immediate abolition was signed by 25,000 inhabitants and the counter-petition calling for gradual abolition received only 1,000 names.[61] Other major cities soon followed. Aberdeen decided to petition on 27 October, Paisley on 1 November and Glasgow on 11 November. Zachary Macaulay in the *Anti-Slavery Reporter* observed 'with great satisfaction, that this cause has been advocated by the ministers of religion, in that country, both of the established Church and other denominations' and, noting that they had kept the issue apart from party politics, he reported that the clergy had 'come forward prominently at this important conjuncture, to instruct and arouse the people under their charge to petition the legislature'. Macaulay detailed the activity of the three Church of Scotland synods and eight presbyteries but he added: 'it is but justice to notice that the United Synod of the Scottish Secession Church, representing upwards of three hundred congregations, led the way, as a religious body, in this work of justice and mercy'.[62]

Nearly a third of the secessionist congregations petitioned. Petitions also came from dissenting congregations in Perth, Tillicoultry and Pittenweem, five Independent churches, thirty-two Methodist and three Baptist congregations. They were joined by fifty towns and villages. Eight petitions were sent by dignitaries in the community from Kirkwall to Ayr, one from a political union in Auchtermuchty and two from the Ladies of Inverurie.

The Secession Presbytery of Cupar pre-empted the Synod in August of that year by passing a motion that called on Parliament for 'immediate and extensive abolition of slavery' and urged that members would 'use their influence to interest their respective neighbourhoods in the same great cause', thus spreading the pressure for abolition.[63] By November, the word 'immediate' was inserted more frequently in petitions from secessionist congregations, those from Crail, St Andrews, Dunblane, Kirkwall and Edinburgh Potterrow combining it with the words 'utter extinction' and 'total'. The Stirling congregation spoke of 'sweeping away that abomination slavery' because this was the only right course 'due to the common feelings of humanity and to those eternal laws of justice, the observance of which can alone exalt a nation.' There was a slightly different tone from some parts of the country deeply involved in Caribbean commerce. The petitions from Leith Kirkgate and Aberdeen cautiously spoke of preparing the way for emancipation 'as soon as shall be practicable', and Peterhead spoke of abolition being achieved 'consistently with the interests of all parties concerned'. But far from being concerned about protecting the interests of the planters' party, some congregations expressed scepticism over the now openly discussed proposals for compensation. St James's Paisley, added to its petition the hope that 'no claim of compensation shall be conceded by this House on any pretended right of property in the slave' and that 'no compensation shall be awarded on any ground or pretence whatsoever, 'till the abolition of slavery has been effected and the system of free labour honestly and fairly tried'.

Civic petitions tended to be more cautious than those from the churches. Arbroath's Town Council asked for a 'feasible plan for emancipation' to be devised within the present Parliament, and the inhabitants of Tames in Aberdeenshire requested 'more decisive measures than have hitherto been taken' to 'convince the colonists that slavery must quit'. The Magistrates of Dunfermline, a town known for constant petitioning on slavery, felt it necessary to preface theirs with a concern for the interests of all parties.[64]

The 1830 General Assembly did not find any place to discuss slavery, but clear calls were made between October and November from the largest synods and a number of presbyteries for urgent steps to be taken towards emancipation. The Synod of Glasgow and Ayr sought 'the most decisive and effectual measures' to secure slavery's 'early and utter extinction', action that was commended at Glasgow's public meeting several days later.[65] The Presbytery of Brechin later in the month called for 'immediate measures for a speedy and effective abolition' and on the same day that of Tain, from where the West Indian interest had publicly showed itself in 1824, petitioned both Houses for 'early and total abolition'. Forres lamented the resistance of the planters to any improvement, declared the system directly opposed to natural rights and 'the spirit of the holy religion of which they are teachers'. The petitioners prayed to God and invited 'all their people to unite with them' to 'direct and incline' the nation's rulers to adopt the best methods of 'speedily delivering the captive from his miseries' and the nation from its guilt in continuing a system of 'such aggravated injustice and cruelty'.[66]

Most petitions were agreed without any controversy. An exception was the Synod of Lothian and Tweedale, which agreed on 9 November to petition both Houses of Parliament. The Synod incorporated seven presbyteries, including that of Edinburgh, and many of its members were present at the public meetings in the city. When Andrew Thomson moved that Synod petition Parliament 'to adopt without delay such measures as in their wisdom they may deem requisite for effectually securing the abolition and extinction of slavery', Dr John Inglis, minister of Old Greyfriars, moved an amendment praying for Parliament to pass a bill abolishing slavery 'with as much expedition as may be consistent with a due regard to the well being of the parties concerned'.

Prior to Dr Inglis' motion another attempt was made to counter Andrew Thomson. Rev. John Elliott of Peebles argued that in the present excitement on reform, it would be irresponsible to stir up another issue in Parliament; and Rev. James Robertson of Livingston seconded him on the grounds that Church of Scotland ministers had no right to 'meddle in politics' – they should confine their activities to the kingdom 'not of this world'. Inglis argued that God's permitting slavery by the Jews meant that the theological rejection of any grounds for property in men was invalid. He was totally opposed to slavery and had campaigned against the trade, but rejected any pressure for immediate abolition. Despite this opposition, Thomson's original motion was carried by twenty-three votes to seven. Following the vote, dissent was recorded by Dr Inglis, Dr John Sommers of Mid-

Calder and Rev. John Somerville of Currie on the grounds of an unwillingness to declare slavery as an offence to God that involved national guilt and the danger of premature emancipation before the interests of slaves and planters were guaranteed.[67]

Zachary Macaulay's observation that the most prominent activists in the campaign were clergy, was also born out in the public meetings that took place on the other side of the country. The principal speakers at the Glasgow meeting were Dr Ralph Wardlaw, a leading Independent minister, who was to play a major role in the Glasgow Emancipation Society in the 1830s and Dr Patrick Macfarlane whose remarks led to the dispute with James McQueen in the columns of the *Glasgow Courier*. In Paisley the key figure was Dr Robert Burns of St George's, later prominent in campaigns against American slavery and one of ten ministers on the newly formed Committee of sixteen charged with petitioning.[68] These ministers, along with Andrew Thomson and John Ritchie, were targeted by sectors of the press that were hostile to immediate abolition.

William Motherwell, who succeeded McQueen as editor of the *Glasgow Courier*, maintained the same pro-slavery policy and, according to one author, replaced the lack of McQueen's first-hand knowledge with 'imagination and rhetoric.'[69] The *Courier* prefaced its report on the first Edinburgh meeting by describing it as 'a stain upon the character of the nation – a stain upon her church establishment', and suggested that it was perhaps not surprising that 'in a city disgraced by the systematic murders of Burke and Hare, a miserable fraction of its population would be found to proclaim robbery and massacre as law and religion.' The main attack focused on John Ritchie. Ritchie's anti-slavery activity in his previous charge in Kilmarnock had brought him into conflict with McQueen and Motherwell here declared that the man who seconded resolutions to 'deprive the British subjects of their lawful property without consent and without compensation' was 'our old Anti-colonial friend who properly removed from Kilmarnock to Edinburgh for a higher stipend.' Two days later, the *Courier* reviewed a sermon preached by Ritchie on the death of George IV, commenting that 'he expatiates at considerable length and in his usual rough and violent way on the thread-bare evils of slavery' and that his radical changes proposed in the light of the St Domingue experience either show that he is 'ranting ignorantly' or 'gives proof of a hardness of heart and a misanthropic feeling, which ill accords with the character of a divine'.[70]

Ritchie had of course seconded the 'gradualist' resolutions on

6 October and had asked Thomson to withdraw his amendment. He had also apologised to the Lord Provost, an action that Thomson saw as unnecessary. On 19 October, Ritchie sat next to Thomson on the platform and moved a congratulatory address, using it to explain his change in position. He had been willing previously, he said, to take the lesser good when the greater could not be obtained, but now 'when he saw that 20/- in place of 10/- in the pound had been offered' he needed to accept the larger sum. This had represented for him not so much a shift as an awakening, which he attributed to Andrew Thomson for whom he felt, in his own words, 'an admiration only short of idolatry'.[71] The mantle was to fall on his shoulders all too soon, with the sudden death of his mentor.

Andrew Thomson was always the focus of the strongest press attacks, although he was staunchly supported by *The Scotsman*. The *Courier* claimed, on the authority of the *Edinburgh Evening Post*, that he had 'filched his anti-slavery speech' from papers of Lord Erskine and spoke of 'literary plundering'. It also focused on Paisley Presbytery and on the speeches by Burns there and in the town. In its report of the public meeting, the editor noted that the Provost and civic officials had declined to be present and commented: 'elsewhere it will be seen that in *slavish* imitation of the big-wigs of Edinburgh, the smaller ones of Paisley have had a meeting on negro emancipa-tion . . . to us it seems incredible that just dealing and right feeling men should lend their support'. As if to buttress that, a letter from 'A lover of Justice as well as Humanity' was published in the paper the next month. It was given the editorial heading 'Observations on the Paisley Presbytery Intermeddling with the Slave Emancipation Question', and the author repeated the call for clergy to refrain from discussing political questions in church courts whilst painting a picture of slaves living in the West Indies in conditions far superior to workers in the cotton mills, 'who are loud in their calls and petitions for emancipation'. He complained that the *Courier*, in reporting the Presbytery Meeting, had given prominence to Dr Burns. Far from being 'a tool in the hands of Dr Thomson', the writer claimed that Burns deemed himself as great a man as Thomson or Chalmers, and that his proposals in Presbytery were a platform to secure 'a hitch for a Glasgow or Edinburgh Church'.[72]

The Paisley meeting and the discussion surrounding is a good guide to the temperature and effectiveness of the abolition debate in 1830. Paisley had a strong tradition of petitioning against the slave trade and slavery, combined with a formidable number of radical political and trades groups. All this led to caution on the part of the burgh leaders, although an immediatist position was taken by the church-men in the majority on the Anti-Slavery Committee. Burns' uncom-promising position did not command the support of them all. He admitted that he differed from many of his best friends on the ques-tion of compensation and pled for a strengthening of the resolutions which, in order to gain the support of many at the meeting, were in danger of extracting from them 'the very pith and marrow' of their purpose. In the end, the petition from Paisley called for 'immediate amelioration of the state of the slaves and for the speedy and entire abolition of slavery' – hardly the most radical call in Scotland.[73] It therefore reflected the distance still to be travelled. Although Andrew Thomson's call for 'immediate abolition' marked a watershed from which there could be no return, and those churchmen who followed were to form the key leadership of the campaign, there was still much work to be done.

THE WIDER PICTURE – ANTI-SLAVERY IN THE CONTEXT OF POPULAR CAMPAIGNING

In her analysis of Britain in the long eighteenth century, Linda Colley claimed that the ending of the war with France freed Britons to con-sider fundamental changes in the political system. Many issues that had been suppressed in the interests of patriotism and a united front against the common threat now came to the fore. The Union with Ireland in 1800 inevitably raised the question of citizenship rights for the majority of the population there, and in turn challenged the con-tinuing legal disadvantages suffered by Roman Catholics in Britain. Parliamentary reform and the extension of the franchise beyond the limited few citizens with the wealth and property to qualify had been suppressed during the war years, but now surfaced again. In an expanding Empire, which many saw as extending the benefits of British values to millions worldwide, the question of how British sub-jects could also be slaves needed to be addressed.[74]

All three issues were addressed by legislation within a space of four years. Catholic Emancipation was secured in 1829, the Reform Bill passed in 1832 and slavery in the British Empire was abolished in 1833. It would be tempting to see all these as the results of a common groundswell of public fervour for democratic progress that translated itself into an unprecedented volume of petitions to Parliament from most corners of the United Kingdom. But the pattern was much more complex and at times contradictory. These three issues were not the only ones attracting a substantial expression of public opinion. At the same time that petitions against the European slave trade were flooding in, nearly two hundred others sought Government support for the establishment of Christian missions in India, a cause which Wilberforce and the Clapham Sect promoted with even more fervour than abolition of the slave trade. Moreover, on one issue the tide went the other way. In 1829, three times as many petitions against Catholic Emancipation reached the House of Commons as those in favour of it, and many came from the same churches and trades guilds that had called for the abolition of slavery. This was not a purely Scottish phenomenon. Despite a strong reaction to Catholic Emancipation in Scotland – which included numerous petitions from Glasgow and Dundee, two from Church of Scotland synods and seven from presbyteries – Scotland's share of the petitions from the United Kingdom totalled a mere two per cent, a far smaller proportion of the national total than in most of the petitioning years on slavery.

There was, though, perhaps more common ground on reform and anti-slavery. For all the reports of mass meetings for reform throughout the country, the figure of approximately 3,000 petitions to Parliament in the session 1830–1 was more than matched by those in excess of 5,000 praying for the abolition of slavery. Certainly Scotland's 231 reform petitions to the House of Lords in the 1830–1 session over against 174 for abolition represented a higher percentage of those from the whole of the United Kingdom. But there were significant differences in origin and content.

The petitions from Scotland in 1830–1 that advocated reform came overwhelmingly from the leading civic figures such as burgesses, councillors and magistrates, and from the trades guilds. Although there were a few that were generally from the inhabitants of towns, none came from churches and there was very limited evidence of the clergy being involved. The petitions for reform exemplified what Stana Nenadic has described as a collective approach of the middle-class, using an orderly and business-like method that avoided 'an overt threat to the interests of property'.[75] By contrast, the anti-slavery petitions came overwhelmingly from congregations, and secessionist and dissenting ones at that. A fair proportion of them were from inhabitants of towns and some from political unions. Although many of these would also have been middle-class in origin, those who signed indicated a much wider spectrum than that.

Second, despite the dispute between gradual and immediate abolition, the anti-slavery petitions all shared a common goal in seeking the
end of that institution. The principles of humanity enunciated and
demands for justice made were espoused by all, except in petitions
from those who had property or commercial interests, in the West
Indies. By contrast, the issues of reform and the franchise directly concerned personal and group interests, and these varied greatly. Few
from Scotland argued for a general reform of Parliament. That was
perhaps hardly surprising, though. Bruce Lenman has pointed out that
the bulk of Westminster attention was directed to the English Reform
Bill and Scotland's parallel bill involved a more radical shake-up of the
system, with the franchise monopoly of the old town councils being
ended.[76] A number petitioned for amendments to the Scottish Royal
Burghs, with several, such as Peebles and Selkirk, expressing anxiety
about losing their MP and declaring themselves opposed to the current
proposals. The Universities of Edinburgh and St Andrews also sought
additional representation for themselves.

By the early 1830s, the anti-slavery movement in Scotland was in
as good shape as anywhere in the United Kingdom. It never reached
the heights of the 1792 petition campaign, but it played a significant
part in the British campaign. In the light of all the other issues pressing their claims in the political realm, and the renewed attack by West
Indian interests in Scotland, that was no small achievement. Although
it is true that in 1829 no petitions for abolition from Scotland were
received by Parliament, only six were sent that year from England,
Wales and Ireland. The seven petitions in 1832 would seem to indicate a falling away of interest, but they still represented 5 per cent of
the British total. That was the year of election for the first reformed
Parliament, when considerable activity took place in securing pledges
on slavery from prospective MPs. The next avalanche of petitions
would follow in the first Parliamentary session in 1833. A slave revolt
in Jamaica was forcing Scottish missionaries there to be more forthright on slavery and, as Andrew Thomson had predicted, widespread
talk of compensation at home signalled the inevitability of emancipation. Yet the compromises made in order to secure the passage of
the bill in 1833 were to result in further obstruction to real emancipation. Even after 1833, a new combination of theological decon-
struction, political organisation, public meeting and debate and
parliamentary pressure was needed finally to rid the West Indies of
slavery.

Notes

1 This handwritten note is in my possession.
2 *Substance of the Debate in the House of Commons on the 15th May 1823 on a Motion for the Mitigation and Gradual Abolition of Slavery throughout the British Dominions* (London, 1823), p. 21.
3 *EEC*, 10 Jul 1823.
4 *Substance of the Debate on Abolition*, pp. 11, 19–20.
5 F. J. Klingberg, *The Anti-Slavery Movement in England* (New Haven, CT, 1968), pp. 211–17.
6 Klingberg, *The Anti-Slavery Movement*, pp. 228–9.
7 *GCH*, 15 May 1823.
8 William Wilberforce, *An Appeal to the Religion, Justice and Humanity of the Inhabitants of the British Empire on behalf of the Negro Slaves in the West Indies* (London, 1823).
9 Synod of the United Associate Church, Minutes, 14 May 1823. NAS CH3/298/1.
10 *JHC*, 20 Jun, 2 Jul, 10 Jul 1823.
11 *CM*, 27 Mar 1826.
12 Synod of Merse and Teviotdale, Minutes, 26 Apr 1826. NAS CH2/265/6; Presbytery of North West England, Minutes, 11 Apr 1826. NAS CH2/367/1.
13 *JHL*, Vol. 60, 11 Jul 1828.
14 *EEC*, 10 Jul 1823, *JHC*, Vol. 79, 15 March 1824.
15 Edinburgh Society for Promoting the Mitigation and Ultimate Abolition of Negro Slavery, *First Annual Report* (Edinburgh, 1824), pp. 8, 9.
16 *EA*, 3 Feb 1826.
17 *The Slave Colonies of Great Britain or A Picture of Negro Slavery drawn by the Colonists Themselves* (London, 1826).
18 *SC*, 4 Feb 1826.
19 *Considerations on Negro Slavery with a Brief View of the Proceedings Relative to it, in the British Parliament* (Edinburgh, 1824), pp. 3, 4.
20 *The Necessity of Abolishing Negro Slavery Demonstrated* (Edinburgh, 1826), p. 4.
21 *GC*, 22 Apr 1826.
22 *SC*, 28 Jan 1826. The Aberdeen Society had been founded early in 1825.
23 United Associate Secession Synod, Minutes, 15 May 1830. NAS CH3/298/1.
24 *GCH*, 22 May 1823.
25 *SC*, 24 May, 28 May 1823.
26 *EA*, 27 May 1823.
27 Edinburgh Society, *First Annual Report*, p. 3.
28 *GH*, 27 Feb 1826.
29 *Aberdeen Almanack and Northern Register* (Aberdeen, 1826), p. 258.

30 *SC*, 9 Oct 1830.

31 *EA*, 12 Oct 1830.

32 Jean. L. Watson, *Life of Dr Andrew Thomson* (Edinburgh, 1882), p. 111.

33 A. McNair, *Rev. Dr John Ritchie*. Script of articles for the *Kilmarnock Standard*, 25 Oct. 1913–3 Oct 1914. NCL, Edinburgh (Special Collections), p. 79.

34 Henry Cockburn, *Memorials of his Time* (Edinburgh, 1856), p. 468.

35 *SC*, 16 Oct 1830.

36 *EEC*, 23 Oct 1830.

37 *SC*, 30 Oct 1830.

38 *EEC*, 14 Oct 1830.

39 *EEC*, 20 Oct 1830.

40 A. Thomson, *Slavery not Sanctioned but Condemned by Christianity* (Edinburgh, 1829), p. 3.

41 A. Thomson, *Substance of the Speech Delivered at the Meeting of the Edinburgh Society for the Abolition of Slavery* (Edinburgh, 1830), pp. 27–8.

42 Thomson, *Substance of the Speech*, p. 14. The upas tree is described in *Chambers Dictionary* as 'a fabulous Javanese tree that poisoned everything for miles around'. The word in Malay means poison. 'The Friends of Humanity Laying the Axe to the Upas Tree of Slavery' is the theme of a lithograph produced by Valentines of Dundee and forms the front cover of this book.

43 Thomson, *Substance of the Speech*, pp. 31, 32, 33.

44 Thomson, *Substance of the Speech*, p. 3.

45 Thomson, *Slavery not Sanctioned*, p. 6.

46 *CI*, Vol. 30, 1831, p. 66.

47 Thomson, *Substance of the Speech*, p. 18.

48 Thomson, *Slavery not Sanctioned*, p. 10.

49 Thomson, *Substance of the Speech*, p. 6.

50 Thomson, *Substance of the Speech*, p. 4.

51 Thomson, *Substance of the Speech*, p. 39.

52 *SC*, 20 Oct 1830.

53 C. Duncan Rice, *The Scots Abolitionists*, (Baton Rouge, LA, 1981) p. 26.

54 Rice, *The Scots Abolitionists*, p. 23.

55 David Brion Davis, 'The Emergence of Immediatism in British and American Anti-Slavery Thought', *The Mississippi Valley Historical Review*, Vol. 42, No. 2 (Sep 1962), p. 221.

56 Henry Duncan, *Presbyter's Letters on the West Indian Question addressed to Rt. Hon. George Murray* (London, 1830), pp. 11, 13, 17–19, 26, 27, 29, 30, 38–43, 40–50, 58, 61, 71, 81, 122.

57 *CI*, Apr 1831, p. 259.

58 *CI*, Jan 1831, pp. 53–4, 57, 61, 63–4.
59 *CI*, Apr 1831, pp. 261, 263–4, 266–7.
60 *CI*, Sep 1831, pp. 664–6, 650–2.
61 *CM*, 11 Nov 1830.
62 *ASR*, Jan 1831, pp. 34, 39, 40.
63 Presbytery of Cupar, United Associate Secession Church, Minutes. NAS CH3/65/1.
64 *JHL*, Vol. 62, 1830–31 – 26 Nov 1830, 10 Dec 1830, 16 Dec 1830.
65 *JHC*, Vol. 86, Part 1, 8 Nov 1830; *ASR*, Jan 1831, p. 34.
66 Presbytery of Brechin, Minutes, 24 Nov 1830. NAS CH2/40/14; Presbytery of Tain, Minutes, 24 Nov 1830. NAS CH2/348/13; Presbytery of Forres, Minutes, 30 Nov 1830. NAS CH2/162.
67 Synod of Lothian and Tweeddale, Minutes, 4 May, 5 May, 9 Nov 1830. NAS CH2/256/16.
68 R. Burns, *Speech Delivered at the Anti-Slavery Meeting held at Paisley on the 1st November 1830 by The Rev. Dr Burns, Paisley* (Paisley, 1830).
69 R. M. W. Cowan, *The Newspaper in Scotland – A Study of its First Expansion 1815–1860* (Glasgow, 1946), p. 375.
70 *GC*, 12 Oct, 14 Oct 1830.
71 McNair, *Rev. Dr John Ritchie*, p. 68.
72 *GC*, 12 Oct, 2 Nov, 18 Nov, 30 Nov, 14 Dec 1830.
73 Burns, *Speech Delivered at Anti-Slavery Meeting*, Preface, pp. 2, 5.
74 Linda Colley, *Britons: Forging the Nation 1707–1837* (London, 1992), pp. 340–341.
75 Stana Nenadic, 'Political Reform and the Ordering of Middle Class Protest', in *Conflict and Stability in Scottish Society*, ed. T. M. Devine (Edinburgh, 1990), p. 74.
76 Bruce Lenman, *Integration and Enlightenment*, Scotland 1746–1832 (Edinburgh, 1981), p. 162.

7

EVANGELISM IN JAMAICA, THEOLOGY IN SCOTLAND, BUT FREEDOM DEFERRED

❧

Such associations, we trust, will be multiplied in every corner of the realm, and will never intermit their united and strenuous efforts, until by exposition, petition, remonstrance, and every legal method of intervention, they wipe out this foul stain from the character of their country, and deliver themselves from all participation in a system which, as has now been demonstrated, involves the violation of every acknowledged principle of the religion of Christ.

Zachary Macaulay, *Negro Slavery*, 1823

By the early 1830s, it was becoming obvious even to the staunchest defenders of West Indian planter interests that the system of slavery would soon be brought to an end. The abolition campaign in 1830 had produced an unprecedented number of petitions to both Houses and a future reformed House of Commons would be much more dependent on popular support. Scotland accounted for a rather more modest proportion of these petitions than in the latter days of the campaign against the slave trade, but the churches still featured prominently in the petitioning campaign, as did churchmen in the public meetings held to generate enthusiasm. By 1833, most of the leading anti-slavery ministers were not Church of Scotland, but came from the United Secession Church, with Methodists, Baptists and Independents adding their voices to the movement. The Scottish Missionary Society, although supported by both the established and secession churches, drew its missionaries in the Caribbean from the Secessionists and their attitude to slavery tended to be rather different from that of their brethren at home.

The theological position on slavery adopted publicly by the majority of churches and civic bodies followed Andrew Thomson's calls for immediate abolition, but there were cautious notes from some who called for safeguards. Scots missionaries in Jamaica were working within a slave society and were unable or unwilling to challenge its basis, choosing instead to work within it. They were given strict instructions by the Scottish Missionary Society to remain silent over slavery. At the same time, the West India Association mounted a strong campaign to delay abolition and to include many conditions within it. In their concern to push through emancipation, the Government and to some extent the abolitionists, accepted compromises on compensation for the planters and on an Apprenticeship Scheme, which continued to bind the majority of slaves to their former masters. This tempered the abolitionists' celebrations and after a brief period it became obvious that this was slavery by another name, necessitating a further campaign of petitioning and lobbying to bring full freedom in 1838.

Scots Missionaries in Jamaica – in the Pockets of the Planters?

On New Year's Day 1827, Rev. George Blyth gave a glowing account of the last year's work in Jamaica to the Scottish Missionary Society, and included in it a table indicating the steady growth in numbers of communicant members, baptisms and marriages on the various plantations. He claimed that he had experienced neither any personal opposition from planters or overseers, nor heard of any instances of slaves being punished for attending his communicant's class. On the contrary, he said, the classes were encouraged and he had been met by the planters with 'friendship and good wishes.'[1] Blyth, a minister of the United Secession Church, had come to Jamaica after service with the London Missionary Society in Russia. Two Scottish plantation-owners in Trelawny, in the north-west of the island, had invited the Scottish Missionary Society to send someone to minister to their slaves, and it was to that area that Blyth first went. The Society claimed that the positive feeling of the Jamaican planters towards Presbyterianism was evidenced by the grant made by the island's Assembly in 1814 towards establishing a Church of Scotland congregation in Kingston, and by the proposal by the same body in 1822 to establish a fund to provide for a minister recommended by the Presbytery of Edinburgh.[2]

The Kingston congregation had been founded by Scots in Jamaica in response to the overwhelming dominance of the Church of England on the island. Rev. James Wordie was ordained in Jamaica in 1823 and served as minister there until 1842. The Church of Scotland congregation in Kingston sought to serve the needs of whites alone. In evidence to the House of Commons select committee in 1832,

Rev. Peter Duncan, a Methodist minister, said that he had frequently attended it, and had never seen a slave there.[3] An early attempt by the Scottish Missionary Society to send missionaries to the island had resulted in the death of one and the defection of the other. Rev. John Brown had been ordained in 1818 by the Presbytery of Edinburgh to serve in Jamaica, but he died of fever with months of arriving on the island. George Blyth was therefore the first Scottish missionary who survived or stayed long enough and was enthusiastic enough to undertake work on the plantations. Scots planters may have preferred a Church of Scotland minister, but Blyth later was to report that secessionists were acceptable, since 'the greater part of the respectable people in the country are Scotsmen, who universally favour the Presbyterian form of government'.[4]

A study of the churches in Jamaica at this time described the Anglican Church as 'a true colonial creation' instructed 'to maintain in the colony, the same model of social and political arrangement'.[5] From 1748 to 1824, Anglicans were under the authority of the See of London, and despite the efforts of Bishop Bielby Porteus in the late eighteenth century to encourage the Christian education of slaves, little of that was done. One historian claimed that the Anglican clergy in Jamaica provided the planters with the formalities required at birth, marriage and death, whilst disregarding the spiritual needs of the slaves. These were, in the church's eyes, 'generally regarded as a necessary appendage to white society'.[6] The most glaring example of this was the notorious and violent Rev. George Bridges, a spokesman for the planters, who published a rejoinder to Wilberforce, and founded and ran the Colonial Church Union, which gave ecclesiastical approval to the reprisals after the 1831 slave uprising.[7]

By contrast, the Methodist, Moravian and Baptist missionaries set up churches and educational programmes for slaves. Methodist and Moravian leaders were almost exclusively European missionaries, but out of the Baptist church developed a plethora of groups known as 'native Baptists'. Despite frequent prohibition by the Jamaican authorities, these groups survived and expanded, developing religious forms that met the needs of slaves more effectively than those of the parent mission church. The 1831 rebellion was led by one of the native Baptists, Sam Sharpe, and although some would argue that the Baptist missionaries betrayed their 'native' brethren, the whites were to regard them as the most culpable of all at a time of national emergency.

Both the Methodist and Baptist Missionary Societies gave strict instructions to their ministers to avoid any reference to slavery in their work. Recognising the delicate state of relationships between planters and missionaries, they urged that everything be done to secure the right to preach the gospel. The Wesleyan Society told its missionaries that their 'sole business' was 'to promote the moral and religious improvement of the slaves to which you have access without in the least degree in public or private, interfering with their civil condition'. Baptist instructions to missionaries were similar. They were warned scrupulously to avoid any political issue and to remember that 'the object is not to teach the principles and laws of an earthly kingdom . . . but the principles and laws of the Kingdom of Christ'. That included obedience to masters.[8]

The advice given by the Scottish Missionary Society was no different. Candidates were required to 'yield all due respect and subjection to the civil authorities' and to 'abstain from all interference in the political concerns of such country'. It was acknowledged that missionaries could not remain totally detached, but they were told firmly to avoid any interference. 'Maintain the strictest neutrality' was to be their watchword, and if pressed to speak, 'state distinctly that it is the spiritual interests of the negroes you have come out to promote'.[9]

Winston Lawson considered that Presbyterian missionaries identified with the planters on slavery. The whites, he maintained, 'regularly used Mr. Blyth, the Presbyterian, as their henchman'.[10] That judgement overall is too harsh, even if Blyth's correspondence home seems to justify it. Although in 1824 he reported privately to the Secretary of the Scottish Missionary Society about barriers he encountered when visiting sick slaves and received a reply urging 'extreme caution',[11] his letters home generally demonstrate unbridled optimism over his work. The only despondent notes refer to slaves whom he found 'very ignorant and superstitious', with irregular attendance at Baptist meetings, but even that was balanced by the improvement noticed after considerable preaching and teaching. Blyth accepted without comment the drop in the numbers of his Sunday congregation during the period of sugar production in 1827, when the slaves were permitted no free time. The following year, when a slave confessed that he had taken a little sugar from the boilerhouse to appease his hunger, Blyth told him that this was certainly sinful and he should promise not to do it again.

The missionaries who came later were less uncritical of slavery. In 1827, James Watson and John Chamberlain arrived on the island, followed by Hope Masterton Waddell in 1829. The first two were sent to coastal areas that were outside the patronage of Scottish planters. For that reason, Watson claimed that it had taken him three years to obtain permission to preach to and teach the slaves on four estates. John Cowan, a later arrival still, observed that he would have to become better known before he could ask leave to go 'and instruct negroes on estates which have not been visited hitherto'.[12] Their letters were the first suggestions that the planters were anything other than sympathetic to mission work with the slaves. But Waddell was apparently much more forthright. In 'crop-time', when the sugar was being processed, he encountered objections to admitting slaves from surrounding plantations. 'I replied', he wrote, 'that I could keep out none who came to hear the word of God and behaved properly, for my house was God's house and must be a house of prayer for all people.' Waddell accepted the need to be careful in entering new estates to give religious instruction, but he complained of the trouble given by overseers on most plantations and described several encounters in which he had had to hold his ground and insist on time and space to do his work. In contrast to Blyth's picture of the plantations, Waddell's first impression was that of 'whited sepulchres', where a style of living was marked with excess and vice, and where the picture of prosperity and happiness often painted was in fact was 'a murderous system which unceasingly ground down the people to death'. This was not a description given by Waddell in his reports to the Society, however. It was printed in his memoirs decades afterwards.

In January 1831, the *Christian Instructor* published a letter from a correspondent who had recently returned from Jamaica. 'A' detailed the dissolute life of whites on the plantations and the conditions there for the slaves. He claimed that Blyth had himself been prevented from instructing slaves and that overseers had arranged work to coincide with his visits. 'Mr. Blyth', he wrote, 'is highly esteemed and deservedly so, in Jamaica. He is faithful in the discharge of his duties as it is possible for any minister of the gospel to be in a country where slavery is upheld by the law.' But, he concluded, 'I believe it to be a moral impossibility to instruct the black population of Jamaica till slavery is completely ameliorated, if not totally abolished.'[13]

Blyth, now on leave in Scotland, responded in July with a vigorous refutation of 'A's letter. He restated the excellent reception of missionaries, commended overseers whom he knew and claimed that on a number of properties 'the use of the whip is abolished'. 'A' responded with amazement that the missionary had no word of sympathy for the slaves. He accepted that Blyth had been well received by the planters, but insisted that he himself had heard widespread contempt expressed by them for religious instruction and for missionaries.

Other letters appeared in the *Christian Instructor* in support of 'A'. 'Perthensis' was astonished that Blyth was so anxious to do justice to the planters, and that he 'guardedly refrains from allowing any protestation against the debasing and demoralising evils of slavery to escape his pen'. 'Fifeshire' drew the attention of the Scottish Missionary Society to the fact that its agent's defence of the planters had been published in the pro-slavery *Glasgow Courier*, and he threatened to withdraw his aid from the Society if it did not call Blyth to account.

George Blyth, who was about to return to Jamaica, responded that if he had not been silent over slavery he could not prosecute the work of salvation that was in his view 'a far higher object than even the emancipation of the slaves'. He strenuously denied that he was a defender of slavery and recognised that the age of freedom was approaching, but concluded his letter by warning of the dangers of immediate emancipation.[14]

It is true that Blyth was simply following the Society's instructions to the letter and his deference to the planters and overseers may well have been a necessary condition for the opportunity to evangelise, which he would not put at risk at any cost. Even so, at times the letters to him from the Society show even more willingness on its part to defer to the slave-owners' conditions for missionary work. Blyth's own letters, however, show a genuine concern for the spiritual welfare of slaves and for their moral and educational improvement. In this, he did not differ from other Scottish missionaries, nor from most Methodists and Baptists. Nevertheless, when he permitted himself to be used publicly in support of the status quo, it was not only correspondents to the anti-slavery *Christian Instructor* who were unhappy. In a statement in the Scottish Missionary Society's *Register*, the directors defended strongly the position of missionary silence on issues of slavery and expressed regret at what they saw as inaccuracies in the *Instructor*. But privately the Secretary wrote to Blyth when he returned to Jamaica, expressing the hope that there would be 'no more publications on this subject either in this country or Jamaica', since this would only harm the cause of mission'.[15] Blyth's commendation in the *Glasgow Courier* led them to state that they were persuaded that he, 'from a natural and laudable zeal for the cause of missions in Jamaica, was betrayed into the use of too general and unguarded expressions in representing the facilities for instructing the negroes on that island'.[16]

Clearly there was a very wide gulf on the issue of slavery between the Edinburgh-based Scottish Missionary Society and the Edinburgh

Abolition Society. The former's official silence on the matter contrasted strongly with the immediatist approach the latter had embraced, following Andrew Thomson's speeches in 1830. Both Societies included ministers of the United Secession Church and the Church of Scotland on their Committees, but the only director of the Missionary Society who also served on the Abolition Committee was an Edinburgh lawyer, Dr James Greville.[17] By contrast, the Methodist and Baptist missionary organisations based in England by the 1830s had become much more allied to the anti-slavery movement at home. In 1832, the Wesleyan Methodist Missionary Society's magazine, *Missionary Notices*, declared itself for abolition, and in June of that year an eloquent plea by Rev. William Knibb, recently home from Jamaica, brought the annual meeting of the Baptist Missionary Society to the same position as their Methodist brethren.[18]

All this resulted from the dramatic events of 1831–2 in Jamaica. A severe drought had affected the island in 1831 and the decrease in the number of slaves meant that conditions suffered by the remainder were worse. Reports had reached the island of anti-slavery agitation at home and many slaves became convinced that their masters were thwarting a freedom conferred on them by the British Parliament. On 27 December 1831, several native Baptist leaders under the direction of Sam Sharpe started a rebellion in the northern parishes, many of which had Baptist, Methodist and Presbyterian missions. Twenty thousand slaves took part, over one million pounds' worth of damage was caused, and fourteen whites and several hundred slaves were killed in a two-month military operation that cost the Government over £160,000 pounds.[19]

The Jamaican authorities' response to the rebellion was ruthless: 626 slaves were tried, of whom 312 were executed. Waddell commented that, for the slaves, 'their labours were increased and means of support diminished, their complaints no longer heard'.[20] Many of the leaders of the rebellion came from estates on which missionary churches had been established, including Blyth's district of Hampden. The Colonial Church Union was formed immediately after the rebellion. Rev. George Bridges defined its tasks as expelling the missionaries, destroying what he regarded as 'sectarian' denominations and taking armed resistance against the threat of abolition.[21] It gained support from leading whites and from overseers and bookkeepers, who saw their jobs threatened by the collapse of the sugar market and the prospect of emancipation. Throughout the north of the island, mobs of whites and units of militia started to attack Methodist and

Baptist chapels. James Watson visited the ruins of a Baptist chapel in Lucea and heard of a proposal to destroy his own Presbyterian church.[22] Waddell reported that a conspiracy to 'tar and feather' Watson had led to him being confined to his house for weeks, and that two unsuccessful attempts had been made to burn down Hampden Church.[23] During martial law many Baptist missionaries and several Methodists were arrested. Rev. Thomas Burchell, Sam Sharpe's own minister, had to be escorted off the island by the army to save him from a lynch mob, and a Moravian missionary was court-martialled on charges of supporting the rebellion.

Even before the rebellion, the Scottish missionaries had warned their congregations about the dangers of an uprising. Blyth returned from Scotland days before it began and in Hampden on Christmas Eve he urged the slaves to return to work after the holidays and wait for freedom in a legal manner. He reported that 'many were not only disappointed, but offended with me on account of this information'.[24] Waddell, at the nearby Cornwall mission, gave the same message and assured his congregation that a false move would bring the power of the mother country on them and lose them many friends there. The slaves' reaction was similar to those at Hampden, as they declared 'minister give against we'.[25]

But such cautious advice was not limited to Scottish missionaries. The Baptist missionary at Falmouth, William Knibb, already well-known for his defence of slaves, told his congregation on 27 December 1831 not to believe the reports of abolition and to return to work rather than being 'led away by wicked men'. The previous day, Methodist slaves in Hannover were given a similar message. They too felt that their ministers had deserted them. One Baptist minister turned informer, testifying against slaves, something that no Presbyterian did.[26] The day after martial law was declared on 1 January 1832, a magistrate visited Blyth and Waddell and advised them to join the militia, informing them that they were not above suspicion and that such demonstration of loyalty would help to reassure the authorities. They affirmed their loyalty, but refused to join. However, in Lucea, James Watson was ordered by the soldiers to report to the barracks and had to go on sentry duty alongside the Methodist missionary, Henry Bleby.[27]

No Presbyterian missionaries joined the Colonial Church Union, although the Union sought to co-opt them into the island church establishment on the same footing as the Anglicans. An offer by the Union to erect 'Scotch kirks' in the parishes, often on the ruins of others, was firmly refused. Waddell reported that the Scottish missionaries had no desire to be separated from other missionaries, neither by an alliance with the Presbyterian minister in Kingston (the only representative of the Church of Scotland in the country), nor by siding with the established church in the colony. In his view, it was this firm refusal that led to the denunciation of the missionaries as 'Scots Sectarians' in some of the island's newspapers.[28]

Certainly there is evidence that the particular standing of the Scottish missionaries enabled them, in the early days of the rebellion at least, to intercede in order to save slaves from arbitrary vengeance. Blyth, Waddell and Cowan on 29 December 1831 drew up a memorial to the magistrates in Falmouth in an attempt to secure protection for slaves who had not committed violence and were prepared to return to work.[29] Blyth and Waddell presented a similar plea at Trelawny, deprecating 'excessive and indiscriminate severity towards the disaffected slaves' and arguing that fear rather than rebellion kept many away from work. Both were received sympathetically.[30] On 7 January, Blyth offered to bear witness in favour of a slave in his congregation arrested on suspicion and three days later made a general visit to prisoners, successfully interceding for five of them with the colonel of militia and standing surety for another member of his congregation.[31]

Shortly after the end of the rebellion, fired by these small successes, the Presbyterian missionaries presented a petition to the Jamaican House of Assembly protesting at the harshness of the response to the rebellion. Waddell claimed that they believed, at a time when the colonists were so ill-disposed to missionaries, that the Scots were better placed than others. They requested an extra day per week (apart from Sunday) for the slaves to attend to their own grounds and markets, in order to feed themselves and still attend worship. The petition was read and laid on the table of the House, with varying reactions. Some press reports referred contemptuously to 'Scotch Anti-Slavery Parsons' and 'Anti-Colonialists', and one stated of the Scottish missionaries:

> They are leagued with our enemies, are our worst enemies. We denounce them to the country and call on those who have estates to beware how they permit men, evidently under the late talented Dr Thomson of Edinburgh, to instruct and preach to our slaves.[32]

In 1833, the directors of the Scottish Missionary Society published two leading articles in the *Register* entitled 'Apology for the Scottish

Missionaries in Jamaica'. A letter in the *Glasgow Chronicle* of 30 January, signed by 'Anti-Humbug', had accused Scottish missionaries of laxity in admitting to the Lord's Supper slaves who had worked on their provision grounds on the Sabbath, and thus failed in their church attendance. A lengthy reply to this by Waddell was printed in the July issue of the *Register* and the directors cited George Blyth in emphasising that, for many slaves on the estates, it was a choice of being absent from church on a Sunday or starvation. The petition to the House of Assembly was given as evidence of the missionaries' zeal to see the Sabbath observed and the consequent vilification as evidence of their persecution.

In September, the second 'Apology' related to the 'suspicion entertained by many that the Scottish missionaries in Jamaica have been less faithful than those of other denominations, particularly the Baptist and Methodist missionaries'. The Society admitted that Scottish missionaries enjoyed the special favour of Scottish whites on the island and noted that their persecution was limited. In a twelve-page detailed report, the directors took care to instance all the threats made to Scottish missionaries and mission property, quoting Blyth's most recent communication, in which he wrote: 'there are not a few whose mouths are continually filled with vituperation against me, calling me worse than the Baptists, as the worst epithet they can apply to me'.[33]

Several charges had been made that the Scottish missionaries were allied to the Colonial Church Union. A letter in the *Christian Record*, a Church of England evangelical magazine, suggested as much, and the directors received a report from a minister in the West of Scotland citing correspondence from George Blyth that was sympathetic to the Union. In response, quotations were provided from Blyth, Waddell and Chamberlain not only disassociating themselves from the Union, but condemning it. 'I was', wrote Blyth, 'well known as one of the enemies of that Union by its friends and foes. No one has ever asked me to join it and I am happy to say that none of my members connected themselves with it.'[34]

The final issue raised was that of support for Methodist and Baptist missionaries when they were attacked and arrested. The directors cited the text of a letter to William Knibb from Waddell and Blyth showing concern for his safety and expressing willingness to go to Montego Bay and witness to his character. They reported that Blyth had attended Knibb's trial and offered to speak for him, but the charges were dropped.[35] Waddell and Blyth had taken their families for safety to

Falmouth in January 1832 and lodged with Knibb overnight, sharing the same fate as the Baptist missionary in having horses 'borrowed' by the troopers and then taken by vigilantes as a warning not to attempt to rebuild what the planters had destroyed.

Prior to 1831–2, it might have been reasonable to conclude that the Scottish missionaries in Jamaica had accepted a role of dependence on the planters. Certainly a recent study of their letters supports the contention that they did less to oppose the slaveholders than some Scottish supporters of mission wished, even after the rebellion, and that they alienated some slaves in Jamaica.[36] But several factors need to be set alongside even that cautious judgement. The priority of saving souls was taken as read by all mission agencies, and in building up Christian congregations of slaves the Presbyterian record is comparable to the Methodists, Moravians and Baptists, for all the greater lay leadership in the latter. Scottish concern for education was evidenced by the early establishment of Sunday schools and other groups. There was ample clear water between this approach and the mass baptisms employed by many Anglicans on the plantations, which were neither prefaced by instruction nor accompanied by any expectation of regular worship. The distancing of Scottish missionaries from the Church of Scotland congregation in Kingston, the rejection of invitations to join the Colonial Church Union and the pastoral concern not only for Knibb and other missionary colleagues, but also for slaves in the aftermath of the rebellion, was sufficient to place them firmly with the foreign missionaries rather than with the churches of the planters.

Nevertheless, the strict adherence to silence over slavery, not just in Jamaica, but after their return, contrasts with Knibb and others, who threw their weight behind the anti-slavery cause when their societies recalled them. Knibb was strongly supported in this by the Baptist Missionary Society, as were the former Methodists missionaries in Jamaica. But Blyth, Waddell and the Scots missionaries were answerable to a Society that, even after the Baptist War (as the 1831–2 rebellion in Jamaica had become popularly known), continued to avoid the subject of slavery and they were certainly not brought in on the abolitionist cause. A letter from a number of Edinburgh and Leith secessionist ministers was published early in 1833. It complained of the persecution of missionaries in Jamaica and called upon all Christians to use every constitutional means to bring colonial slavery to an end. Amongst the signatories were Ebenezer Halley, James McGilchrist and George Johnston, all members of the Scottish Missionary Society's committee.[37] But the Society itself, by its official silence even at this late date, was clearly at odds with many strands of opinion in the Church and country at large.

THEOLOGIANS AND ACTIVISTS AT HOME

By 1833, there was only one Church of Scotland minister on the Edinburgh Committee for the Abolition of Negro Slavery, Dr Robert Gordon of St Giles. Rev. Edward Craig, who also served on the Committee to aid Moravian Missions and the Church of England Missionary Society, was Episcopal rector of St James's, Edinburgh.[38] Most of the other activists were ministers of independent or secessionist churches. In the same way, the theological attack on slavery in the early 1830s passed from leading Church of Scotland ministers such as Andrew Thomson to others. Three who played a significant role in this, as in active campaigning, were James Douglas of Cavers, thought by many to be the most influential lay Congregationalist of his time; Dr Ralph Wardlaw, the Glasgow Congregationalist minister whose lectures on slavery were attended by a young David Livingstone; and Dr John Ritchie of Edinburgh.

'An evil which since I have been able to judge it, has been considered by me as the foulest blot on our national character,' said Ritchie, echoing the mood of many of the anti-slavery petitions.[39] The damage done to the nation by slavery was taken up by all three polemicists. 'Britain', said Douglas, 'in addition to a new load of guilt has a new load of taxes', and he continued by quoting the mortality figures of British soldiers deployed to defend slavery in the West Indies.[40] Wardlaw, in his celebration of the emancipation bill, claimed that national honour was restored and that he breathed more lightly, 'as if the heavy sulphurous atmosphere of a gathering storm of divine retribution had been dispelled over the land of my fathers' sepulchres'.

Despite the strong emphasis on national guilt, the theological attack on slavery was much wider than this. Douglas and Wardlaw strongly defended the God-given natural right to freedom. 'Nothing short of a direct divine permission', said Wardlaw, 'can warrant its violation.'[41] For Douglas, it was overwhelming fear that drove every action of a slave, totally destroying his liberty to exercise the 'variety of movements' that are from God. If this was accepted, for him it followed that enslavement was theft not just from man but from God. Striking directly at what was accepted as sacrosanct, Douglas declared that to assert the right of property in man was no more ethically valid than the claims that the Edinburgh criminal Burke might make 'in the victims he stole for anatomical purposes', and for him the fact that Africans were traded alive simply increased their sufferings.[42] Both men quoted Exodus 21:16 ('And he that stealeth a man and selleth him, or if he be found in his hand, he shall surely be put to death'), and Wardlaw followed this with the Deuteronomic prohibition against returning runaway slaves.[43]

Given such strong statements, Wardlaw and Douglas needed to address the obvious fact that slavery existed amongst the people of God in the Bible. Wardlaw dealt with this by emphasising the jubilee, and its announcement on the Day of Atonement. He took this same message from the New Testament when he cited the reading by Jesus in the synagogue of the passage from Isaiah 61:1, declaring liberty to the captives. Israel, he claimed, was in slavery to sin and had lost its 'patrimony', but through Jesus, in a new time of jubilee, the nation was ransomed and restored.[44] Wardlaw's broad sweeping of slavery within the fall, the apostasy of the chosen people and the redemption bought by the crucified Jesus, did not examine the details of slavery in the Old Testament. That was done by Douglas, who claimed that slavery within the chosen people was very mild compared with that of the West Indies, and that Abraham's slaves were part of his family, differing 'little from a clan under their patriarchal head'. He went on to maintain that, far from the Bible sanctioning slavery, 'it only sanctions its mitigations and restrictions.' For him, the law of Moses did not establish slavery. Instead, it tempered it and in many instances terminated it.[45]

By the early 1830s, many of the planters, recognising the inevitability of abolition, were pressing for compensation. Ritchie suggested that the very idea was not to be entertained for a moment, and that money should rather be given to the injured slaves.[46] Douglas compared those who made such claims with Shylock demanding his pound of flesh, and expressed astonishment that compensation is demanded 'for relinquishing a system fraught with nothing but misery and guilt to all involved in it'. He affirmed that, far from seeking compensation, they should 'rather esteem themselves emancipated by the same act that emancipates their slaves.' [47] However, Wardlaw, perhaps in acceptance of what was by then a *fait accompli*, agreed with the principle of compensation on legal, rather than moral, grounds. To those who took a stand in opposition to it, he responded by asking 'whether would you prefer having the twenty millions in the exchequer and the eight hundred million slaves in bonds?'.[48]

Ralph Wardlaw not only preached and wrote on slavery, he put his West George Street chapel, a prestigious venue in the city, at the disposal of the Glasgow Anti-Slavery Society for meetings and for a series of debates on the question of immediate or gradual emancipation. However, it was only after the 1833 Act, when the anti-slavery campaign was reorganised, that he became an active campaigner. In December 1833, Glasgow formed an Emancipation Society with the aim of abolishing slavery throughout the world, and with a particular emphasis on the United States. Wardlaw was asked to become senior Vice-President and he remained active within the Society for the next eight years. In 1836, he memorialised Lord Melbourne on conditions in Mauritius, and in 1838 he was nominated alongside two United Secession ministers from the Committee, Dr James Heugh and Rev. David King, as Glasgow delegates to the London meeting that marked the final push to abolish apprenticeship.[49] By this time, Ralph Wardlaw had become perhaps the leading abolitionist in Scotland. George Thompson, the London anti-slavery lecturer, was described as his 'protégé'. Wardlaw went on to host a visit in 1840 by William Lloyd Garrison, the leading American abolitionist, and in 1853 by Mrs Harriet Beecher Stowe, author of *Uncle Tom's Cabin*.

In Edinburgh, John Ritchie assumed the mantle of Andrew Thomson, having been convinced of immediatism by Thomson in the first of the meetings in October 1830. As Moderator of the United Associate Secession Synod, Ritchie had been appointed convenor of a committee to prepare a petition on slavery. A complaint was received at the April 1831 meeting that he had not waited to receive the last Synod's minute, but was 'so anxious for the immediate abolition of slavery that he transmitted the resolutions of the Anti-Slavery Society by the post, by coaches, in short in every possible way, to the members of the court'. The move to find Ritchie's behaviour 'irregular', failed by only 3 votes in a Synod of 158 delegates, with 20 abstaining.[50] The results of such 'irregularity', meanwhile, were impressive. A total of 83 petitions were sent to the Commons and 102 to the Lords in 1830–1 from United Associate congregations, building on a strong record of petitioning from that source throughout the 1820s.

Given the debate in the Synod of Lothian between gradualism, and immediatism and the reputation Ritchie had as a supporter of radical causes, it is hardly surprising that he had enemies. He was at the centre of many a dispute within his church. Yet it was that very same stubborn refusal to compromise that made him effective as an anti-slavery leader, and not only in Edinburgh. His commitment had been honed

Figure 11   *Dr John Ritchie of Potterrow. By kind permission of the Ritchie family*

by Andrew Thomson, but it began in Kilmarnock, where he had preached in favour of the abolition of slavery.[51] On moving to the Potterrow congregation in Edinburgh, Ritchie became active in the Edinburgh Society's Committee, moved the resolutions at the Society's meetings in the Assembly Rooms in January 1833 and again in

April, and was nominated from that meeting as a member of a three-man delegation appointed to attend the great Anti-Slavery Convention in London. Thereafter he played a leading part in the campaign to abolish apprenticeship, chairing the meetings addressed by George Thompson in 1836, moving resolutions again in Edinburgh in 1838 and attending the much more powerful Glasgow Emancipation Society Committee. In April 1840, he was made an Honorary Vice-President of 'L'Institut d'Afrique', the French successor to 'Les Amis des Noirs'.[52] He also became active in support of the radical abolitionists in America, and joined those who attempted in 1844 to force the Free Church to return money donated from the slave-owning southern states.

In the petitions on slavery sent to the House of Lords in 1833, there were a cluster of ten from Roxburghshire. Lilliesleaf United Associate congregation had petitioned the Commons in 1823, and the towns of Kelso and Jedburgh had done likewise in 1824 and 1826, but otherwise there had been little sign of activity in this part of the country. In 1833, the inhabitants of Lilliesleaf were joined by Sprouston, Hopkirk, Roberton, Southdean, Oxnam, Eckford, Howham, Askirk and Cavers.[53] The last perhaps provides the clue to this phenomenon deep in the Scottish Borders, for James Douglas of Cavers in his preaching and teaching within that collection of small and remote villages had obviously galvanised them to action on one of the great issues of the time.

THE 1833 CAMPAIGN – THE FINAL PUSH?

Between 1830 and 1833, the political map of Britain was significantly and irreversibly altered. Early in 1830, Sir George Murray, the Tory Colonial Secretary, had assured the West Indians that the 1823 resolutions should be seen as 'an opinion' and that the Government had no intention of interfering with slavery in the chartered colonies. The return of the Whigs to power later that year, however brought the prospect of Parliamentary Reform nearer, with a promise to extend the franchise to many amongst the middle class who supported the abolition of slavery. But for abolitionists in Parliament, and in the country, there were still many battles to be fought. In April 1831, at the annual meeting of the London Anti-Slavery Society, the policy of seeking immediate abolition was agreed and members encouraged to make emancipation a major issue for candidates in the 1832 election.

Earlier that year, the news of the persecution of missionaries and the ruthless suppression of the slave insurrection in Jamaica led Lord Grey's administration to authorise committees of both Houses of Parliament to investigate West Indian slavery. Ironically, this was what many of the petitions on behalf of the West Indian interest demanded as a tactic for delaying emancipation, and they seemed to have been successful, since no less than eight slave-owners were appointed to the select committee of the House of Lords. Thomas Fowell Buxton remarked bitterly that 'the advocates of the negro have met with opposition and desertion'.[54] Certainly Lord Howick, under-secretary for the colonies, was preparing an amended order in Council that would make fiscal privileges in the West Indies dependent on adoption of ameliorating measures. Yet far more significant for abolitionists was the Reform Act of 1832. In the election of December 1832, the extended franchise produced a House of Commons that reduced West Indian representation to thirty-five, while at the same time including over one hundred members pledged to immediate abolition.

But the cause of emancipation in 1833 was still to involve a struggle. The former Tory Prime Minister, the Duke of Wellington, had warned that, whatever the Commons might decide, the Lords would defeat any precipitous move for the expropriation of private property. At the same time, frustration amongst some abolitionists at the Government's seeming failure since taking office to initiate meaningful steps on slavery led to a radicalisation of part of the abolition movement. A new group arose under the leadership of the Liverpool merchant and Quaker abolitionist, Joseph Cropper. This 'Agency Committee' raised funds to employ agents who would address nationwide meetings to arouse the public in much the same way as Clarkson and Dickson had done in 1792. At first its independent action was regarded with suspicion by the London Committee, but by the end of 1832 the latter was committing funds to the Agency Committee. Two of the most effective agents, in this respect were the returned Baptist missionary William Knibb and a Methodist laymen George Thompson, both of whom were to contribute substantially to the campaign in Scotland in early 1833.

Knibb spent several months addressing meetings in Scotland and told the Edinburgh Anti-Slavery Society at a large public meeting in January 1833 that he rejoiced to see public opinion gaining ground. He had, he said, 'met with a hearty response from the descendants of Knox, from those who knew well how to defend their rights and liberties'.[55] That meeting was chaired by Rev. Edward Craig, but the

Glasgow gathering, which Knibb addressed two days later, was presided over by a local member of Parliament, Sir John Maxwell, and the *Glasgow Herald* noted that 'notwithstanding the unfavourable weather, long before the hour of meeting the chapel [Wardlaw's] was crowded to excess'.[56] Knibb commented that, 'throughout the hills and dales of Scotland', he had told the facts of slavery and everywhere had met 'a hearty response'. Perhaps not quite everywhere, though, since he admitted in the same speech that he had been represented in Glasgow as a 'gravedigger', a charge he warmed to in seeking to dig the grave of slavery. 'In Jamaica', he said, 'they look to Glasgow as the great den of colonial slavery', a reference to the way in which that cause had been ably served by the West India Association and the *Glasgow Courier*. Knibb desisted from responding to attacks on him by the latter. Instead, he turned to the unrecognised and embarassing legacy of Scots males in the West Indies. 'I plead', he declaimed, 'for thousands of children of Scotsman in slavery, children left by their parents . . . to all the horrors of West Indian slavery.' Abolition, he said, would 'break the bonds of the descendants of Scotsman' and he called on ministers of the gospel to assist. [57]

With such enthusiasm for immediate abolition in Glasgow and Edinburgh, it was to be expected that the West Indian interest would respond. The Association undertook a substantial press campaign in 1833 and appointed Peter Borthwick, a member of a prominent Borders family and MP for Evesham, to be their answer to the Agency Committee's speakers. Early in 1833, there were three debates in Glasgow between Borthwick and George Thompson. These were paralleled in Edinburgh by separate lectures from the two protagonists, and a further lecture series in April by Thompson 'at the express desire of the friends of immediate abolition'.[58] Thompson argued that the planters themselves claimed that it was impossible to have Christianity and slavery together, that no preparation had been made for freedom in the West Indies and that 'gradual emancipation, in honest and plain truth, meant everlasting slavery'.

Borthwick based his response on claims of improvement. The use of the whip, he insisted, was greatly exaggerated, much religious and other education was now being provided by the planters, and in one area of Jamaica no less than 376 young slaves had been catechised. On the other hand, the destruction of property in Jamaica demonstrated the danger of immediate abolition. Borthwick challenged the abolitionists' claim that slavery was a sin. He put the blame on the British government that had introduced slavery. It had, he noted, taken two thousand years of Christian teaching to realise that slavery was evil. In reply, Thompson cited other missionary sources to detail the continuing physical abuse of slaves and discouragement of religion. At the close of the third debate, the Chairman's call for a show of hands led to an overwhelming majority in favour of immediate abolition. [59]

On 9 April 1833, the Edinburgh Anti-Slavery Society held a meeting in Dr Brown's chapel in Broughton Street at short notice. The meeting was in response to what Dr R. K. Greville described as 'the desperate efforts' of the 'colonial party to thwart the measures about to be introduced to Parliament for the immediate abolition of slavery'. It appointed Greville, Ritchie and the Quaker John Wigham Jnr to represent the Society at a Convention in London, which would go on to lobby Government ministers.[60] Edward Stanley had replaced Viscount Goderich as Colonial Secretary in March, and the abolitionists believed him to be less amenable to emancipation. On 23 April, the West Indians had demanded that compensation be based on the high price of slaves in 1823, and that slaves should serve a forty-one year apprenticeship. The 330 delegates who met in London and paraded to Downing Street on 29 April in their address to Stanley acceded to 'some kind of reasonable measures for relief of the planter', provided it was accompanied by immediate and unconditional emancipation. They were given assurances that their demands would be met when Stanley presented his proposals to the Commons on 14 May.

The first six months of 1833 saw a similar proportion of petitions to both Houses of Parliament, as had been the case in the campaign of 1830–1. Throughout the United Kingdom, approximately 2,500 petitions were sent to the Commons and over 3,000 to the Lords. In Scotland 158 petitions were sent to the Commons and 174 to the Lords. As in 1830–1, the greater number being sent to the Lords indicated that petitioners realised where the real stumbling block to abolition might lie, especially in view of a more representative Commons in 1832. A substantial number of the petitions, around 30 per cent, were sent to both Houses. For Scotland, this meant that 210 different places or organisations petitioned that year.

By far the majority of the petitions came from the United Secession Church, including its Scottish Synod and Presbytery of Perth. Methodists, Baptists, Congregationalists and Independent Dissenters sent petitions, too. The solitary Church of Scotland petition was from Perth's Middle Kirk, although there were ministers from the Kirk involved on committees and no doubt signatory to those from the

'Clergy, Bankers, Merchants and Manufacturers of Glasgow' and the 'Ministers, Merchants and Manufacturers of Paisley'. Most of the remainder were recorded as from the 'Inhabitants' of towns and villages or simply by the place-names. Four petitions to the Commons and three to the Lords were from women in Edinburgh, Dalkeith, Hawick, and Freuchie in Fife.

Tantalisingly, the minutes of congregations and sometimes even synods simply record that petitions were sent, and many do not even do that. Similarly, even burgh records from towns such as Inverkeithing, which petitioned during almost every campaign, scarcely mention this amid the more domestic details of councillors' duties. The volume of petitions reaching the House of Commons meant that its records simply make reference to such categories as 'praying for the abolition of negro slavery' or 'for the immediate abolition of slavery', with a list of petitions attached. However, despite the greater volume reaching the House of Lords, its *Journals* carry selective texts, and from these it is possible to identify some of the issues.

There was an urgency and an uncompromising tone to many of the petitions in 1833 that was missing in 1831. A yawning gap had appeared between the supporters of gradualism, who now included the West Indians, and those pressing for immediate abolition. Inverkeithing's inhabitants warn of emancipation being 'too long deferred', while Selkirk's United Associate congregation echoed John Ritchie in reminding their Lordships that they had declared slavery to 'originate in injustice and robbery'. Kirkcaldy and Abbotshall called on the Lords to 'at once and forever put an end to the pretended right of property of men in their fellow creatures.' Stonehouse Males and Females prayed for 'immediately wiping out the misery of so many of His Majesty's subjects', and Paisley's Committee asked that 'the foul stain of slavery' should forever be 'wiped out' from the British people.

The issue of national sin and moral and religious honour was addressed in the petition from John Ritchie's Potterrow congregation. Its message was echoed by the Arbroath Methodists, who also pled for religious freedom for negroes and their equal citizenship rights. A Glasgow petition recognised the opportunity offered by a reformed Parliament and called on the unreformed Lords to 'imbue' it 'with a moral glory that shall make it the admiration and boast of Britons in every future period of their country's history'.

There were, however, some notes of caution. From Nairn, Kirkwall and Lochwinnoch came calls for 'safety' measures to accompany emancipation, and Kennoway requested 'protection for the whites if necessary'. But for some of the Paisley petitioners, however, the only way to secure 'the safety and tranquillity' of the West Indies was immediately to emancipate the slaves. No recorded petitions argued for compensation, except for the slaves. Strathblane wanted to see compensation paid 'for the floggings, oppressions and mutilations which they have sustained from their masters'. Huntly suggested that allotments from the crown lands be granted to the slaves, 'as a small requital for the wrongs hitherto inflicted'. The Glasgow Political Union expressed anxiety that any compensation for the planters would add 'to the pecuniary burdens of the already impoverished people of this country', and declared its opinion that 'traffikers in the flesh and blood of their fellow creatures are not entitled to any compensation whatsoever'.[61]

Compensation for the planters and a period of apprenticeship were, as the petitioners feared, two central elements in the proposals outlined by the Colonial Secretary to the Commons on 14 May. Stanley's plan included a loan of £15 million to the planters, to be repaid whilst the slaves worked for their freedom over twelve years. It pleased no one. The West Indians demanded compensation without strings and in direct contradiction to the 'immediate and entire abolition' sought by the anti-slavery movement. However, the belief in the sanctity of property was so strong that, despite the petitions against it and the speeches of men such as John Ritchie, the Anti-Slavery Society accepted it, and Buxton did not oppose it in the Commons. He did attempt to overturn the clause instituting apprenticeship, though, and failed in this by only seven votes, which placed enough pressure on Stanley to see the period of apprenticeship reduced from twelve to seven years. Abolitionists were horrified to find that the legislation compensated the planters without freeing the slaves, and although Buxton attempted once more to have compensation withheld until emancipation was secured, he lost heavily. Despite opposition from the Duke of Wellington, who was supported by most of the Bishops of the Church of England, the petitions to the Lords had found their mark and the house passed the bill without any major changes.

THE FALSE DAWN OF APPRENTICESHIP

On 17 July 1833, the Committee of the Edinburgh Anti-Slavery Society sent one of the last petitions to the House of Lords, a few days before the act was passed. It asked for the bill to be rendered a 'safe and equitable enactment' conferring on 'the negro not the semblance but the realities of freedom', to permit free disposal of time and labour with adequate pay, and finally to place 'him on a level as to civil and religious privileges with the other subjects of His Majesty in the colonies and elsewhere'. It was a forlorn attempt to salvage something at the last minute. Although preachers such as Wardlaw rejoiced in the Emancipation Act and the Glasgow West India Association reported to their AGM that it was a capitulation,[62] the terms enabled the planters to claim the enormous sum of £20 million in compensation and keep most ex-slaves bound to them.

The Apprenticeship Scheme was doomed from the start. Although it emancipated all under six years of age, adults were still required to work for three-quarters of the week, with no change in conditions. James Stephen the younger, who had drafted the Emancipation Act, realised that Jamaica's proposed legislation to implement it was in fact converting apprenticeship back into slavery, and he unsuccessfully urged Edward Stanley to veto this. The abolitionists' agreement to give ground over continuing white control and certain punishments for idleness led Jamaica's Governor, Lord Sligo, to justify the treadmills and 'houses of correction' over which he had no control.

Sligo sent a despatch to London at the end of 1834 indicating the success of the scheme. There had been no uprising or destruction of property, he claimed, Christmas had passed peacefully, the apprentices worked for their wages and the crop was harvested. The improvement in crime statistics and the development of the plough in farming were points highlighted in an equally optimistic letter sent to Sligo by a Jamaican stipendiary magistrate the following year, though he noted that little had been done for negro education and that the 'benevolent feelings' of masters and managers 'towards the negro are not on the increase'.[63]

However, a rather different report was reaching the Glasgow Emancipation Society. Both the Glasgow and Edinburgh Anti-Slavery Societies had regrouped after the Emancipation Act and set their sights on the ambitious task of abolishing slavery elsewhere in the world. Their focus was intended to be mainly on the United States, but for the next few years energies were divided between this area and unfinished business in the British colonies. At the June 1835 meeting of the Glasgow Committee, members expressed their view that the essential aspects of the Act 'intended for the protection of the apprentice' had been defeated by the measures of the colonial legislatures, and that the system of flogging continued even towards females, a direct contradiction of the Imperial Act'. The *Annual Report* for that year cited evidence from the Jamaican House of Assembly on the unwillingness of the slaves to work the expected sixteen-to-eighteen hours per day, six days a week. At all this, the Committee declared that they were 'grieved but not surprised', since they had protested strongly against both compensation and apprenticeship. They declared their support for Thomas Fowell Buxton in his intended call for a parliamentary inquiry into the working of the Apprenticeship Scheme.[64]

In 1836, the Annual Meeting supported a petition for the abolition of apprenticeship. This was moved by John Ritchie of Edinburgh and seconded by James McCune Smith, a free African-American from New York who had been in Glasgow as a medical student since 1832 and had been active in the Society since its inception. The petitioners rejoiced in the recent emancipation proclaimed in Antigua and the Bermudas and deplored the compensation given to slave-owners instead of slaves. They also insisted that, 'since the Apprenticeship Scheme had totally failed in its design and is more productive of evil than good', Parliament should abolish it and bring complete emancipation to the slaves. The petition was then entrusted to Committee members to procure signatures and forward it to both Houses. By the end of the month, 29,830 Glaswegians had signed and James Oswald, nephew of Richard Oswald of Bance Island and one of the two MPs for the city, agreed to support it.[65]

Although there were other societies active in the cause of abolishing the apprenticeship scheme, Glasgow's contribution was outstanding. The Society's Committee was now sixty strong, including eighteen clergy. It was almost an international society whose corresponding and honorary members included Arthur Tappan and William Lloyd Garrison, the American abolitionists; Washington Lafayette and Victor de Tracey from the French Committee; George Thompson; and Joseph Sturge, the Birmingham industrialist whose investigative report on the Apprenticeship Scheme was to play a significant role in its premature end.[66]

In 1836, Sturge went on a private visit to six West Indian islands to assess the effects of apprenticeship. He reported that abolition in Antigua had 'succeeded beyond the expectations of its most sanguine advocates'. By contrast, in Barbados, for him, 'the planters have succeeded in moulding the apprenticeship into an almost perfect likeness of the system they so willingly relinquished'. Even worse was Jamaica, where apprentices could be flogged and tortured in the workhouse without legal restriction.[67]

When Sturge's report reached Britain it was given wide coverage by the abolitionists. On 19 June 1837, the Glasgow Emancipation Society organised a public meeting in Wardlaw's chapel calling for the 'immediate and unqualified abolition of the negro apprenticeship system in the British Colonies'. Ralph Wardlaw reported that Sturge had met fifteen missionaries before leaving the island and that he had been totally convinced that the scheme made 'a mockery of freedom'. Rev. George Cheever from the United States, supported by James McCune Smith, called for a united campaign against slavery in America and the West Indies, and George Thompson claimed that a returned magistrate, Mr Brown, had admitted that the law officers 'ate with the planter, hunted with the planter, got drunk with the planter' and were totally unable to administer justice. Thompson proposed an open-air meeting of the citizens of Glasgow on 'the public green' to press for abolition.[68]

In the same month, the Edinburgh Society held a public meeting in St Cuthbert's Church, rehearsing the failures of the Apprenticeship Scheme and proposing to petition the House of Lords for abolition. The meeting had added significance since the minister of St Cuthbert's was Dr David Dickson. Dickson had been since 1833 the Secretary of the Scottish Missionary Society. His was the signature over which the petition was transmitted and reports of meetings in the following years show him taking a prominent part in the proceedings of the Society. In the meantime, the *Scottish Missionary Register* throughout 1837 and 1838 ignored the clamour for abolition, confining itself to an appeal for negro schools and expressing grievances at the alleged misrepresentation of Scottish missionaries by Joseph Sturge in Birmingham in June 1837. Sturge later satisfied them that he had been misreported, had never met any Scottish missionaries in Jamaica, but had heard glowing testimonies there to their zeal and devotion.[69]

The pressure on apprenticeship grew over the course of 1837 and 1838. The Glasgow Society's fourth *Annual Report* listed ten meetings of the Committee since the third report: five public meetings, three petitions to Parliament, two Memorials to the Government, a Memorial to the Queen and three delegations to London to join with other delegates from the United Kingdom.[70] That indicated the groundswell of opinion that developed between the publication of the Sturge Report in mid-1837 and the final victory in July 1838. In the first half of 1838, 200 Scottish petitions reached the Commons and 173 were sent to the Lords. Many were common to both Houses, but marginally the greater pressure was exerted on the Lower House, possibly because the opposition from the Lords was not thought to be as much of a threat to emancipation as in 1833.

The text of most petitions simply called for the abolition of the scheme and for 'full, unqualified and unconditional freedom', as one Glasgow petition put it. Dumbarton, identifying a familiar delaying tactic used by the planters, pressed their Lordships to 'refuse all demands for further enquiry', and Kilsyth made a similar plea to 'take care that their [the slaves'] avaricious and cruel taskmasters shall not have it in their power to render their lives more miserable in time coming'. The United Associate Secession congregation of Muckart made the intriguing request that 'Mr. George Thom[p]son, the invaluable advocate of the victims of colonial slavery', might be heard at the bar of the House of Commons.[71]

An estimate of how many people were involved in petitioning is not easy. Many petitions were signed by civic or church leaders on behalf of a community, a congregation or, in some cases, a large public meeting that agreed to petition. Reports of meetings sometimes referred to numbers attending and occasionally referred to the length of the scroll presented to the House. In March 1838, *The Scotsman* reported that the total number received by the Commons from all over Britain was 518 and the number of signatures over 169,000, but that does not tell the full story. [72]

The Scottish overall contribution to this last petitioning period did not seem to be as impressive as in previous campaigns. Nearly seven thousand petitions came from the British Isles, of which Scotland's proportion was slightly under 6 per cent. Yet many single Scottish petitions came from town and city meetings, indicating the support of far more citizens than a village or small congregation. Moreover, there were other ways of exerting pressure. Although women's petitions were few in number and confined to the main towns, a remarkable spread of signatures from sixty-nine places throughout Scotland were gathered in an Address to the Queen in 1837. One hundred and thirty five thousand women pressed Victoria to end apprenticeship and their narrative focused on the condition of women and children in the colonies. This figure represented nearly one third of that sent by the women of England.[73]

All this was in the teeth of much opposition amongst Scotland's Members of Parliament. On 29 March 1838, Sir George Strickland, the Yorkshire reformist MP, attempted to persuade the Commons to abolish apprenticeship. Delegates from throughout the land met at Exeter Hall on 27 March, and were addressed by Henry Brougham in what some considered to be the best speech of his career. After a two-day debate in the Commons, the vote for abolition was lost by 269 to 205. Scotland had 55 Members of Parliament in the House, including the Speaker, the Hon. J. Abercromby; 10 voted for Strickland's motion and 31 against. Two months later, another attempt was made to abolish apprenticeship. On 22 May, Sir John Eardley-Wilmot, MP for Warwickshire North, carried the motion 'That it is of the opinion of this House that Negro apprenticeship in the British Colonies should immediately cease' by 96 votes to 93. Out of Scotland's 53 MPs, 36 were absent and only 4 voted for the Wilmot motion.[74] Lord John Russell declared that ministers would resist any bill founded upon that resolution. The *Glasgow Herald* predicted that what they called 'further agitation' of a question that would be resolved in two years' time would only result in evil for all concerned. [75] But six days later, Sir George Grey sought a further debate and in a House of 432 members defeated the earlier resolution by a majority of 72. This time, 37 Scottish members were present and only 6 voted for abolition.

It may be true, as one historian claims, that opponents of emancipation in Britain were primarily from rural seats and small towns, while supporters were from urban, industrial and shipping constituencies, but this does not entirely fit the pattern in Scotland.[76] Sir George Sinclair in Caithness was firmly in favour of abolition, as was James Duff in Banffshire. Alexander Chisholm in Inverness was only in the chamber for one vote, but it was in favour of the Strickland motion. In the major cities, there was a more mixed pattern. Edinburgh had three members of Parliament, including W. G. Craig, who in April had signed a Memorial to the Queen. They voted three times for abolition, but Sir John Campbell supported the Government in resisting the Wilmot resolution. Glasgow's John Dennistoun supported the Emancipation Society, but Lord William Bentinck, the other member for the city, voted against the Strickland resolution. There is evidence that popular pressure did have some effect on the vote, though. The number of petitions along the Moray Firth may well have influenced Duff in Banffshire, and Captain Wemyss from the well-known landed family would not have been unaware of the consistent plethora of petitions against slavery that came every time from the Kingdom of Fife. By contrast, Paisley's radical tradition and widespread anti-slavery stance was not reflected in Archibald Hastie's two votes against emancipation.[77]

The details of each vote were published in the press, but these were not always accurate. *The Scotsman* omitted the names of three

Scottish members who voted against the Strickland motion and the *Edinburgh Evening Courant* failed to record two members from Berwick who stood by the Government in its resistance on 28 May. But, intended or not, the publication of names was a boost to the abolitionists. At a meeting in April called by the Edinburgh Emancipation Society, Mr Gibson-Craig, one of the city's members, was commended for his positive conduct. By contrast, Sir John Campbell's absence from the vote [he voted against abolition in the other two divisions] was subject to considerable satire. Rev. William Alexander of Argyll Square Congregational Chapel provoked laughter when he speculated on the important business which took Sir John out of the chamber at exactly the moment when the discussion on slavery started. He had, said Alexander, declared himself so far 'on our side', and that 'we have opened his eyes', but he questioned, amid laughter, whether the best use of Sir John's eyes lay in such an early exit.[78]

In early June 1838, a table was printed in *The Scotsman* of the voting record of every Scottish MP over the three divisions. In contrast to earlier (and less accurate) reports of the votes, this one was prefaced by a report of a meeting on 28 May attended by delegates in response to the action of Government ministers who 'unhappily succeeded in setting aside the recent solemn decision of the House of Commons for the immediate extinction of the apprenticeship scheme, thereby continuing for two years the crime and the evils of slavery'. The resolution at the meeting was that those MPs who supported the Government in 'their cruel policy, in disregard of the opinions and wishes of their constituents and in palpable violation of the dictates of humanity and justice, are unworthy of the support of a free and Christian people'. The analysis of members' voting was clearly divided into geographical areas, and an alphabetical list of Scottish constituencies and their members was appended.[79]

This is perhaps the first instance in the press of a 'name and shame' campaign. The petitions continued to flow ceaselessly throughout June, but events were soon to overtake the Government. The Glasgow Emancipation Society's Committee commended the minority of eleven in the Jamaica Assembly who voted to abandon the scheme, and shortly afterwards rejoiced to hear that the same Assembly had agreed unanimously on 16 July to finish apprenticeship on 1 August. Other islands followed swiftly, and when the British Government finalised its own legislation the Society's Committee was already preparing services of thanksgiving throughout the churches.

THE FINAL DEATH THROES OF CARIBBEAN SLAVERY

In the end Caribbean slavery was to die with a whimper, yet this state-ment on its own is deceptive. The planters bowed to the inevitable, but they did so, as the Glasgow Emancipation Committee continually pointed out, after securing compensation which represented over thir-teen times the collective annual profits of sugar, rum and coffee on West Indian property.[80] Even if the Williams theory with which this book started and the protestations of the West Indians that the prof-itability of sugar plantations was severely curtailed are accepted, there is no doubt that the last years of Caribbean slavery saw some of the strongest resistance to abolition, necessitating strenuous and sus-tained work for final emancipation. From 1833 onwards, there were rival priorities occupying the energies of churchmen who remained the mainstays of the abolition movement. In the late 1830s, complacency over the victory of 1833 and the shifting of focus to American and world slavery meant that it needed a particularly focused effort to complete the task by ending the Apprenticeship Scheme.

The hostile reaction of planters and other whites in Jamaica towards even the mildest suggestion of reform of slavery proposed by the missionaries, indicated that they were taking seriously the advice of the *Glasgow Courier* that 'West Indians can save themselves only by resisting to the death this wholesale scheme of confiscation'.[81] George Blyth's favourable comments on the character and conduct of the planters in Jamaica and Henry Duncan's assertion that conditions for the slaves had improved, found wide coverage in the *Courier* which sought to show that abolition was unnecessary. In June 1833, only six weeks before the abolition bill was passed, the Glasgow West India Association's London representative, Mr Campbell, attempted to guarantee a longer period of apprenticeship which would extend slavery for some until 1851.[82]

By 1833, it was no easy task for the churches in Scotland to main-tain their momentum on anti-slavery. The year 1829 ushered in a decade that saw a fierce controversy reminiscent of the Covenanting days two centuries before, when many had resisted the imposition of Episcopalian government on the Church of Scotland. The Voluntary movement sought an end to the privileged position of the Church of Scotland and to its state connection. Naturally, it was a cause that excited dissenting churches above all. They felt a strong sense of injus-tice, although they never suffered the same disadvantages as did Dissenters down south in relation to the Church of England. It was not, however, a simple issue on which denominations were divided. Voluntarism also found a good deal of support amongst members of the Kirk, who often added their names to petitions for disestablishment. A further element in the churches, ferment was that part of the enthusiasm for disestablishment arose from the fear that Catholic Emancipation would lead to the replacement of Protestant ascendancy in Ireland, and that Roman Catholicism might be regarded as the established church. This was the theme of the sermon by a Secessionist minister who launched the Voluntary movement in April 1829.[83]

All this might have made anti-slavery in Scotland a low priority for churchmen. However, not only did the congregations and church courts provide nearly one half of all the Scottish petitions in the early 1830s, but two of those most deeply involved in church controversies were also leading anti-slavery campaigners. John Ritchie of Potterrow has been described as the most outspoken and radical voice in the Voluntarist cause, and Ralph Wardlaw of Glasgow, who made a unique contribution to the latter part of the emancipation campaign, publicly argued that disestablishment would emancipate the Kirk from what he saw as the thralldom and indignity of state control.

Internal concerns about church and state relations in Scotland were not the only diversions for churchmen who might be active at this time in the anti-slavery cause. The increasing enthusiasm for overseas mission was not as helpful to abolition as might be thought. One of the key points in the petitions against the slave trade had been that the trade had obstructed the spread of the gospel. Yet this argument was hardly used in the campaign against slavery itself, although many petitions condemned the refusal of colonial planters to allow the religious instruction of their slaves. Two aspects of missionary enthusiasm worked against abolition. First was the contention that strict neutrality on issues such as slavery was necessary to keep the door open in the colonies for the prime task of evangelism. Any challenging of the social order was seen as not just a diversion, but as a potential threat to the goodwill of colonists which enabled the prime task of evangelism to take place. Although in the early 1830s many ministers were active in the committees of the Scottish Missionary Society and the Abolition Societies, there were very few who served on both.

Second, the idea that the religious education of slaves and their conversion to Christianity, as well as objectives in themselves, were steps on the road to civilisation and citizenship seemed useful to the cause

Figure 12   *The reverse of a British medallion commemorating the Abolition of Slavery in 1834. A dance of joy round a palm tree by a group of jubilant slaves. A slightly premature jig, since there would be another four years before compulsory apprenticeship would be ended.*

of amelioration of slavery. Equally, however, it could be a barrier to abolition, since it easily translated into a gradualist argument. It was a short step to argue for the delay of emancipation until it was thought (by whom was never made clear) that the slaves had reached a certain level of education. The *Scottish Guardian*, a newspaper sympathetic to evangelism, articulated this in 1833, when it claimed that slaves in the West Indies were not yet ready for freedom.[84]

Three further factors made the task of the abolitionists in Scotland harder in the late 1830s. Although apprenticeship turned out to be slavery by another name, and most abolitionists opposed it, the celebrations in 1833 and 1834 fixed in the public mind the conviction that the job of emancipation had been achieved. Commemorative medals issued at the time showed slaves dancing round palm trees and hailed the abolitionists and even King William IV, who had opposed abolition, as heroes. Even after the Sturge report, a government that had been sympathetic to abolition nonetheless felt that it could not change an agreement made with the colonies. The *Glasgow Herald* pointed out the dangers of interference with the scheme and they were not alone amongst the press.[85] The *Glasgow Chronicle* complained that supporters of the Committee of the Glasgow Emancipation Society were exploiting its columns by using them for its propaganda. The *Glasgow Argus*, a supporter of abolition, was later to express its anxiety about interference with even 'scoundrally' assemblies such as Jamaica's.[86] Finally, much of the enthusiasm for abolition of slavery after 1833 focused on world slavery, and especially on the growing links with the American campaign, as yet in its early stages. The international support for the Glasgow Emancipation Society did, of course, benefit it. But the dilution of resources and efforts on a wider front was a real danger, and the Society constantly had to remind its supporters that there was unfinished business in the Caribbean.

Given the many limiting factors facing the anti-slavery movement in Scotland in the 1830s, it is remarkable that so much was achieved. The sustained attacks of a very powerful body representing West Indian interests; the ambivalence of much of the media and hostility from some of it; the lack of sympathy for the cause from the majority of Scotland's MPs; and the turbulent and diverting concerns in the churches – all might have combined to muzzle public protest. The fact that approximately 5 per cent of the total number of petitions from the United Kingdom and Ireland came from Scotland in 1833, and 6 per cent in 1838, might not seem very impressive, especially compared to Scotland's huge contribution in 1792. But they were the result of resilient and committed leadership alongside widespread religious and humanitarian revulsion at an institution whose victims had evoked those same feelings in Ayrshire, Fife and Perthshire nearly eighty years before.

Notes

1 *SMPR*, May 1827, p. 213.
2 *SMPR* Jul 1823, pp. 290–2; Sep 1823, pp. 430–1.
3 Minutes of Evidence taken before the Parliamentary Select Committee on Slavery, 20 Jun 1832, p. 1502.
4 *SMPR*, Jun 1832, p. 242.
5 Winston Lawson, *Religion and Race: African and European Roots in Conflict* (New York, 1998), p. 58.

6 M. Turner, *Slaves and Missionaries: The Disintegration of Jamaican Slave Society 1787–1834* (Chicago, 1982), p. 10.

7 G. W. Bridges, *A Voice from Jamaica, in Reply to William Wilberforce* (London, 1823).

8 Lawson, *Religion and Race*, pp. 73, 150–85.

9 *SMPR*, May 1832, pp. 4, 5.

10 Lawson, *Religion and Race*, p. 135.

11 Scottish Missionary Society, Correspondence Book. W. Brown to G. Blyth, 2 Oct 1824. NLS MS. 8985.

12 *SMPR*, Jun 1825, p. 244; May 1827, p. 211; Apr 1828, p. 148; Jan 1831; 6 Jun 1832, p. 243.

13 *CI*, Jan 1831, p. 14.

14 *CI*, Jul 1831, p. 493; Sep 1831, pp. 619–20, 622–30, Nov 1831, pp. 765–67.

15 Scottish Missionary Society, Correspondence Book. 2 Jun 1832.

16 *SMPR*, May 1832, pp. 195–6.

17 *The Edinburgh Almanack*, 1833, pp. 371, 379.

18 Turner, *Slaves and Missionaries*, p. 171.

19 Lawson, *Religion and Race*, p. 150.

20 H. M. Waddell, *Twenty-Nine Years in the West Indies and Central Africa* (London, 1863), p. 70.

21 Turner, *Slaves and Missionaries*, p. 166.

22 *SMPR*, May 1832, p. 199.

23 Waddell, *Twenty-Nine Years*, p. 78.

24 *SMPR*, Mar 1832, p. 98.

25 Waddell, *Twenty-Nine Years*, p. 52.

26 *CI*, Jan 1831, pp. 14, 165.

27 *SMPR*, May 1832, pp. 197–8.

28 Waddell, *Twenty-Nine Years*, p. 76.

29 *SMPR*, Mar 1832, p. 100.

30 Waddell, *Twenty-Nine Years*, p. 56.

31 *SMPR*, May 1832, p. 49.

32 Waddell, *Twenty-Nine Years*, pp. 75–6.

33 *SMPR*, Jul 1833, pp. 251–60; Sep 1833, pp. 339, 343.

34 *SMPR*, Sep 1833, pp. 344, 349.

35 *SMPR*, Sep 1833, p. 350.

36 J. H. Proctor, 'Scottish Missionaries and Jamaican Slaveholders', *Slavery and Abolition*, Vol. 25, No.1 (Apr 2004).

37 *SC*, 16 Jan 1833.

38 *Edinburgh Almanack*, 1833, pp. 371, 379.

39 J. Ritchie, *A Discourse Suggested by the Demise of King George the Fourth* (Edinburgh, 1830), p. 43.

40 J. Douglas, *Address on Slavery, Protection and Church Reform* (Edinburgh, 1833), pp. 2, 21–2.

41 R. Wardlaw, *The Jubilee: a Sermon Preached in West-George Street Chapel on Friday August 1st 1834 the Memorable Day of Negro Emancipation in the British Colonies* (Glasgow, 1834), pp. 6, 26.
42 Douglas, *Address on Slavery*, pp. 7, 9.
43 Douglas, *Address on Slavery*, p. 14. Wardlaw, *The Jubilee*, pp. 8, 9.
44 Wardlaw, *The Jubilee*, pp. 12, 13, 15, 16.
45 Douglas, *Address on Slavery*, pp. 11, 13.
46 Ritchie, *A Discourse*, p. 45.
47 Douglas, *Address on Slavery*, pp. 31–2.
48 Wardlaw, *The Jubilee*, p. 27.
49 Glasgow Emancipation Society, Minutes, Dec 1833; Mar 1838.
50 Synod of the United Associate Secession Church, Minutes, 19 Apr 1831; *SC*, 20 Apr 1831.
51 A. Ritchie, 'The Life and Political Career of Rev. Dr John Ritchie, early-Victorian Radical Dissenter and Activist'. MSc, unpublished dissertation, University of Edinburgh, 1998, p. 10.
52 A. McNair, *Rev. Dr John Ritchie*. Script of articles for the *Kilkdrock standard*, 1913–14, p. 81.
53 *JHL*, Vol. 88, 1833.
54 *ASR*, May 1832, p. 144.
55 *SC*, 19 Jan 1833.
56 *GH*, 21 Jan 1833.
57 J. H. Hinton, *Memoir of William Knibb, Missionary in Jamaica* (London, 1847), pp. 156–8.
58 *SC*, 6 Apr 1833.
59 W. R. McPhun, *Speeches of Messrs Thom[p]son and Borthwick on the Question of Negro Slavery as delivered in Dr Wardlaw's Chapel* (Glasgow, 1833), pp. 4, 7, 12, 13, 17, 22.
60 *SC*, 10 Apr 1833.
61 *JHL* 4, 8, 11, 12, 28 Mar; 1, 3, 18, 22 Apr; 6, 14, 15, 20 May; 1 Jun 1833.
62 Glasgow West India Association, Minutes, 22 Jan 1834.
63 Quoted in Michael Craton, James Walvin, David Wright, *Slavery, Abolition and Emancipation: Black Slaves and the British Empire: A Thematic Documentary* (New York, 1976), pp. 330–5.
64 Glasgow Emancipation Society Committee, Minutes. MLG, 891502, Reel 2, 1835, Smeal Collections, pp. 61, 62. Glasgow Emancipation Society, *Annual Reports*, pp. 19–20.
65 Glasgow Emancipation Society Committee, Minutes, 28 Mar 1836, p. 85.
66 Glasgow Emancipation Society, *Annual Reports*, 1836, p. 6.
67 J. Sturge and T. Harvey, *The West Indies in 1837, being the Journal of a Visit to Antigua, Montserrat, Dominica, St Lucia, Barbados and Jamaica undertaken for the Purpose of Ascertaining the Actual*

Condition of the Negro Population of those Islands (London, 1838), pp. 70, 153, 168.

68 Glasgow Emancipation Society, *Annual Reports*, 1837, pp. 125–38.

69 *SMR*, March 1837, pp. 48, 49; Dec 1837, pp. 177–9.

70 Glasgow Emancipation Society, *Annual Reports*, 1838, pp. 8–16.

71 *JHL*, Vol. 70, 1838. 26 Feb, 8 Mar, 23 Mar.

72 *SC*, 31 Mar 1838.

73 *GA*, 13 Nov 1837.

74 *GA*, 26 May 1838.

75 *GH*, 28 May 1838.

76 Izhak Gross, 'Parliament and the Abolition of Negro Apprenticeship, 1835–8', *English Historical Review*, Vol. 96 (Jul 1981), p. 560.

77 *SC*, 4 Apr, 26 May 1838; *EEC*, 2 Jun 1838.

78 *SC*, 25 Apr 1838.

79 *SC*, 9 Jun 1838.

80 F. J. Klingberg, *The Anti-Slavery Movement in England* (New Haven, CT, 1968), p. 287.

81 *GC*, 14 May 1833.

82 Glasgow West India Association, Minutes, 25 Jun 1838.

83 S. J. Brown, 'Religion and the Rise of Liberalism: The First Disestablishment Campaign in Scotland, 1829–1843', *Journal of Ecclesiastical History*, Vol. 48 (Oct 1997), pp. 686, 687, 692.

84 *SG*, 23 Jun 1833.

85 *GH*, 1 Jun 1838.

86 *GC*, 6 Aug 1838; *GA*, 9 May 1839.

8

EYES ON THE PRIZE – FOCUS, FAITH AND FERVOUR

~

What more need we say, to enforce the propriety and necessity of immediate abolition? Interest, humanity, justice, religion, all plead for the emancipation of the slaves without delay . . . emancipation the slaves will have,
even if we refuse it; but that emancipation will be written in characters of
blood.

James Douglas of Cavers, *Address on Slavery, Sabbath Protection and
Church Reform*, 1833

In the American Civil Rights movement of the mid-twentieth century,
one of the most popular songs had the refrain 'keep your eyes on the
prize, hold on, hold on'. Amidst setbacks and disappointments, there
was a pressing need for a sharp focus that avoided other distractions
and concentrated on the urgent need to destroy the system of racial
segregation. Above all, in what was to prove a long and uncertain
haul to freedom, the quality of tenacity was absolutely crucial. So it
was in the struggle against slavery in the previous century.

A STRONG REVULSION AND A BASIC SENSE OF RIGHT

During the 1820s, the numbers of petitions against slavery from
Scotland were fewer than 200, but they still represented nearly 13 per
cent of the British total. In the great campaigning years of 1830–1,
1833 and 1838, Scotland sent over 1,200 petitions to Parliament. Yet
numbers of petitions alone cannot be the index of the nation's anti-
slavery involvement. From the aftermath of the battle of Culloden
through to the time of the Highland Clearances in the early twentieth
century, an increasing number of Scots moved to the great urban
areas. Therefore one petition from the citizens of Glasgow, Edinburgh,
Aberdeen or Dundee might not only carry a large number of signatures,
but would also encompass a highly populated area. Similarly, a petition from a presbytery or synod would be held to be representative of
many Kirk Sessions and congregations who, as the minutes of these

courts frequently record, had been consulted on, or at least informed about, the issue. A synod such as that of Glasgow and Ayr, although it might send only one petition to each House of Parliament, would represent a large number of church members and would communicate the concerns of the court from many a pulpit in the west of Scotland.

We have seen that many of the ideas of the Scottish Enlightenment informed the Scottish petitions at this time. The philosophical and poetic challenge to slavery, from Francis Hutcheson to Robert Burns, laid a strong foundation for the ideas expressed in these. There was a considerable change in attitudes in Scotland to slavery in the second half of the eighteenth century, from a previous uncritical acceptance of the institution. The presence of black slaves undoubtedly assisted in this. Gradually, slavery was perceived as uncivilised, unchristian and simply wrong in a country that one judge in the Knight case described as 'the land of freedom'. This perception is evident in the arguments found in the Scottish petitions from the late eighteenth century onwards, and it was also a particular element in the contribution made to abolition by the London Scots. They combined a basic humanity with a steely determination to move the cause forward and a directness of purpose that was to enervate the rather more cautious and, at times, legalistic approach of Wilberforce and the other London abolitionists.

This Scottish contribution to the anti-slavery movement was made in the face of considerable and widespread Scottish opposition to emancipation. Petitions to delay or abandon emancipation came from Tain and Wick in the far north to Irvine and Ayr in the west, from Fortrose on the Black Isle to the central town of Stirling, as well as from the Clyde and Forth ports. This indicated a much wider Scottish resistance to abolition than those opposition voices in England, which tended to be limited to the slaving ports of Liverpool, Bristol and London. The amount of Scottish opposition to emancipation was not surprising, given the extensive involvement of Scots in West Indian commerce. Planters and bookkeepers, tradesmen and professionals, whose livelihood depended on the continuation of the West Indian slave system, would be cautioning their relatives and friends at home against any change that might threaten this. News from Scots in the West Indies found its way into the newspapers, and not just to the avowedly pro-slavery *Glasgow Courier*. In a tightly knit society, the word of Scots 'on the spot' in the Caribbean, who assured those at home that the 'agitators' did not have the true picture, proved to be a difficult message for abolitionists to counter. The Glasgow West India

Association was also ever ready to support this pro-slavery 'information' from the colonies, for all that its actual effectiveness was less than its potential.

It has been claimed that anti-slavery activity in Scotland was directly related to the Evangelical revival throughout the churches and the decline of the Moderate party in the Church of Scotland. The truth, though, is not as straightforward as that. William Robertson, the first leader of the Moderate party, was regarded by William Wilberforce as a strong supporter of anti-slavery, and many of the ministers described by William Dickson in his 1792 diary as 'zealous' for the abolition of the slave trade were Moderates. It is certainly true that some of the most strident opposition to presbytery petitions on the slave trade came from the Moderate leader George Hill of St Andrews and on 'premature emancipation' from John Inglis of Edinburgh. It is also true that many of those who led the abolitionist movement in the 1830s, such as Andrew Thomson and Ralph Wardlaw, were prominent evangelicals. On the other hand, the opposition to immediate abolition in the speeches and writings of the evangelical minister of Ruthven, Henry Duncan, gave comfort to the advocates of slavery.

The idea that abolition of slavery was a Christian duty did not go unchallenged. There may have been few who justified slavery on scriptural grounds, such as 'Senex', who wrote in the *Glasgow Courier* in 1792, or the Aberdeenshire minister noted by William Dickson in the same year; but many others, such as Henry Duncan, simply baulked at seeing slavery described as a sin against God. Some argued that the identification of the Kirk with an anti-slavery stance could compromise its relationship with the state. James Lapslie warned Glasgow presbyters in 1792 of the risks involved in taking a political position on the slave trade, while 'D.C.' in the *Glasgow Courier* in 1831 reminded prominent abolitionists in the same city that the money for their stipends depended on the profits made for the city on the plantations.

None of this stemmed the rising anti-slavery tide. In all the shifting ecclesiastical, political and social sands of early nineteenth-century Scotland, no issue involved more people in adopting a clear moral position than did slavery in the British Empire. Even the 'gradualists' felt the need to give assurances of their strong desire to see this 'stain' removed. There was an attractiveness about the simple definition of abolitionism as a crusade against evil. It brought together the values of decency and humanity embraced by the Enlightenment and the fundamental imperative of the Christian gospel to show love and compassion to all. It had strong roots in the Scottish distaste for distinctions of rank and the general affirmation of common humanity. It was perhaps best expressed in an anti-slavery petition by the Bonnetmakers and Dyers of Edinburgh, who asked the House of Lords in 1833 to ensure 'equal rights for black men indiscriminately with white'.[1] Yet that sense of justice alone was not enough to sustain the campaign throughout so many years of uncertainty and discouragement. The general feeling in church bodies that they must declare their opposition to slavery 'as men and Christians' (as the early petitions put it) needed the backbone of a focused theological and biblical attack on the institution to make it effective.

SLAVERY AS THE ANVIL FOR HAMMERING OUT OTHER CONCERNS?

Twenty-five years ago, Duncan Rice contended that slavery became a platform to allow evangelical churchmen to address the theological issues that really concerned them. Rice drew on the first two *Problem of Slavery* volumes by David Brion Davis to argue that evangelical enthusiasm for abolition was simply part of a complex network of anxieties and self-doubts in a changing and increasingly industrialised society, where the traditional restraints on authority no longer held. These anxieties, he claimed, could all 'readily be erased by channelling them into a symbolic aggression against slavery',[2] which would serve as a convenient crusade on a wide variety of fronts. The importance for evangelicals of liberty to slaves, said Rice, was that it was 'conflated with national redemption', and the frontal attack on slavery 'provided a means of releasing the energies and tensions incidental to evangelical commitment'.[3] He further claimed that 'if slavery had merely been cruel or unjust or at odds with the golden rule, it might well have been left alone.' Rice was quite willing to admit that human pity and horror of cruelty played its part in generating opposition to slavery, and he specifically denied making any charge of hypocrisy; but the tenor of his argument was that humanity and concern for physical freedom of slaves were sidetracked or subsumed by other issues. 'In Christian terms', wrote Rice, 'slavery's long standing metaphorical connection with sin made it a vehicle for resolving the tensions of evangelical generations whose primary interest was in the wider problems of guilt, accountability, free agency, declension and personal salvation.'[4] As evidence of this, Rice pointed to the writings of William Innes, James Douglas of Cavers and Ralph Wardlaw, and to the printed speech and sermon by Andrew Thomson. His analysis of the theological motivation behind Scottish

anti-slavery has provided a challenge to the simplistic view of abolitionism that was current-coin in the era of heroes. There certainly
appears to be some evidence for the theory that anti-slavery was used
in the service of other concerns, if we consider the detachment with
which slavery was often discussed in the Scottish Enlightenment's academic circles. It was possible then to see it as an interesting subject
for discussion without being moved enough by its inhumanity to take
action on it. Slavery was used by David Hume and Adam Smith to
provide examples for their philosophical or economic theories, all of
which represented a distancing from the implications of the very
moral and human values that were represented in Enlightenment
thought, an attitude strongly criticised by the Aberdeen philosopher
James Beattie.

But the contention that anti-slavery campaigners meant something
quite different from a basic concern for humanity is much more ques-
tionable when we examine the writings of Innes, Douglas, Thomson
and Wardlaw, those theologians whom Rice cites in support of his
arguments; for the matters addressed in these men's writings and
speeches were echoed in many of the petitions sent by communities, civic bodies, trades guilds and citizens, as well as from churches.
Certainly these petitions frequently included references to the national
guilt and shame brought about by the continuation of slavery, the conflict between the institution of slavery and the values of an enlightened
and Christian society, and the offence which it gave to God bringing
the possibility of divine retribution. But these were not themes unique
to the utterances of evangelicals torn by their own inner conflicts. They
were threaded throughout popular statements coming from all kinds
of group petitions, and they assisted, rather than diluted, the effectiveness of those statements and petitions. Far from reflecting a
complex variety of moral concepts, the Scottish petitions are mainly
focused and unambiguous. That is perhaps the reason that they are
frequently to be found quoted in full as a representative sample in the
parliamentary journals.

The Barman Declaration of the Confessing Church in Germany in
1933 was a powerful evangelical response to Hitler's Jewish decrees,
a theological repost that challenged the racial philosophy of Naziism
at its roots. It became the inspiration for another theological assault
fifty years later on the South African doctrine of apartheid by church
leaders there such as Dr Allan Boesak and Archbishop Desmond Tutu.
Their uncompromising analysis of the sinful nature of apartheid, the
impossibility of the reformation of evil and the urgency of their call

for its destruction was almost a replication of the theological attack on the institution of slavery in the early nineteenth century. Rather than anti-slavery becoming simply a vehicle for other concerns, the evangelical revival meant that theological insights were brought to bear in the service of abolition. The fervour and moral certainty that characterised the evangelical position may have been unwelcome in some quarters, but this fervour and certainty frequently provided the fuel for action. Roger Anstey pointed out that it was the clarity of their philosophy that made evangelicals so formidable a force when they turned to political action against the slave trade.[5]

There are a number of particular areas in which, far from anti-slavery being sacrificed to theological concerns, theology was able to effectively serve the abolition movement in a unique way by providing a radical challenge to slavery. One such was a theology of creation that affirmed that all human beings were formed in the image of the creator. This challenged the overemphasis on the categories of civilisation, beloved by some Enlightenment thinkers, that could be used to support racial subordination. It also challenged by implication the rigid Calvinist doctrine of the elect that could be used to justify the permanent inferiority of certain races. Montesquieu's cynical statement about the threat to our comfortable dominance if slaves were regarded as human was well exploited by Macaulay, Thomson and Ritchie.[6] This doctrine struck at the very concept of 'property in human beings', and its proponents went on to argue that to claim such 'property' was to commit robbery from man and God. It followed that there could be no compensation for thieves, and this logic provided a radical plank in the anti-slavery platform, albeit one that was ultimately to prove unsuccessful.

The evangelical abolitionists often focused on the Exodus story as a model of freedom, but refused to be bound by biblical literalism in their interpretation of the law of Moses, or of Paul's seeming acceptance of slavery in his epistles. In contrast to the more fundamentalist claims of the apologists for slavery, they took an approach to the Bible that allowed for reinterpretation in the light of contemporary conditions. They focused on the broad teaching of the Christian gospel and the example of Jesus. Much of the Baptist William Innes's pamphlet on the slave trade, for example, with its emphasis on 'benevolence', could have been written by a Moderate churchman. Andrew Thomson's argument that slavery was 'insupportable' to the 'feelings of Jesus' also reflected an emphasis that sat easily within Enlightenment values.[7]

Although evangelicals are often perceived as subordinating communal action for justice to individual salvation, the Scots abolitionists rejected the demands of their opponents that their sole concern should be a 'spiritual' one, divorced from social and political realities, demands that were indeed laid on the missionaries in Jamaica. Andrew Thomson firmly rejected the idea that Jesus's promise that 'the Son shall make you free' was in any way 'abstract' and insisted that it pointed to a very concrete freedom. Ralph Wardlaw's sermon on 'The Jubilee' in 1833 was not simply a celebration of an 'act of propitiation for national guilt'[8] though it was all of that. Wardlaw knew well that the biblical jubilee was an unambiguous command for the physical freedom of those in bondage, and when the Emancipation Act failed to deliver that in 1834, he threw himself into the leadership of the struggle in Scotland to end the Apprenticeship Scheme.

A key idea evangelical theology brought to the struggle against slavery was that of fallen humanity and the inevitable abuse of power by sinful humans. The doctrine of original sin has often been used to oppress the weak with guilt, but conversely it can challenge the powerful by pointing to their moral frailty before God. When applied to slavery, this was to take the argument beyond mitigation and to undermine the comfortable idea that slavery could be beneficial even when there were just, or even benevolent, masters such as Mr Joshua Steele in Dickson's *Letters on Slavery*. In this it parted company with a dominant strand in Enlightenment thought, that human nature was essentially good. As Andrew Thomson put it: 'knowing as we do, from all our experience of human nature, that absolute power must be abused . . . where those who are subject to it are continually exposed to its caprices and resentments'.[9] This was a frequently repeated argument in the petitions in the 1830s, but we can find it much earlier. In a pamphlet published at the start of the abolition campaign, Zachary Macaulay wrote: 'after all that can be said in favour of the slaveholders is admitted, we would ask, is it possible to expect that such power as theirs should not be abused? . . . To suppose this, would be to suppose the planters of Jamaica to be angels and not men.'[10]

Coming out of sin 'by degrees' was firmly rejected by Thomson. The emphasis on slavery as sin and an offence to God was fundamental to the immediatist approach. Sympathetic gradualists such as Henry Duncan or George Combe were unable to identify themselves with the full weight of the sinfulness of slavery, and still argue for a staged approach to abolition. It was the acceptance of the gravity of the sin of slavery in both individual and corporate terms, however, that provided an urgency to abandon it that could not brook delay. It recognised, moreover, the need for those involved in the whole business of slavery, and indeed the nation itself, to have this burden lifted from them. It offered a theological counter to those whose caution became a tool in the hands of the West Indians, with their tactics of seeking to delay abolition indefinitely. It had a directness and an urgency that could never have been carried by the Moderates or by philosophers of the Enlightenment, with their belief in the inevitable march of human progress. Immediatism needed the energy of a full-bodied theology of sin to drive it forward.

FOCUS ON THE GOAL AND FUSION OF PHILOSOPHIES

The dangers of sinful human power and the urgency of abandoning defiance of God were significant theological contributions to the Scottish campaign for abolition, but they were not static doctrinal positions hampered by biblical literalism. They were rooted in Christian doctrine and were capable of being translated into the political sphere, therefore they permeated a whole variety of contributions made by individuals and bodies far beyond the evangelical or secessionist churches. In a recent study, David Brion Davis argued that there was a confluence between American enlightenment and evangelical Protestantism on slavery that laid a strong emphasis on benevolence and gravitated 'towards a humanitarian and reformist criteria for interpreting God's law'.[11] Of course that was soon to contrast sharply with the defence of slavery from the Southern churches, but in other respects it would be a fair description of the Scottish movement.

The abolition movement in Scotland not only faced considerable opposition; it also risked having its fervour diverted and weakened by other issues. We have seen how Catholic Emancipation and parliamentary reform competed with the abolition of slavery for the attention of local communities, and the amount of petitioning on slavery is a credit to the ability of the abolitionist societies to arouse and sustain interest in the face of other causes. Two parallel issues at that time took up a great deal of attention within the Presbyterian tradition – the Voluntary Controversy and the dispute over patronage in the appointment of Church of Scotland ministers. In 1831, the year when the Voluntary Controversy began, 455 anti-slavery petitions were sent from Scotland, just under 50 per cent of which came from

Presbyterian congregations and church courts. In 1833, 152 anti-patronage petitions were sent to Parliament from Scotland, but those seeking the abolition of slavery more than doubled that total, with 30 per cent of these coming from Presbyterian sources.

Despite heated internal controversies, the contribution of the churches to the anti-slavery movement in Scotland was strong. In 1792, the Church of Scotland's presbyteries and synods provided 32 petitions against the slave trade compared with 39 from the very much larger Church of England. Even in the difficult days of 1831, the national church in Scotland provided 5 per cent of the Scottish petitions, whilst the Church of England contributed just over half that proportion in England.[12] As in England, however, the 1820s and 1830s saw a shift away from the prominence of the national church in petitioning on slavery, with secessionist and dissenting churches playing a much more significant part. It would, however, be a mistake to judge the Church of Scotland's influence on anti-slavery simply by the proportion of petitions from its courts. In the early 1830s, more than half of the Scottish petitions arose from gatherings of citizens and public meetings in which the parish church and its minister would certainly be involved.

At this time, Scotland saw a plethora of petitions, meetings, sermons, speeches and pamphlets employed in the anti-slavery cause, in addition to providing leading figures for the abolition campaign at home and in London. It was not that such a contribution itself was unique or, except in the early years, that it substantially outweighed those from other parts of Britain. What was distinctive was the fusion of Enlightenment thought and evangelical passion that was able to take root in a culture theologically tuned to it. This inspired men such as James Ramsay to give his life for the cause, Andrew Thomson to dedicate much of the last year of his life to it and Zachary Macaulay to spend his life in its service. That combination of the rational and the emotional, of theological passion and humanitarian feeling, was the foundation laid in the first half of the nineteenth century that would subsequently be employed by other Scots in the struggle against slavery in the United States and in the Africa of David Livingstone or Mary Slessor. In spite of heavy commercial pressures and strong resistance from certain quarters to abolition, a small nation whose own history was bedevilled by internal fractures and an endemic lack of self-confidence was nonetheless able to make a significant contribution to the long struggle against one of the greatest crimes against humanity.

Notes

1 *JHL*, 26 Feb 1833.
2 C. Duncan Rice, 'Controversies over Slavery in Eighteenth and Nineteenth Century Scotland', in *Anti-Slavery Considered – New Perspectives on the Abolitionists*, S. Lewis and R. Feldman, eds (Baton Rouge, LA, 1981), p. 26.
3 C. Duncan Rice, *The Scots Abolitionists* (Baton Rouge, LA, 1981), p. 26.
4 Rice, 'Controversies over Slavery', pp. 27, 41, 43.
5 Roger Anstey, *The Atlantic Slave Trade and British Abolition 1760–1810* (London, 1975), p. 199.
6 Baron de Montesquieu, the French philosopher, wrote 'it is impossible for us to suppose these creatures to be men, because allowing them to be men, a suspicion would follow, that we ourselves are not Christians'. *The Spirit of Laws* (London, 1752), Vol. 2, pp. 341–2.
7 Andrew Thomson, *Slavery not Sanctioned but Condemned by Christianity* (Edinburgh, 1829), p. 9.
8 Rice, 'Controversies over Slavery', p. 38.
9 Andrew Thomson, *Substance of a Speech delivered of the Meeting of the Edinburgh Society for the Abolition of Slavery* (Edinburgh, 1830), p. 6.
10 Zachary Macaulay, *Negro Slavery or a View of Some of the most Prominent features of that State of Society as it exists in the United States of America and in the Colonies of the West Indies, especially in Jamaica* (London, 1823), pp 70–1.
11 David Brion Davis, *Challenging the Boundaries of Slavery* (Cambridge, MA, 2003), pp. 55–6.
12 S. Drescher, 'Two variants of Anti-Slavery: Religious Organisation and Social Mobilisation in Britain and France, 1780–1870', in *Anti-Slavery, Religion and Reform: Essays in Memory of Roger Anstey*, C. Bolt and S. Drescher, eds (Folkestone, 1980), p. 47.

BIBLIOGRAPHY

NEWSPAPERS AND JOURNALS

Anti-Slavery Reporter
Blackwood's Magazine
Caledonian Mercury
Christian Instructor
Edinburgh Advertiser
Edinburgh Evening Courant
Edinburgh Review
Gentleman's Magazine
Glasgow Argus
Glasgow Chronicle
Glasgow Courier
Glasgow Herald
Glasgow Journal
John Bull
Journals of the House of Commons
Journals of the House of Lords
Kelso Chronicle
Parliamentary History
Scots Magazine
Scotsman
Scottish Guardian
Scottish Missionary and Philanthropic Register

MINUTES BOOKS, ANNUAL REPORTS AND PUBLICATIONS OF SOCIETIES

Aberdeen Almanack and Northern Register
[The] African Institution, *Reports*
Church of Scotland: Minutes.
All the minutes referred to are to be found in the National Archives of
Scotland, Edinburgh, with the exception of the Presbytery of Glasgow
minutes, which are housed in the Mitchell Library, Glasgow.

Presbyteries

Aberdeen
Brechin
Cupar
Edinburgh
Forres
Glasgow
Hamilton
Kirkcaldy
Kirkwall
North West England
Paisley
St Andrews
Selkirk
Stirling
Tain

Synods

Angus and Mearns
Dumfries
Glasgow and Ayr
Merse and Teviotdale
Moray
Lothian and Tweeddale
Ross

Edinburgh Almanack (Edinburgh, 1833)
Edinburgh Chamber of Commerce, Minutes, Edinburgh City Archives.
[Edinburgh] Society at Edinburgh for the Purpose of Effecting the Abolition of the African Slave Trade, *Abstract of the Evidence Delivered before a Select Committee of the House of Commons in the years 1790 and 1791 on the part of the Petitioners for the Abolition of the Slave Trade* (Edinburgh, 1791)
—, *Evidence on the Subject of the Slave Trade with a Summary view of the Evidence delivered before a Committee of the House of Commons on the part of the Petitioners for its Abolition* (Edinburgh, 1792)
—, *Reprint of Two Petitions from Scotland* (Edinburgh, 1790)
—, *A Short Address to the People of Scotland on the subject of the Slave Trade with a Summary View of the Evidence Delivered before a Committee of the House of Commons on the part of the Petitioners for its Abolition* (Edinburgh, 1792)
—, *Slave Emancipation in the British Colonies* (Edinburgh, 1791)

[Edinburgh] Society at Edinburgh for the Purpose of Effecting the Abolition of the African Slave Trade, bound pamphlets, 6 Feb 1789, 1 Oct 1790 and 14 Oct 1791. NLS

Edinburgh Society for Promoting the Mitigation and Ultimate Abolition of Negro Slavery, *First Annual Report* (Edinburgh, 1824)

—, *Considerations on Negro Slavery with a Brief View of the Proceedings Relative to it, in the British Parliament* (Edinburgh, 1824)

—, *The Necessity of Abolishing Negro Slavery Demonstrated* (Edinburgh, 1826)

Glasgow Society for the Abolition of the Slave Trade, *Address to the Inhabitants of Glasgow, Paisley and the Neighbourhood concerning the African Slave Trade by a Society in Glasgow* (Glasgow, 1791)

Glasgow Emancipation Society, *Annual Reports*. MLG, Smeal Collection

—, Minutes MLG, Smeal Collection

Glasgow West India Association, Minutes. MLG

London Society for the Abolition of the Slave Trade, Minute Books (2 vols). BL

Musselburgh Burgh Council, Minutes. NAS

Scottish Missionary Society, Correspondence Book. NLS

United Associate Church, Synod, Minutes. NAS

United Associate Secession Church, Presbytery of Cupar, Minutes. NAS

Wemyss Parish Church, Baptismal Records. NAS

—, Register of Discipline, Kirk Session. NAS

LEGAL PROCEEDINGS

Court of Session Papers, *Sheddan* v *Sheddan*, *Sheddan* v *A Negro*, *Montgomery-Sheddan* v *Sheddan*, 1756. NAS

—, *Dalrymple* v *Spence or Spens*, 1770. NAS

—, *Knight* v *Wedderburn*, 1773–78. NAS

Advocates Library Session Papers, Campbell's Collection. Vol. 5, 1756. (Printed)

—, Information and Additional Information – John Wedderburn, Joseph Knight. (Printed)

VARIOUS MSS

Ailsa Muniments. NAS

Dickson, W., 'Diary of a visit to Scotland 5th January–19th March 1792 on behalf of the Committee for the Abolition of the Slave Trade'. Friends Library, London

Gordon, Duke of., Discharge Accounts, 1762. NAS

Macaulay, Z., Diaries (5 vols). Private Collection (to be deposited in Trinity College, Cambridge)

McNair, A., *Rev. Dr. John Ritchie*. Script of articles for the *Kilmarnock Standard*, 1913–14. NC

Plymley, K., Diaries 1791–2, Shropshire Records and Research, Shrewsbury.

Ramsay, J., Papers, RHO

BOOKS, PAMPHLETS AND PRINTED MATERIALS BEFORE 1900

Adair, J., *Unanswerable Arguments against the Abolition of the Slave Trade with a Defence of the Proprietors of the British Sugar Colonies* (London, 1790)

Anon., *Arguments from Scripture For and Against the African Slave Trade as stated in a series of Letters, lately published in the* Glasgow Courier (Glasgow, 1792)

—, *A Defence of the Slave Trade on the grounds of Humanity, Policy and Justice* (London, 1804)

—, *History of the Speculative Society* (Edinburgh, 1845)

—, *Marley: or the Life of a Planter in Jamaica; Comprehending Characteristic Sketches of the Present State of Society and Manners in the British West Indies*. ed. Karina Williamson (Oxford, [1828] 2005)

—, *Opinions of Henry Brougham on Negro Slavery* (London, 1830)

—, *The Slave Colonies of Great Britain or a Picture of Negro Slavery drawn by the Colonists Themselves* (London, 1826)

—, *Substance of the Debate in the House of Commons on the 15th May 1823 on a Motion for the Mitigation and Gradual Abolition of Slavery throughout the British Dominions* (London, 1823)

Barclay, A., *A Practical View of the Present State of Slavery in the West Indies or an Examination of Mr. Stephen's 'Slavery in the West Indian Colonies' containing more particularly an Account of the Actual Condition of the Negroes in Jamaica* (London, 1826)

Barrington, D., *Observations on the More Ancient Statutes* (London, 1796)

Beattie, J., *The Letters of James Beattie to Sir William Forbes* (London, 1820)

—, *Elements of Moral Science*, (Edinburgh, 1817)

—, *An Essay on the Nature and Immutability of Truth, in Opposition to Sophistry and Scepticism* (London, 1807)

—, 'On the Lawfulness and Expediency of Slavery particularly that of Negroes' (1788), AUL

Blackstone, Sir W., *Commentaries on the Laws of England* (Oxford, 1786)

Boswell, J., *Life of Johnson*, ed. R. W. Chapman (Oxford, [1791] 1953)

—, *Journal of a Tour to the Hebrides with Samuel Johnson*, F. Pottle and C. Bennet, eds (New York, [1785] 1961)

—, *Letters of James Boswell* (London, 1857)

Bridges, G. W., *A Voice from Jamaica, in Reply to William Wilberforce* (London, 1823)

Brown, M. P., ed., *Decisions of the Lords of Council and Session from 1766 to 1791*, collected by Lord Hailes (Edinburgh, 1826)

Brougham, H., *A Concise Statement of the Question regarding the Abolition of the Slave Trade* (London, 1804)

—, *An Enquiry into the Colonial Policy of the European Powers* (Edinburgh, 1803)

—, *Lord Brougham's Speech in the House of Lords on 29th January 1838 upon the African Slave Trade* (London, 1838)

—, *Selections from the Speeches and Writings of the Rt. Hon Henry, Lord Brougham and Vaux* (London, 1831)

—, *Speeches of Henry, Lord Brougham*, 4 vols (London, 1838)

Burns, R., *Poetical Works*, ed. W. Wallace (Edinburgh, 1902)

Burns, R., *Speech Delivered at the Anti-Slavery Meeting held at Paisley on the 1st November 1830 by The Rev. Dr Burns, Paisley* (Paisley, 1830)

Buxton, C., *Memoirs of Sir Thomas Fowell Buxton* (London, 1850)

Chambers, T., ed., *Biographical Dictionary of Eminent Scotsmen* (Glasgow and Edinburgh, 1875)

Clarkson, T., *The History of the Rise, Progress and Accomplishment of the Abolition of the Slave Trade by the British* (London, 1808)

Cockburn, H., *Memorials of his Time* (Edinburgh, 1856)

Dalrymple, J., Viscount Stair, *Institutions of the Law of Scotland*, ed. D. M. Walker (Edinburgh, [1681] 1981).

Dalzel, A., *The History of Dahomey – an Inland Kingdom of Africa. Compiled from Authentic Memories*, ed. J. D. Fage (London, [1789] 1967)

Dickson, W., *Addresses to Whites, Free Negroes of Barbados and Accounts of some Negroes eminent for their Virtues and Abilities* (London, 1797)

—, *Hints to the People of the United Kingdom in general and North Britain in particular on the Present Important Crisis and some Interesting Collateral Subjects* (Edinburgh, 1803)

—, *Letters on Slavery* (London, 1789)

—, *Mitigation of Slavery* (London, 1814)

Douglas, J., *Address on Slavery, Protection and Church Reform* (Edinburgh, 1833)

Duncan, H., *Presbyter's Letters on the West Indian Question addressed to Rt. Hon. George Murray* (London, 1830)

Dwarris, F., *The West India Question Plainly Stated* (London, 1828)

Edwards, B., *The History, Civil and Commercial, of the British Colonies in the West Indies* (London, 1794)

Equiano, O., *The Interesting Narrative and Other Writings*, ed. V. Carretta (London, [1789]1995)

Ferguson, A., *Essay on The History of Civil Society*, ed. D. Forbes (Edinburgh, [1767] 1966)

Ferguson, *Institutes of Moral Philosophy* (Edinburgh, 1769)

Fielding, J. Penal Laws (London, 1768)

Fletcher, A., 'The Second Discourse Concerning the Affairs of Scotland: Written in the Year 1698', in *Selected Political Writings and Speeches*, ed. D. Daiches (Edinburgh, [1698] 1979)

Forbes, W., *Memoirs of a Banking House by the late Sir William Forbes of Pitsligo* (Edinburgh, 1860)

—, *Life and Writings of James Beattie* (Edinburgh, 1806)

Galt, J., *Annals of the Parish* (Edinburgh,1821)

Harris, R., *Scriptural Researches on the Licitness of the Slave Trade, Showing its Conformity with the Principles of Revealed Religion, Delineated in the Sacred Writings of the Word of God* (Liverpool and London, 1788)

Hinton, J. H., *Memoir of William Knibb, Missionary in Jamaica* (London, 1847)

Home, H., Lord Kames, *Sketches of the History of Man* (Edinburgh, 1813)

Hume, D., *Political Discourses* (Edinburgh, 1752)

—, *Essays Moral, Political and Literary, including 'Essays Moral and Political', 'An enquiry into the Principles of Morality', and 'Dialogues concerning Natural Religion'*, T. H. Green and T. H. Grose, eds (London, 1889)

Hutcheson, F., *A System of Moral Philosophy* (Glasgow, 1755)

Innes, W., *Important and Interesting Observations on the Abolition of the Slave Trade* (Edinburgh, 1796)

Jamieson, J., *The Sorrows of Slavery, a Poem containing a Faithful Statement of Facts respecting the African Slave Trade* (London, 1789)

Long, E., *History of Jamaica* (London, 1774)

Macaulay, Z., *Negro Slavery or a view of some of the most Prominent Features of that State of Society as it exists in the United States of America and in the Colonies of the West Indies, especially in Jamaica* (London, 1823)

—, *Letter to his Royal Highness the Duke of Gloucester from Zachary Macaulay occasioned by a Pamphlet published by Dr Thorpe late Judge of the Colony of Sierra Leone entitled 'A letter to William Wilberforce Esq.'* (London, 1815)

Mackenzie, G. M., *Institutions of the Law of Slavery*, second edition (Edinburgh, 1688)

Marjoriebanks, J., *Slavery, an Essay in Verse* (Edinburgh, 1792)

McPhun, W. R., *Speeches of Messrs Thom[p]son and Borthwick on the Question of Negro Slavery as delivered in Dr Wardlaw's Chapel* (Glasgow, 1833)

McQueen, J., *The Colonial Controversy containing a Refutation of the Anti-Colonialists Addressed to the Earl of Liverpool with a supplementary letter to Mr Macaulay* (Glasgow, 1825)

Millar, J., *The Origin of the Distinction of Ranks* (Edinburgh, 1806)

Montesquieu, Baron de, *The Spirit of Laws* (London, 1752)

Napier, M., ed., *Selection from the Correspondence of the late Macvey Napier* (London, 1879)

Nugent, Lady Maria, *Journal of a Resident in Jamaica*, ed. P. Wright (Kingston, [c.1804] 1966)

Ramsay, J., *An Essay on the Treatment and Conversion of African Slaves in the British Sugar Colonies* (London, 1784)

—, *Objections to the Abolition of the Slave Trade with Answers to which are prefixed Strictures on a Late Publication entitled "Considerations on the Emancipation of Negroes and the Abolition of the Slave Trade", by a West Indian Planter* (London, 1788)

—, *An Examination of the Rev. Mr Harris's Scriptural Researches on the Licitness of the Slave Trade* (London, 1788)

—, *An Address to the Publick on the Proposed Bill for the Abolition of the Slave Trade* (London, 1789)

Ritchie, J., *A Discourse Suggested by the Demise of King George the Fourth* (Edinburgh, 1830)

Roberts, A., ed., *Letters of Hannah More to Zachary Macaulay Esq containing Notices of Lord Macaulay's Youth* (London, 1860)

Robertson, W., *The History of the Reign of the Emperor Charles V*, 2 vols (Dublin, 1762)

—, *The Situation of the World at the time of Christ's Appearance and its Connection with the Success of His Religion Considered* (Edinburgh, 1755)

Schaw, J., *Journal of a Lady of Quality: Being the Narration of a Journey from Scotland to the West Indies, North Carolina and Portugal in the years 1774–1776*, ed. Evangeline Walker Andrews (New Haven, CT, [1776] 1939)

Sharp, G., *A Representation of the Injustice and Dangerous Tendency of Tolerating Slavery in England* (London, 1769)

Smellie, W., ed., *Encyclopaedia Britannica*, 3 vols (Edinburgh, 1771)

Smith, A., *An Inquiry into the Nature and Causes of the Wealth of Nations* (London, [1776] 1884)

—, *The Theory of Moral Sentiments* (New York, [1759] 1966)

Somerville, T., *A Discourse on our Obligation to Thanksgiving for the Prospect of the Abolition of the African Slave Trade with a Prayer delivered in the Church in Jedburgh on 15th April by Thomas Somerville D.D.* (Kelso, 1792)

—, *My Own Life and Times 1741–1814* (Edinburgh, 1861)

Stephen, Sir G., *Anti-Slavery Recollections* (London, 1859)

Stephen, J., *The Crisis of the Sugar Colonies. An Enquiry into the Objects and Probable Effects of the French Expedition to the West Indies and their Connection with the Colonial Interests of the British Empire* (London, 1802)

—, *The Dangers of the Country – We may be Conquered by France* (London, 1807)

—, *England Enslaved by her own Slave Colonies* (London, 1826)

—, 'Memoirs of James Stephen written by Himself for the Use of his Children, commenced 6 June 1819'. BL.

—, *Reasons for Establishing a Registry of Slaves* (London, 1815)

—, *The Slavery of the British West India Colonies Delineated as it exists, both in Law and Practice and compared with the Slavery of Other Countries, Ancient and Modern* (London, 1824, 1830) 2 Vols.

—, *War in Disguise: or the Frauds of the Neutral Flags* (London, 1805)

Stewart, J., *A View of the Past and Present State of the Island of Jamaica; with Remarks on the Moral and Physical Condition of the Slaves and on the Abolition of Slavery in the Colonies* (Edinburgh, 1823)

Sturge, J. and T. Harvey *The West Indies in 1837, being the Journal of a Visit to Antigua, Montserrat, Dominica, St Lucia, Barbados and Jamaica undertaken for the Purpose of Ascertaining the Actual Condition of the Negro Population of those Islands* (London, 1838)

Thomson, A., *Slavery not Sanctioned but Condemned by Christianity* (Edinburgh, 1829)

—, *Substance of the Speech delivered at the Meeting of the Edinburgh Society for the Abolition of Slavery* (Edinburgh, 1830)

Waddell, H. M., *Twenty-Nine Years in the West Indies and Central Africa* (London, 1863)

Wallace, G., *A System of the Principles of the Law of Scotland* (Edinburgh, 1760)

Wardlaw, R., *The Jubilee: a Sermon Preached in West-George Street Chapel on Friday August 1st 1834 the Memorable Day of Negro Emancipation in the British Colonies* (Glasgow, 1834)

Watson, Jean L., *Life of Dr Andrew Thomson* (Edinburgh, 1882)

Wedderburn, R., *The Horrors of Slavery and Other Writings*, ed. I. McCalman (Edinburgh, [1824] 1991)

Wilberforce, R. and S., *Life of William Wilberforce*, 5 vols (London, 1838)

—, *The Correspondence of William Wilberforce*, edited by his sons (London, 1860)

Wilberforce, W., *An Appeal to the Religion, Justice and Humanity of the Inhabitants of the British Empire on behalf of the Negro Slaves in the West Indies* (London, 1823)

SECONDARY SOURCES AFTER 1900

Adams, D., *Montrose – A History of its Harbour, Trade and Shipping* (Tayport, 1993)

Akinjogbin, L. A., 'Archibald Dalzel: Slaver Trader and Historian of Dahomey', *Journal of African History*, Vol. 7 (1966)

Anstey, R., *The Atlantic Slave Trade and British Abolition 1760–1810* (London, 1975)

—, 'Capitalism and Slavery: A Critique', *Economic History Review*, 2nd Series, Vol. 21, No. 2 (1968).

Baker, S., 'Paradox in Grenada – Ninian and George Home, a study of Slave-Owning Scots of the Enlightened Age', unpublished MA (Hons) dissertation, University of Edinburgh, 1999.

Basker, J., ed., *Amazing Grace: An Anthology of Poems about Slavery 1600–1810* (New Haven, CT, 2003)

Bevington, M. E., ed., *The Memoirs of James Stephen* (London, 1954)

Blackburn, R., *The Making of New World Slavery* (London, 1997)

Bolt, C. and S. Drescher, eds., *Anti-Slavery, Religion and Reform: Essays in Memory of Roger Anstey* (Folkestone, 1980)

Booth, C., *Zachary Macaulay, his Part in the Movement for the Abolition of the Slave Trade and of Slavery* (London, 1934)

Brown, S. J., *The National Churches of England, Ireland and Scotland 1801–1846* (Oxford, 2001)

—, 'Religion and the Rise of Liberalism: The First Disestablishment Campaign in Scotland, 1829–1843', *Journal of Ecclesiastical History*, Vol. 48 (Oct 1997)

Burns, A. and J. Innes, eds, *Rethinking the Age of Reform: Britain 1780–1850* (Cambridge, 2003)

Cairns, J., 'The Scottish Law of Slavery', unpublished lecture, University of Edinburgh, 6 Dec 2000

Calder, A., *Revolutionary Empire* (London, 1981)

—, 'Picture of a Hidden Past', *The Herald*, 18 Mar 2004

Carrington, S., 'American Revolution and the British West Indies' Economy', in *British Capitalism and Caribbean Slavery*, B. Solow and S. Engerman, eds (Cambridge, 1987)

Colley, L., *Britons: Forging the Nation 1707–1837* (London, 1992)

Coupland, R., *The British Anti-Slavery Movement* (Oxford, 1933).

—, *Wilberforce* (Oxford, 1923).

Cowan, R. M. W., *The Newspaper in Scotland – A Study of its First Expansion 1815–1860* (Glasgow, 1946)

Craton, M., *Testing the Chains: Resistance to Slavery in the British West Indies* (Ithaca, NY, 1982)

—, 'What and Who to Whom and What, the Significance of Slave Resistance', in *British Capitalism and Caribbean Slavery*, B. Solow and S. Engerman, eds (Cambridge, MA, 1987)

Craton, M., J. Walvin, D. Wright, *Slavery, Abolition and Emancipation: Black Slaves and the British Empire: A Thematic Documentary* (New York, 1976)

Crawford, T., *Boswell, Burns and the French Revolution* (Edinburgh, 1990)

Cunningham, A. S., *Rambles in the Parishes of Scoonie and Wemyss* (Leven, 1905)

Davis, D. B., 'Capitalism, Abolitionism and Hegenomy', in *British Capitalism and Caribbean Slavery*, B. Solow and S. Engerman, eds (Cambridge, MA, 1987)

—, *Challenging the Boundaries of Slavery* (Cambridge, MA, 2003)

—, 'The Emergence of Immediatism in British and American Anti-Slavery Thought', *The Mississippi Valley Historical Review*, Vol. 42 (Sep 1962)

—, *The Problem of Slavery in Western Culture* (Ithaca, NY, 1966)

—, *The Problem of Slavery in the Age of Revolution, 1773–1823* (Ithaca, NY, 1975)

—, *Slavery and Human Progress* (Oxford, 1984)

Devine, T. M., *The Tobacco Lords* (Edinburgh, 1975)

—, 'An Eighteenth-Century Business Elite: Glasgow–West India Merchants', *Scottish Historical Review*, Vol. 57 (1978)

—, *Scotland's Empire* (London, 2003)

Drescher, S., *Econocide: British Slavery in the Year of Abolition* (Pittsburg, 1977)

—, *Capitalism and Anti-Slavery: A Critique* (London, 1986)

—, 'Whose abolition? Popular Pressure and the Ending of the British Slave Trade', *Past and Present*, Vol. 143 (1994)

Edwards, M., *Who Belongs to Glasgow?* (Glasgow, 1993)

Evans, J., 'African/Caribbeans in Scotland, A Socio-Geographical Study'. unpublished PhD thesis, University of Edinburgh, 1986

Ferguson, W., *Scotland: 1689 to the Present* (Edinburgh, 1968)

Forbes, M., *Beattie and his Friends* (London, 1904)

Fry, M., *The Scottish Empire* (East Linton, 2001)

—, 'Commercial Empire: Scotland and British Expansion in the Eighteenth Century', in *Eighteenth Century Scotland: New Perspectives*, T. M. Devine and J. R. Young, eds (East Linton, 1999)

Furneaux, R., *William Wilberforce* (London, 1974)

Gross, I., 'Parliament and the Abolition of Negro Apprenticeship 1835–8', *English Historical Review*, Vol. 96 (Jul 1981)

Hancock, D., *Citizens of the World* (Cambridge, 1995)

Hall, C., *Civilising Subjects: Metropole and Colony in the English Imagination* (Cambridge, 2002)

Hall, D., ed., *In Miserable Slavery: Thomas Thistlewood in Jamaica 1750–1786* (London, 1989)

Hamilton, D., *Scotland, the Caribbean and the Atlantic World 1750–1820* (Manchester, 2005)

Hawes, F., *Henry Brougham* (London, 1957)

Herman, A., *The Scottish Enlightenment – The Scots Invention of the Modern World* (London, 2003)

Hochschild, A., *Bury the Chains: The British Struggle to Abolish Slavery* (London, 2005)

Holland, M., Viscountess Knutsford, *Life and Letters of Zachary Macaulay* (London, 1900)

Hurwitz, E. F., *Politics and the Public Conscience: Slave Emancipation and the Abolitionist Movement in Britain* (London, 1973)

Inikori, J. E., 'Slavery and the Development of Industrial Capitalism in England', in *British Capitalism and Caribbean Slavery*, B. Solow and S. Engerman, eds (Cambridge, 1987)

Jackson, G. and S. G. E., Lythe eds, *The Port of Montrose* (Tayport, 1993)

Karras, A., *Sojourners in the Sun: Scottish Migrants in Jamaica and the Chesapeake 1740–1800* (New York, 1992)

Kay, W., 'The Black History of Scotland', unpublished lecture, University of Edinburgh, January 2004

—, *Scotland's Black History*, BBC Radio Series, 2003.

King, E., *The Hidden History of Glasgow's Women* (Edinburgh, 1993)

Klingberg, F. J., *The Anti-Slavery Movement in England* (New Haven, CT, 1968)

Lawson, W., *Religion and Race: African and European Roots in Conflict* (New York, 1998)

Lenman, B., *Integration and Enlightenment, Scotland 1746–1832* (Edinburgh, 1981)

McInnes, A. I., *Clanship, Commerce and the House of Stuart 1603–1788* (East Linton, 1996)

McIntosh, J. R., *Church and Theology in Enlightenment Scotland: The PopularParty, 1740–1800* (East Linton, 1998)

McGinty, S., 'The Trade in Shame', *Sunday Times Ecosse*, 5 Mar 1998

Midgley, C., *Women against Slavery: The British Campaign 1780–1870* (London, 1982)

Morgan, K., *Slavery, the Atlantic Trade and the British Economy 1600–1800* (Cambridge, 2000)

Nenadic, S., 'Political Reform and the Ordering of Middle Class Protest', in *Conflict and Stability in Scottish Society*, ed. T. M. Devine (Edinburgh, 1990)

Oldfield, J. R., *Popular Politics and British Anti-Slavery: The Mobilisation of Public Opinion against the Slave Trade 1787–1807* (Manchester, 1995)

Orr, W., 'Slave Labours', *The Scotsman*, Weekend (30 Jun 1982)

Pollock, J., *William Wilberforce* (Oxford, 1987)

Proctor, J. H., 'Scottish Missionaries and Jamaican Slaveholders', *Slavery and Abolition*, Vol. 25, No. 1 (Apr 2004)

Rice, C. D., 'Abolitionists and Abolitionism in Aberdeen', *Northern Scotland*, No.1 (1972)

—, 'Archibald Dalzel, The Scottish Intelligentsia and the Problem of Slavery', *Scottish Historical Review*, Vol. 62 (Oct 1983)

—, 'Controversies over Slavery in Eighteenth and Nineteenth Century Scotland', in *Anti-Slavery Considered – New Perspectives on the Abolitionists*, S. Lewis and R. Feldman, eds (Baton Rouge, LA, 1981)

—, *The Scots Abolitionists, 1833–1861* (Baton Rouge, LA, 1981)

Ritchie, A., 'The Life and Political Career of Rev. Dr John Ritchie, early-Victorian Radical Dissenter and Activist'. MSc, unpublished dissertation, University of Edinburgh, 1998.

Robertson, J. I., *The First Highlander-Major-General David Stewart of Garth CB, 1768–1829* (East Linton, 1998)

Scott, H., ed., *Fasti Ecclesiae Scoticanae, the Succession of Ministers in the Church of Scotland from the Reformation*, 7 vols (Edinburgh, 1915)

Shepperson, G., 'Frederick Douglass and Scotland', *Journal of Negro History*, Vol. 38 (1953)

Sher, R. B., *Church and University in the Scottish Enlightenment: The Moderate Literati in Edinburgh* (Edinburgh, 1985)

Sheridan, R. B., *Doctors and Slaves* (Cambridge, 1985)

Shyllon, F., *Black Slaves in Britain* (Oxford, 1974)

—, *James Ramsay – The Unknown Abolitionist* (Edinburgh, 1977)

Small, R., *History of Congregations of the United Presbyterian Church 1733–1900* (Edinburgh, 1904)

Smout, T. C., *A History of the Scottish People* (Glasgow, 1972)

Solow, B. and S. Engerman, eds, *British Capitalism and Caribbean Slavery: The Legacy of Eric Williams* (Cambridge, 1987)

Stephen, L. and S. Lee eds, *Dictionary of National Biography* (London, 1908)

Stewart, R., *Henry Brougham 1778–1868: His Public Career* (London, 1986)

Temperley, H., *British Anti-Slavery 1833–40* (London, 1972)

Thomas, H., *The Slave Trade* (London, 1997)

Thompson, H. W., *A Scottish Man of Feeling: Some Account of Henry Mackenzie Esq.* (Oxford, 1931)

Thomson, J., *The Seasons*, ed. James Sambrook (Oxford, 1981)

Turley, D., 'British Anti-Slavery Reassessed', in *Rethinking the Age of Reform*, A. Burns and J. Innes, eds (Cambridge, 2003)

Turner, M., *Slaves and Missionaries: The Disintegration of Jamaican Slave Society 1787–1834* (Chicago, 1982)

Walvin, J., *The Black Presence: A Documentary History of the Negro in England, 1555–1860* (London, 1971)

—, *England, Slaves, and Freedom 1776–1838* (Jackson, MS, 1986)

—, 'The Rise of British Popular Sentiment for Abolition', in *Anti-Slavery, Religion and Reform: Essays in Memory of Roger Anstey*, C. Innes and S. Drescher, eds (Folkestone, 1980)

—, *Questioning Slavery* (London, 1996)

Watson, D., 'Monklands and the Slave Trade', *The Journal of Monklands Heritage Society*, Vol. 5. (Sep 2000)

Waldman, L. K., 'An Unnoticed Aspect of Archibald Dalzel's '*The History of Dahomey*', *Journal of African History*, Vol.6 (1965)

Williams, E., *British Historians and the West Indies* (London, 1966)

—, *Capitalism and Slavery* (London, [1944] 1964)

INDEX